I0819115

ALSO BY KERRY DOCHERTY

Somewhere, Right Now

SELFISH

HARMONY
NEW YORK

SELFISH

UNLEARNING, RECLAIMING, AND TELLING THE TRUTH

A Memoir

KERRY DOCHERTY

Harmony Books
An imprint of Random House
A division of Penguin Random House LLC
1745 Broadway, New York, NY 10019
harmonybooks.com | randomhousebooks.com
penguinrandomhouse.com

Library of Congress Cataloging-in-Publication Data

ISBN 9780593736340
Ebook ISBN 9780593736357

Printed in the United States of America

1st Printing

First Edition

BOOK TEAM: Production editor: Annette Szlachta • Managing editor: Allison Fox • Production manager: Maggie Hart • Copy editor: Hilary Roberts • Proofreaders: Kate Hertzog, Dan Janeck, Caitlin Van Dusen, Wes Alspach

Book design by Elizabeth A. D. Eno

The authorized representative in the EU for product safety and compliance is Penguin Random House Ireland, Morrison Chambers, 32 Nassau Street, Dublin D02 YH68, Ireland. https://eu-contact.penguin.ie

For Alex

If you don’t break your ropes while you’re alive
do you think
ghosts will do it after?

—Kabir

The Self is not an Individual.

—Prentis Hemphill

There is no you. It’s all for you.

Introduction

My husband and I sat on opposite sides of an unfamiliar leather couch: Alex on the far right and me on the left. It was our first meeting with Bruce Almo, a highly recommended couples therapist whose hourly rate was way more than we could afford.

We were there for one reason only: to negotiate my salary.

Bruce's cozy, dimly lit carriage house in New York City's West Village was immaculately decorated with framed pictures of him and his husband and oil paintings of what looked like Ireland. I scanned his bookshelves and saw a biography of Leonard Cohen, a book on playwriting, and several collections of Buddhist writings. I was already in love with him.

"We have so many of the same books," I said, giving him a wink. I was certain he would like me more than Alex. He smiled kindly, if neutrally, back at me.

"So . . ." he began, fanning his hands out to both of us like a Catholic priest welcoming his parishioners.

I knew not to speak first. Never speak first.

Alex jumped in.

"We're not really here to talk about marriage," Alex clarified. "We're having more of a business issue."

Bruce smiled neutrally again.

This was obviously a marriage issue.

Two years before this session, my husband, Alex, his identical twin brother, Mike, their mother, Ninie, and I started a clothing company named Faherty Brand (after their last name). As members of a family business, each of us relied on the others' skill sets: Alex had a background in finance, Mike's expertise was fashion design, Ninie was an interior decorator, and I had a law degree and also taught mindfulness. I joked that each of us had one-quarter of a brain, but together we might be able to figure things out.

The brand was, and remains, known for its casual designs, sun-washed hues, and signature comfortable fabrics that you never want to take off. We often describe Faherty as "clothing for life's great moments": those moments spent surfing at sunrise, enjoying long dinners with friends, or sitting around a bonfire under the stars. But behind the scenes, I quipped that "every day was Monday," meaning every single day, even Saturday, felt like the start of a week filled with an endless list of problems. We had depleted our savings, owed money to many, and we were illegally airbnbing our apartment to make rent. Every day ignited a fire that needed to be put out, be it production delays, see-through board shorts, or botched photo shoots (to name but a very few).

Before starting Faherty, I had focused on social justice and human rights, but now I was a professional "shuffler of stuff," moving trunks of clothing from trade shows to events to stores. I wore many hats to meet the needs of the business and compensate for the scarcity of employees. I was the social media manager. The PR person and event planner. I was the head of HR, who hired people and then sometimes had to fire them. I was the general counsel, who had to deal with trademark issues and lawsuits and leases and contract negotiations. I was also the fit model and photo shoot creative director, which my friends found hilarious, considering I knew nothing about the fashion industry or upcoming trends. Most days, my personal style was "grandpa chic": oversize old cardigans, beat-up brown boots, and vintage jeans.

People say that working with your spouse can make or break the relationship; but working with your husband, brother-in-law, *and* mother-in-law? The jury was still out. Alex and I had been married only two years at that point, but already our marriage had morphed into the business. Our queen-size bed was essentially our conference room. Conversations about the business were our pillow talk, our good-morning chat, and, dare I say, even our foreplay at times. Faherty was what we fought about most and also what might have been, at that moment at least, the main thing still connecting us.

Bruce didn't know any of this yet.

"We are actually here to negotiate my salary," I said. And then I laughed, knowing the ridiculousness of having a poetry-loving Buddhist couples therapist mediate this decision, and also because I always laughed when I was about to cry.

"Continue," Bruce said.

"Listen, I value Kerry, I do," Alex assured Bruce. "But I should make more money than her. I work more. I care more. I'm the CEO, which means I have to run almost every part of the company to ensure we financially survive. That's a lot of stress on me. Plus, this has been our dream since we were kids." In this instance, Alex's use of the word "our" did not pertain to me and him. Alex often used the plural "our" or "we" to describe himself and Mike as if they were one entity, one brain; as if Mike were his one main life partner. *This is a twin thing,* Alex would say. And I would nod.

Alex wasn't wrong. He did work more than I did, he did care more about the company, and he did manage more people. But the three of us were in this together, fully consumed by the desire and need to make sure Faherty got off the ground. And if salary reflected value, Alex was confirming his belief that I mattered less than he did, and this fucking hurt. Beyond the fact that I spent nearly every waking moment trying to make his and his brother's dream come true, I contributed things to the company that were invaluable, though often unseen: building a healthy culture, forming meaningful relationships with partners and nonprofits, creating an expansive community of customers, and ensuring our family values were reflected in the brand.

What about emotional labor? I wanted to say. *Heck, spiritual labor?*

"And besides," Alex added, "Kerry's just not as committed."

The word "committed" echoed through the silence.

It was true that I wasn't as committed as I used to be—to the business or, frankly, to the marriage. Why, just a few months before, I'd been in Los Angeles for a trade show and then afterward stayed for three days on my sister's couch, where I vented and avoided emails and befriended two musicians, staying up until 3:00 A.M. drinking tequila, singing songs around a fire, and declaring them both to be my new soulmates. I was supposed to return to New York for an investor meeting on Monday, but instead I drove up to Ojai on Sunday night and checked myself into a spiritual retreat center, where I sat with a book and my journal and cried while walking through the nearby blossoming orange groves. I filled pages of my journal with ideas and dreams outside the brand: creating a music and meditation event series, writing a book of poetry, hosting retreats, starting a farm, running away. Basically, anything other than what I was doing. All this dreaming infused me with hope. A hope that life could be different. That I could be different.

Bruce looked at me. I looked back.

Alex kept talking. "And anyway, you're not like you used to be. You're not the woman I married."

We weren't talking about money anymore, but Alex had nailed one of the main issues at hand.

I finally chimed in.

"Well, you're exactly like you used to be, Al. You're the exact man I married."

This was our shared problem: I wanted a man who would evolve, and he wanted to wake up next to the girl he fell in love with when he was nineteen years old. The one who was reliable. Who pleased people. Who never got angry.

"And now," Alex said, closing his opening statement to Bruce, but staring at me, "you just do what you want."

I paused, trying to decide whether this was an insult or a compliment. Where was the problem?

"Why don't you do what *you* want?" I asked.

"Because I'm not selfish," he said.

The word lingered in the air.

He had said it.

The *S* word.

SELFISH

One

I wasn't always like this. Selfish, that is. But when you're born with a vagina, an unspoken thing happens. A chipping away begins, like a sculptor to clay, to ensure you fit a certain mold. It begins early, with well-meaning people commenting on your appearance, your outfits, your adaptability, your generosity, your kindness, your smile, your ability to give. And then one day you look down and realize you're contorted into a shape that is entirely misaligned with who you are: contoured into a figure that doesn't reflect your true essence.

You literally cannot find your Self.

~

GROWING UP, I WAS the dutiful, well-behaved middle child. The determined, happy-go-lucky sister. The Enneagram 9, also known as the "Peacemaker." I also loved being seen, jumping into the frame of my mother's video camera to showcase my newest dance move while my sister and brother stood in the background. I wanted to be a star. And in many ways, I was. I accumulated accolades with acceleration and ease. My résumé through high school was extensive and nauseating: three-sport captain-athlete, All-American lacrosse player, and taker of AP classes. My sister joked that if I hadn't been so hilarious and humble, I would have been entirely unlikable. I was actively recruited to play Division I lacrosse by a range of colleges and accepted early at Yale University.

I entered college a good, obedient, unsensual, competitive, high-achieving virgin.

I MET ALEX ON our first day of college. More specifically, in Spanish 101, in the basement of an eighteenth-century Gothic building on Yale's campus. As the other students quietly settled into oak desk chairs, I categorized them: the Legacy, the International Genius, the Musician, the Young Prodigy. To get into Yale, you didn't need to be particularly well-rounded; you simply had to be exceptional at one thing. And I was the Athlete, dressed as I would be dressed most days—in monochromatic lacrosse sweats and a messy side ponytail.

Ten minutes into class, the door opened and a boy with thick, wavy brown hair walked in. He had a surfer's tan and wore an Incredible Hulk tank top, floral board shorts, and flip-flops. Basically a Jersey Shore Ken doll: flawlessly handsome, confident, and smiling. I pegged him as a fellow Athlete and likely—like me—in this early-morning section because of an inflexible afternoon practice schedule.

"Alejandro Faherty," our professor said, looking down at her attendance sheet. "*Adelante, adelante.*" He sat down at the empty desk next to me.

He smelled of metal.

The professor soon sorted us into pairs to introduce ourselves through rudimentary introductions in Spanish. Alex and I were put together.

My name is Kerry. I am from Buffalo. I play lacrosse. I want to be in the FBI when I grow up.

My name is Alex. I am from New Jersey. I play football. When I grow up, I want to have a clothing company.

Clothing company, huh, I thought to myself, surprised to hear this last answer. I'd only been at Yale for a week, but already knew that most of the male athletes would go into finance. (Spoiler alert: Upon graduation, Alex went into finance.)

After class, we walked out together.

"See you tomorrow," he said, giving me a fist bump.

"*Hasta mañana,*" I said, giving him a pound back.

OVER THE COURSE OF that first semester, Alex and I slowly got to know each other better. After class, we would head to the dining hall, and as we chewed greasy, protein-packed food, I learned about his childhood: He grew up in a small beach town and had an older brother, an identical twin, and four half siblings. He loved surfing and Bruce Springsteen and drove a beat-up yellow Xterra. His mom, Ninie, had an open-house policy and cooked for everyone who walked in the door: big dinners of paella and prime rib and strawberry angel food cake with hand-beaten whipped cream. His dad, Roger, was a charismatic and handsome entrepreneur who wore impeccable custom suits during the week and colorful Hawaiian shirts on the weekend. He loved sports and Sea Breeze cocktails and never talked about his feelings.

"There was a lot of fighting at home," Alex said.

"That must have been hard," I said, waiting for him to say more.

He didn't. Instead, he shrugged.

I thought comparatively about my childhood. We were not fighters in our family, which didn't mean we didn't have disagreements, but rather that most things simply weren't discussed. When my brilliant and witty brother, Brendan, started getting brain freezes—a mental paralysis that made it impossible for him to finish his homework and surely related to the pressure to get into a great college—the word "depression" was whispered between my parents but then dismissed.

"Don't say anything to anyone," my dad said to me one night as I heard Brendan sobbing from the next room over. I agreed to keep the secret. But later that night, I brought Brendan a slice of American cheese and a glass of ice water—the way he always did for me growing up—and asked him how I could help.

When my sister, Shannon, started throwing up after she ate, my mom asked me what to do. "I don't know, Mom," I said. "I'm fifteen."

"Please don't talk about it at school," she added before ending the conversation, and I agreed. But later that night I knocked on Shannon's door, offered to clean her room, and asked her how I could help. Several years later, when I finally confided in my parents that I was worried Shannon was struggling with addiction, I was again asked not to talk about it with anyone.

When my dad got cancer and had to get weekly radiology treatments at the hospital, he made my mom swear to not tell my siblings and me. My mom promised to keep his illness a secret, which she did, even abiding by his request to not wait in the waiting room as he got his treatment. Heaven forbid someone recognize her. It wasn't until years later that my sister read one of my mom's journals and confronted her and my dad about the discovery (*Hello, Dad, you had cancer?!*). My dad dismissed the fact that it was a big deal, saying, "I didn't want to worry you all. And you don't need to tell anyone about it."

Secrets. Secrets. Secrets.

I learned pretty quickly growing up, both in the pews of the Catholic church we attended every Sunday and within the walls of our suburban Buffalo home, that some parts of ourselves were *good* and made to be shared, and some parts were *not good* and meant to be hidden. Parts like depression, addiction, lust, anger, sadness, or sickness were off the table for discussion. The word "shame" was never spoken, but even as a kid, I learned what it felt like to be buried in the body: sticky, blood red, and solid. It wasn't a conscious decision, but somewhere along the line I decided to be the sibling who was always fine. I wouldn't burden anyone with my needs or wants. I'd be better than fine: I would be successful! Happy! Helpful! Need-free! Selfless!

I did not tell Alex any of this over our scrambled eggs, of course. Instead, I changed the subject to sports and told him what I thought was a funny story about how my high school basketball coach called me by the wrong name for four years: "Terry."

"You let him call you by the wrong name?" Alex asked, incredulous.

"I think he liked calling me Terry," I said laughing, "because it went so well with 'Terrible, Terry, terrible,' which he said every time I missed a layup. And I missed a lot of them."

Alex laughed. "Talk about being easygoing," he said.

I smiled at the compliment. It was true that I didn't take things personally. I went with the flow.

"Easygoing and a subpar basketball player," I added.

Alex laughed again, and then gazed a little more deeply into my eyes. "Do you know that I don't have any friends who are girls?"

"Am I your friend?" I asked.

"First one," he said, smiling.

"Lucky me," I responded, my stomach flipping.

SO I KNEW ALEX liked me as a friend, but I couldn't tell if he found me attractive or not.

When I was growing up, my mom found obsession with beauty boring, which to this day I'm deeply grateful for but which put me at a disadvantage in terms of knowing the requisite commodification of a college woman's sex appeal. The only beauty products in my childhood house were unwaxed floss, economy-size jars of Vaseline, Nair hair-removal cream, and Jolen bleach that I used on my upper lip and occasionally in my hair for a DIY highlight. While most teenage girls spritzed their skin with the 1990s signature scent Cool Water, I used Coppertone sunscreen as my coconutty perfume, slathering it on in the winter to smell like a tropical breeze. Sometimes I frequented an indoor tanning bed, but this was less about getting tan (which my pale Irish skin never did) and more of a desperate attempt to combat seasonal affective disorder during Buffalo's seven-month-long winters. Apart from these things, I didn't spend much time thinking about how I looked. I did not pluck my eyebrows or the scraggly hair around my nipples; I didn't moisturize my legs, trim my pubic hair, or wear makeup.

But a few months into that college freshman year, my roommates and I learned that in order to be hot and wanted, you needed to look a certain way. We replaced our chino pants and V-neck T-shirts with "going-out outfits": a uniform made up of shiny and skimpy and flammable clothing like polyester halter and tube tops, tight, stretchy jean skirts, and large fake-gold hoops from Claire's that would undoubtedly turn our earlobes green. We sported smoky eyes, blond highlights, and bare legs—even in freezing temperatures—and wrapped our fingers around red Solo cups full of vodka and packets of calorie-free Crystal Light. We carried fake IDs and fake confidence.

On Wednesday and Saturday nights, my friends and I frequented a New Haven bar called Toad's Place, which was known for its signature acrid odor of stale beer and piss. Too lazy to leave their perches at the bar, many male athletes just unzipped their flies under their stool and let it rip. These were some of the same men who gathered during fraternity rush week, around a fountain honoring the first class of women students, to chant, "No means yes, and yes means anal."

Rape culture was not only out in the open but celebrated, and while, yes, my friends and I found it disgusting and outrageous, it was also the dirty water we swam in. We squealed when R. Kelly's notorious signature song "Ignition" came over the loudspeakers, despite hearing the rumors that he pissed on and trafficked young girls. One particular night, there was an art installation on campus where sexual assault survivors hung T-shirts on a clothesline that shared their stories of abuse, and a group of male athletes ripped the T-shirts off the line and mockingly and pridefully wore them out to the bar. We had heard that Ivy League men were the nation's best and brightest, but I was beginning to wonder about the standards for measuring such things.

Looking back, I see now that the message we were getting from the media and music and clothing industries and the men at our prestigious Ivy League school was that women were made for men's consumption. And yet each night my friends and I went out, we waited to be chosen, hoping that one of our crushes—even if he was toxic and obnoxious—would buy us a one-dollar beer or a vodka soda. Hoping we were worthy.

ALEX AND I STARTED dating early in our sophomore year. Over our freshman year summer, we had occasionally emailed: I filled him in on my lacrosse coaching gig and my wakeboarding escapades, and he told me how he was making a killing buying discounted velour sweatpants at Marshalls and then upselling them on eBay. (Truly a burgeoning fashion CEO in the making.) He signed off one of his emails with a "miss ya!" and that's when I knew: We were 100 percent going to fall in love.

Our first make-out in college happened after a night out at Toad's (of course). On my dorm room single bed, I undressed for Alex like I had seen in the movies: making serious eye contact while taking off my shirt to the background beat of Mariah Carey's "Always Be My Baby." As I fumbled to unclasp my bra, Alex asked me curiously why my bra and underwear didn't match. I looked down at my Victoria's Secret pink polka-dotted full-coverage underwear and my white stretchy Gap Body bra. I knew socks should match. But underwear? I made a note to myself to invest in black padded bras with matching black polyester thongs whose lace would undoubtedly make my labia itch.

As the make-out turned hotter and heavier, Alex made a comment that confused me.

"Say that again?" I asked, my underwear around my ankles.

"That's a lot of hair down there," he said sheepishly, maybe even with concern.

"Oh!" I said in surprise. Clearly, I had missed a memo. "Thank you for telling me."

THE NEXT DAY AFTER lacrosse practice, I studied my teammates' naked bodies in the locker room shower, where sixteen of us at once cleaned up after workouts and scrimmages. Candidly, I can now say that that locker room was more educational than all Ivy League college curriculum. It was where secrets were revealed through the steam: who was sleeping with their teaching assistant, which frat guys were still in the closet, and how much sugar was in the cafeteria's homemade granola. We didn't usually discuss calories, but there's no doubt that most of us compulsively thought about them. Our female coach often commented on our bodies, and while we were supposed to be strong, as evidenced by our deadweight lifting routine, we were also supposed to be slim. "Look good, play good" was the unofficial motto of the team, and while many of us recited it jokingly, there was an underlying truth at hand. I was already waking to the particular cruelty of the conflicting expectations that female athletes should be physically strong to succeed on the field and physically small to be worthy of the male gaze. Many of the girls on my team developed eating disorders.

Per Alex's feedback, as my teammates and I stood naked, washing the sweat off our bodies in the stall-less, open shower, I assessed the diversity of vaginal decor. I had never been aware of the vast possibilities of pubic grooming: There was the bikini wax, the Brazilian wax, the full wax, the trimmed and shaved, the just trimmed, the shaved with red bumps, and the all-natural. I suspected that a woman's vaginal maintenance correlated with personality type, but I couldn't quite articulate how.

I looked down at my own unruly hairs coiled like soft, wiry weeds spreading from my vulva toward my inner thighs and stretching up toward my belly button. Naturally expansive and messy. *Oh my god,* I thought to myself. *I am too much* woman. Of course, I had seen myself naked in the mirror thousands of times, but I had never studied my own womanhood in contrast to others'. In high school, my friends and I were coy and strategic when we changed, so as not to flash our familiar female private parts. Embarrassing! The only exception to this was before one of my basketball games when I was unable to figure out how to put in a tampon, and a teammate had knelt down below me as I sat wide legged on the toilet. "You are not playing with a maxi pad," she said, inserting a paper Tampax up my vagina with two fingers. "We're wearing white uniforms, for God's sake."

When I got home from lacrosse practice that night, I took my nail scissors into a bathroom stall, straddled the toilet, and slowly snipped away the long curls of hair I'd accumulated since I was fourteen, forming a close-to-the-skin, highly trimmed goatee. It felt symbolic of something, a rite of passage to the new version of me, one that was up to the standard of socially acceptable beauty.

~

A FEW NIGHTS LATER, I whispered, "I think I'm ready," in Alex's ear. The admission that I was finally ready to have sex made me nervous. While we were growing up, after our third teenage babysitter got pregnant, my mom had warned my siblings and me that "sex is fun, but not *that fun*," and thereafter often repeated catchy sayings to encourage abstinence: "No ringy, no dingy," she would say, holding out her ring finger. "No glove, no love!" she'd yell out the car window as she dropped me off at a friend's house, while making a fist and pretending to put a condom over it.

"Okay, Mom!" I would yell back, noting that lust and pleasure came with insurmountable risks. The word "abortion" was never uttered.

"Are you sure?" Alex asked, wide-eyed and hopeful upon hearing me assert my readiness.

I nodded. While bracing for impact, I prayed to baby Jesus that I wouldn't bleed. Though monthly bleeding was the most guaranteed fact of having a uterus, bleeding was *gross*. At least that's what we were taught. It was why I always *whispered* when I needed a tampon; why I snuck that tampon inside the cuff of my sleeve on the way to the bathroom; and why I lowered my eyes at CVS when the cashier put my tampons in a nondescript paper bag. Menstruation was a crime—all evidence of bleeding must be hidden. I wasn't menstruating now, but I knew that virgins often bled. I hoped that the three horseback riding classes I took when I was thirteen (before I realized I was allergic to hay) had broken my hymen.

When it was over, I felt a deep relief wash over me: I had crossed the threshold with a man who cared about consent and my feelings, a celebratory feat in the college market. I was no longer a virgin.

"I literally waited years for that?" I asked as he lay on top of me, our breathing synchronizing between our chests. And then we burst out laughing. I lay on my side as Alex wrapped his arms around me from behind. "It gets better," he promised.

Then, with my back nestled into his chest, I heard him whisper, "I think I love you."

My eyebrows rose, and my mouth opened in happy surprise. But before I could say anything back, he shot out of the bed.

"I can't believe I just said that. I need to take a walk," he said, starting to put on his clothes. He looked pale. I could see the panic constricting his throat. He was having feelings, and they overwhelmed him, making him feel like he needed to flee. I offered to come with him, but he told me to stay back. He returned fifteen minutes later, less pale, although still sweaty, and crawled back in bed.

"Do you feel better?" I asked sleepily. I had fallen asleep in his absence.

"Yeah, thanks," he said.

"I love you too," I added with certainty, touching my head to his forehead.

THE SUMMER AFTER OUR sophomore year, Alex came to visit me at our family summer cottage on the shores of Lake Erie in Canada. The cottage was my happy place, where I'd spent long summer days tubing, sucking back freeze pops, and eating s'mores around a bonfire with my thirteen cousins while our grandparents led sing-alongs of Irish trad music. It is where I realized I had a "fun" family, who indulged in day drinking and night drinking and late-night dance parties in the kitchen. (Years later, I'd learn that—surprise!—a lot of the so-called family ragers were actually familial symptoms of alcoholism.) The cottage was also where I learned that I could kill things: catching baby toads with my hands, placing them in neon pink plastic buckets, saran-wrapping the top, and waking up to find them dead. It was where I captured fireflies and put them in mason jars and watched their light fade away. It was where I plucked the feathers off the carcasses of dead seagulls and put them in cotton bags to make my own homemade pillows. (I realize now that this is a deeply disturbing and problematic health concern.) It was also where I found washed-up treasures, spending hours walking up and down the beach looking for sea glass—browns, greens, whites, occasionally a blue, and, only once, a yellow.

On the first night of his visit, my siblings told Alex stories about me from childhood. Shannon recounted how I once dug a four-foot-deep hole, made her sit in it, buried her up to her neck with sand so she couldn't move, and then ran away, leaving her stuck there. She shared how I used to make her drink "refreshing potions" made from Coke, hot sauce, toothpaste, ketchup, and pickle juice, and how I loved cruel pranks like donning a ski mask and peeling in and out of my friends' driveways while they were home alone.

Brendan shared a story about the mudpuppies. In 1996, he had spotted something in the lake that looked peculiar: a bloated-looking fish with feet. Given that he had a photographic memory and could name every dinosaur according to their respective extinction dates, he thought this dead specimen was a significant scientific find. He scooped it into a mason jar filled with rubbing alcohol and made our dad drive us to the Buffalo History Museum. "We found the missing link," we said solemnly to the receptionist.

"This is a dead mudpuppy," she said, pushing the mason jar back at us. The next day, we found more washed ashore. And then more: hundreds of decomposing mudpuppies dotting the shore. My brother told Alex how I had methodically dissected one rubbery stomach after another with a plastic butter knife to try to diagnose what had killed them. (My conclusion? Poisonous pollutants of course.) And then, to ensure they had a proper, dignified funeral, I stacked them in a huge hole, covered them up with sand, then spelled out *RIP* with small rocks on top to mark the burial ground.

"Gross," Alex said matter-of-factly. He didn't know that ten years later we would get married right over that mass mudpuppy grave.

"Kerry has a dark side," Shannon warned.

"But she's a great lacrosse player!" my dad caveated. He was notorious for inserting my accomplishments into conversations, reciting non sequiturs and unimportant statistics from high school basketball games or recalling how many ground balls I had at a national lacrosse tournament. He was a supportive dad!

"When Kerry was a child, *she was very, very good, and when she was bad, she was horrid,*" my mom chimed in, alluding to the infamous Henry Wadsworth Longfellow poem.

"Wow, thanks, everyone, for the kind words," I said. "I'm so glad Alex knows this side of me now."

"I'll sleep with one eye open," Alex said, laughing, and everyone else laughed too. I could already tell he got the Docherty stamp of approval.

My family wasn't wrong, however, to warn Alex about my dark side. I always felt as if there were two of me, at odds at all times, competing for different needs and interests. One side was sunshiny, optimistic, extroverted, obedient, and ambitious, and the other one was cynical, rebellious, slightly reclusive, and morbid. I had always been obsessed with death, inventorying the names of every dead person I knew before I went to bed at night and writing different versions of my obituary every year since I was twelve. I filled my childhood journal—written from within my safe and privileged bedroom walls—with ruminations on hard life experiences I never endured. I wrote poems with titles like "Alone in a Prison Cell," "The End of the World," "Why, Why, Why?," and "When Papa Comes Home," a sonnet about an abusive father. When my poems were proudly displayed on the walls of my seventh-grade classroom, my dad expressed embarrassment at Parent Night: "Ker, you are sunshine. Why are you writing and sharing poems like this?"

I didn't answer what I now know to be true: that even sunshine burns the skin.

OUR LAST NIGHT IN Canada, before Alex and I crawled into my sandy, squeaky single bed, Alex scanned my bookshelf filled with collected sea glass, bleached animal skulls, and several books from the Chicken Soup for the Soul series—anthologies about how small acts of kindness can change the world. He then pulled out a book titled *In a Dark, Dark*

Room and Other Scary Stories, which, per the title, featured spooky parables.

"Read 'The Green Ribbon,'" I said as he flipped through the pages.

"What's that?" Alex asked.

"You don't know 'The Green Ribbon'?" I said, aghast. I questioned whether I could date someone whose Rolodex of scary stories was so limited. Was he cultured enough for me?

"Nope," he said.

I recounted the story about a girl named Jenny, who, for as long as anyone could remember, wore a green ribbon around her neck. Jenny later met a boy named Alfred, and Alfred wanted to know why she wore the ribbon, but she refused to tell him. Even after they got married, she wouldn't say a word. *Tell me, tell me why you wear it,* Alfred would plead. *When the time is right,* Jenny would respond.

It was not until Jenny was on her deathbed, old and frail, that she let Alfred untie the ribbon . . . and her head fell off.

Oh, how I jumped in glee at this surprise ending. There was so much I loved about the story: that Jenny kept the secret all those years—both taunting and visible around her neck—an obvious reminder that there was a part of her that remained unknowable to the person she loved most. A secret that she was, quite literally, holding on to by a thread. I wondered then, even as a child, if each of us carried hidden aspects of ourselves that could never be fully understood by others; if we needed to disguise the most seemingly scary parts of ourselves for the comfort of the people we loved.

Why hadn't Jenny told Alfred the truth about such a key part of her identity? Did she, herself, know the truth of why she wore it? She must have. Was she selfish for not sharing the reality of her situation? Or was she selfless for not burdening

Alfred with her fragility? Did Alfred feel betrayed when he found out? Would he have married her if he knew? How brave Jenny was to harbor a secret for so long. And how heartbreaking that she never felt safe to share the truth of who she really was to those around her.

I let Alex process the punch line about her head falling off, watching his face closely to see if I could tell what he was thinking. His eyebrows furrowed, and his lips pursed into a grimace.

"Creepy," he said.

"Totally," I confirmed in satisfaction.

ALL IN ALL, ALEX was a great college boyfriend: He was kind, empathetic, and rarely moody. We laughed a lot. We danced a lot. We loved spending time together. He seldom annoyed me, which was a rarity, because though I loved people deeply, I also got very sick of them. Alex didn't ask for much and didn't appear to have many needs, which was convenient because it meant I didn't have to attend to them. He reminded me of my dad in that way: always deferring to whatever others wanted. He scratched my back before I went to bed, brought me coffee in the library, and volunteered to be the ball boy at my lacrosse games. I, in turn, cleaned his room on a weekly basis, removed Gatorade bottles from his bedside filled with yellow piss from the night before, and joined him and his football friends at their weekly all-you-can-eat Chinese food buffet dinners.

One night after dinner, Alex told me that he didn't want his future wife to work: "I loved having a mom who did everything for us: who cooked dinner each night, made pancakes in the morning, helped us with our homework, and came to all our games." I knew what he meant, because my mom did the same. Yet as he shared this, I burst into tears: It was an expectation that suffocated the possibility of what it would be like to be his wife. I loved my mom but didn't want her life. Should you break up with your college boyfriend because maybe in ten years you'd have different ideas of the roles a spouse should play in a marriage?

One Valentine's Day, I wrote him a five-page rhyming poem that chronicled our favorite memories: road-tripping to South Carolina, pranking each other, tubing in Lake Erie, and spending long mornings in bed playing the game DSquaredS (aka Deepest Darkest Secrets). In return, he got me a card with Barney the Dinosaur on the front that said "Te Amo" on the inside. He left it unsigned. "You didn't write in it," I said, laughing, when I opened it, blinded by the white blank space of unsaid adorations.

"I didn't need to," he said. "'Te amo' sums it up."

"Classic," I said with a twinge of disappointment, but grateful that at least he gave me a card. Some men didn't give cards. Our relationship wasn't particularly romantic anyway, I justified. We were best friends who got to sleep together: a deep reciprocity of love and support. Maybe romance was overrated.

SENIOR YEAR, DAYS BEFORE graduation, I told Alex that I could see us being together for a long time.

"Maybe forever?" he asked.

"Maybe forever," I said.

Two

"We need to sell more clothes," Alex said when I walked into the small art studio, slightly panting from the effort of walking up five flights of stairs. I was holding two cold brews—one for him, one for Mike. Alex's eyes were locked on an Excel spreadsheet and his fingers moved across the keyboard of his PC swiftly, like a pianist playing a sonata. *Clickity clack clickity clickity clack,* CTRL + C3 = AGGREGATE SUM.

"'Sell more clothes' is the mantra for the rest of your life," I said, handing Alex his coffee, but not before I sucked down a shot of it for myself. I was tired from a day of teaching meditation workshops, zigzagging under the city on the subway to a law firm, a home on the Upper West Side, an all-boys school on the Upper East Side, and then finally to an all-girls charter school on the Lower East Side. All that breathing and focusing on the breath and being present. Shouldn't I be enlightened by now?

I hadn't initially planned on teaching mindfulness full time. After college, and to deal with my own stress during law school, I signed up for mindfulness classes at UCLA's Mindful Awareness Research Center, where I sat in a room with strangers and learned to pay attention to my breath and my thoughts and ask myself questions like *What am I noticing in my body right here, right now?* It was the first time I started to notice how feelings *actually felt* in my body: soft or hot, piercing or tight, pulsating or relaxed; I began to sense the color, the shape, the texture of how emotions manifested in physical form. It was also the first time I noticed the flavor of the mind between thoughts. What was it like to sit and wait for a thought, to observe that thought, and then to let it pass by like a cloud wafting across the sky?

Following law school, I got a clerkship with a federal judge in Brooklyn and one day the judge asked me to teach mindfulness to a group of nonviolent criminal offenders, many still in their teenage years, who were part of a program that provided an alternative to incarceration if the participants completed vocational, mental health, and drug treatment offerings.

When I took a seat at the large conference table in the courtroom and asked the group if anyone had ever meditated, one of the boys told me he had met the Dalai Lama years ago in a youth program that he was in. "I got to shake his hand," he said.

I reached across the table with my palms open, and he put his warm palms on mine. "Thank you," I said, giving his hands a squeeze. "Looks like through you, I too have touched the Dalai Lama's hand." He squeezed back.

I guided the group through some simple breathing exercises, and before we ended, we did a loving-kindness meditation where we recited, *May I be healthy, may I be happy, may I be free of worry, may I have peace.* When I opened my eyes, all of our faces, including mine, were wet with tears. I wanted to stay with them and hear their stories: to ask what it felt like to be them, what they dreamed of at night, and who was the cause of their mothers' suffering. But our time was up. When I walked back into chambers, I dragged my half-written applications to law firms into the trash folder. I appreciated the importance of legal advocacy, but I didn't want to spend my time sitting behind a desk writing legal opinions anymore. I wanted to sit side by side with people in pain and collectively find ways of fostering healing.

A few months after my clerkship ended, I officially launched my mindfulness coaching business offering simple, practical, and ancient tools to return to our bodies in a way that lowered stress. I taught classes at charter schools, law firms, and tech start-ups, and built curriculums for colleges and courts. Regardless of who I spent time with, it was always the same conversation: *How are you doing? How do you know? And what does the breath feel like in your body?*

I HELD OUT THE second cold brew for Mike.

"Mike, here's yours." I had to say it three times before he grabbed it, his back turned away from me, deep in thought as he stared at the floor-to-ceiling mood board he had created. Smack in the middle of the wall was a large Faherty Brand logo composed of a sun and waves with "Clothing for Life's Great Moments" handwritten below it. Surrounding the logo were photos of girls in bikinis licking Popsicles and surfers catching waves and French women in striped linen shirts; there were also a few wicker hats, fabric swatches of 1940s work-wear denim, sun-washed tees, a pair of kids' overalls, and a Peruvian sweater pinned to the wall. A few Native-looking blankets were draped over a wooden hanger. A sample hangtag read "A Guarantee of Quality: If you don't see the sun and waves, you're not getting the best."

Mike put down the cold brew and picked up an indigo swatch and massaged it through his hand, feeling the weight of it, the wash, and the hand feel of its texture. He obsessed over garments the way chefs obsess over ingredients, and I knew that level of obsession often yielded one-of-a-kind fabrics you wanted to rub on your cheek.

"Wow, coming together," I said, thoroughly impressed by how the brand concept was taking shape. The idea for Faherty had started decades back when Alex and Mike were two young towheaded surfers on the Jersey Shore. Mike always had a knack for style, setting Alex's clothes out each morning for him and studying their dad's tailored suits and custom ties, noticing the weight of the perfect cashmere sweater, the silk lining of a suit, the slight stretch of a pant, and a perfectly finished seam.

When it came time to apply to college, Mike wrote his application essay on starting a clothing brand that offered laid-back surf styles in beautiful, high-end, sustainable fabrics. He went on to attend Washington University, where he majored in fashion design and played basketball, alternating between early mornings at the gym and long evenings sewing women's dresses. His first job out of college was at Ralph Lauren, where he spent the next ten years learning the ins and outs of fashion design and manufacturing. Alex meanwhile spent the ten years after Yale in private equity, learning the financial expertise necessary to run a business.

Soon after Alex and Mike both quit their jobs, Faherty Brand became a real company in that there was an official website and a makeshift warehouse (aka a former indoor lacrosse rink) that the boys' mom, Ninie, set up as a shipping facility complete with metal shelves, a printer for UPS labels, and baskets of bikinis and board shorts. Ninie and a friend now spent their afternoons following Mike's extensive instructions for packaging every order: Each bathing suit was to be wrapped in thin tissue paper with a hand-drawn map on it and then placed in a reusable blue tote shipping bag with one of three beautiful postcards. Given that we had no formal customer service department, Alex had now personally received countless emails from customers stating they received the wrong string bikini.

"Mom," Alex had said, "you have to read the labels better."

This comment had made Ninie angry. "This is your fault. If you didn't make so many different styles and prints, it would be easier to fulfill the orders correctly."

She had a point. It was true we had too many styles. We also had *too* many units of *too* many styles. Months before, again while looking at an Excel spreadsheet, Alex had asked Mike and me how many units we should make for our women's swim order. I had thought about this for a moment. There were a lot of people in the world. Things went viral all the time. Mike had designed some great bold prints in saturated colors that were good quality and made from low-impact materials like recycled polyester. We knew a lot of people. How hard could it be to sell bathing suits?

"Maybe, like, ten thousand?" I suggested. Mike agreed.

"Yeah, that sounds right," Alex said.

This was our first major mistake, one that would continue to haunt us. We had ordered too much inventory. Way too much inventory. Despite the fact that a month after the launch Faherty had garnered some great press with features in *Vogue, Harper's Bazaar,* and *InStyle,* we still had 9,457 remaining bathing suits to sell. To this day we still have string bikinis left from that initial order hidden in every crevice of every drawer in our basement.

Mike took another swig of his cold brew. "Thanks, Ker. Needed this. Gonna be a long night."

I sighed, knowing that once again I would walk home to our empty apartment as Alex and Mike continued working. *Our* apartment, meaning Alex's, Mike's, and mine, now that we all lived together.

TWO WEEKS AFTER OUR wedding over the mudpuppy grave, and months before Faherty Brand became official, Alex and I moved into a small two-bedroom apartment in Alphabet City *with* Mike.

"Is this a twin thing?" my mom asked, concerned.

"Interesting choice," my therapist, Colleen, said when she found out. She had just gotten her license and charged only half the market rate, but she was already annoying me, sitting cross-legged in her chair and sipping loudly out of a large reusable water bottle straw that made a whizzing sound when she sucked the water through her pursed lips.

"It makes sense financially," I had said, minimizing this strange newlywed living configuration and regurgitating Alex's reasoning. Alex was using his private-equity savings to pay

Mike's bills, and while my mindfulness business was growing quickly, it wasn't growing quickly enough to cover my portion of the rent, which meant that Alex was providing for both Mike and me. Now that I mention it, Alex was helping Ninie out financially too.

Right after he graduated from college, Alex's parents suddenly separated after thirty years of marriage. Alex nominated himself to take over the financial needs of the family and helped Ninie buy a house in a small town on the Jersey Shore, which meant his roster of financially dependent people amounted to three.

Colleen took another sip from her straw, which made the ice clank in the bottle. I shuddered.

"Marriage signifies the start of you and Alex starting your *own* family," Colleen said. "A time to focus on *your* partnership and build new ways of doing things outside your family of origin. There must be boundaries."

"It is what it is," I said, shrugging.

I TRIED TO MAKE our newlywed *Three's Company* situation work, making a home for Mike, Alex, and me in our small East Village apartment. I made dinners most nights, grocery shopped at Trader Joe's, packed kale salads for them to take to the office, and decorated Mike's bedroom walls so it didn't look like a frat room. I threw away the used contact lenses that they flung from their corneas onto the carpet. I washed their dirty, sweaty tees and socks, rinsed and recycled their coconut water cartons, and put the caps on their toothpaste. I washed their dirty pots and pans when they drunkenly made gluten-free mac and cheese after a night out. And I occasionally made breakfast in the morning for the girl that Mike was dating. *Would you like avocado or peanut butter toast?* I'd ask hospitably, holding out her breakfast as she tiredly wiped her smeared eyeliner onto the back of her hand.

At night, the three of us would all watch shows together: *Friday Night Lights, Nashville, Anthony Bourdain: Parts Unknown.* One night we watched the psychological thriller *Gone Girl,* in which a doting wife mysteriously disappears on her fifth wedding anniversary. Spoiler alert: The wife had arranged for her disappearance to look like a murder, while setting up her husband for the crime. She returns weeks later, after having an affair with a bad ex-boyfriend.

"You remind me of the wife," Mike said when it ended. I couldn't tell if he was joking.

"Thank you so much?" I said, unsure if he was referencing that I too was white and blond or that I too was manipulative and psychopathic.

Anyway, I was a very good wife. To two men, no less! Whenever people would ask what it was like being married, I would refer to Alex—my husband—as "they/them" to be inclusive of Mike.

~

AS MIKE AND ALEX finished their cold brews and I cringed at the sound of Alex chewing his ice, I listened to them plan their upcoming monthlong cross-country Faherty road trip. Mike had been inspired by the food truck movement and recently commissioned a store on wheels, essentially a tiny wooden beach house that sat on the flatbed of a semitruck. It opened up on hydraulics into a twenty-by-twenty-foot fully functioning pop-up shop, replete with shelves and hanging racks, a sound system, rotating fans, solar panels, and wifi. The Mobile Beach House, as we called it, was officially Faherty's first store. Everyone had been telling Alex and Mike that brick-and-mortar storefronts were dead, that a "DTC" (direct-to-consumer) online strategy was the best: *Sell online! Sell online!* But how was anyone going to find our clothing on the World Wide Web? If someone searched "bathing suit" or "casual clothing company," Faherty wouldn't be found until page 845, and no one scrolled past the first pages of Google. So yes, we could market online, but avenues for that were very, very expensive. Intuitively, Mike wanted to have a store where people could touch the clothes, feel the fabrics, and learn first-hand about the brand's backstory. Which was why Alex and Mike were now planning to take the Mobile Beach House across the country for a month.

"What's the itinerary for the tour?" I asked, grabbing a vintage pillow from the oversize chair that sat in the corner of the studio and pulling out one baby bird feather after another from it. It was a nervous habit.

"New York City, D.C., Virginia Beach, Charleston, Atlanta, Dallas, maybe Phoenix, San Diego, LA, San Francisco, then back," Alex said. "And anywhere else along the way where we can open the trailer and sell clothes."

"Should I come with you?" I asked, surprised by the tremble in my own voice.

I don't know why I was so nervous to ask this. I hadn't admitted to Alex yet how much FOMO I had watching him and Mike spend hours building something together. Teaching mindfulness was rewarding but lonely. I had no cofounder to bounce ideas off of. No one to help me cocreate a marketing plan or help me run the business. And I felt awkward having to constantly promote myself, specifically around "selling" meditation—a practice that was so sacred to me. Plus, although I loved talking about other people's feelings, a lot of my mindfulness sessions had turned into straight-up therapy sessions, which drained me emotionally.

Selling clothing felt less personal, less serious, and more fun.

And, if I went one step deeper, I was starting to feel disconnected from Alex, which worried me so soon into our marriage. Alex and Mike were in their own entrepreneurial world, and I was by myself in my meditative one.

I thought of the Sunday before as an example: Mike and Alex had run to the East River track for a workout of burpees and sprints, met their friends for brunch, and then gone to the local sports bar to drink copious amounts of a drink named Transfusion, made of vodka, 7UP, and grape juice. Meanwhile, I had spent the morning at the progressive Middle Church's antiracism workshop listening to Dr. Jacqui Lewis lecture on radical love and righteous anger, read a few chapters of *Confessions of an Economic Hit Man* for my human rights book club, worked on my mindfulness blog, and then met Alex at the bar before fleeing ten minutes later. The noise at the bar alone was a recipe for a panic attack: competing sports broadcasters on the TVs, "Sex on Fire" blaring over the speakers, draft beer glasses clanking, and boozy-breathed small talk. I didn't like noise. I didn't like crowded rooms. I didn't like small talk. And I certainly didn't like small talk with people who I could barely hear and who were three drinks deep. I hadn't yet psychoanalyzed how my sister's struggle with alcohol in college instantly put me into a fight-or-flight response around drunk people, but that was certainly a contributing factor to my panic.

"I gotta get out of here," I shouted into the ear of the girl next to me.

"I wish I could leave too," she shouted back, a pang of desperation in her eyes that I interpreted as *don't leave me.*

"Why can't you leave?" I asked, throwing my vintage XL Buffalo Bills sweatshirt over my head and putting down my half-drunk beer on the sticky table.

"I don't want to disappoint him." She nodded her head to her boyfriend, whose eyes were locked on the screen over the bar. I knew with utmost certainty he would not notice she was gone until the game was over, but I didn't say that. I also suspected that she was clearly disappointing herself in choosing to stay.

"Good luck," I said, pulling her in for a hug, and then yelled across to Alex, "I'm out! Sorry to be a fun assassin."

"Ker's a fun assassin!" someone yelled after me, repeating my own insult as if it were his own, as unoriginal as he was loud. I found the best way to quell people's persuasions to not leave a party was to make fun of yourself before someone else did. It always worked.

Alex's eyes turned downward as I waved goodbye. I knew he didn't want me to leave, and yet I had been leaving his friends' social settings with increasing frequency. "Why don't you come? All the other girlfriends will be there," he would ask, time and time again, as I politely declined an invite to another party.

"Because I don't *want* to," I would respond. That was a good enough reason, wasn't it?

I grabbed my leather tote, blew Alex a kiss from across the bar, and mouthed to him, "Sorry. Love you." He waved disappointedly back.

On my walk back to the apartment, I stopped at a coffee shop to write in my journal, picked up some fresh flowers, and then once home, watered my plants, ordered gluten-filled takeout, and later crawled into bed by myself.

I didn't want to be living in separate worlds so soon after our marriage.

"Should I come with you guys on the trailer tour?" I asked Alex again, as I rubbed the plucked feather from the pillow between my thumb and index finger.

"If you want to, Ker," Al said, eyes widening as he looked back at me. Were his eyes hopeful? I couldn't tell if he was trying to play it cool and wanted me to come on the tour with Mike and him or if he honestly didn't care if I joined them.

"I'll decide tomorrow," I said, fluffing the pillow back to its shape and giving Alex a kiss on the forehead before walking out alone. It was starting to get dark, and I already had an appointment on the books for the next day that I knew would be, shall we say, *informative.*

~

MY MOM TAUGHT ME at a fairly young age that when in doubt—when you needed advice—there were two places to turn: Oprah or a psychic. Maybe in my early years it would have been Jesus too, but somehow every time we left Sunday Catholic church as a family, we were worse off than we came. We'd pack into the car, Brendan would withdraw into his Game Boy, Shannon would start hitting me, I would yell, "*I am Gandhi, I practice nonviolence,*" which would make her hit me more, which then would make my mom yell, "*We just went to church, goddamnit!*" Meanwhile, my dad zoned out as he loudly chewed his glazed donut (a sound that did actually make me want to be violent).

I noticed my mom's inclination of leaning on psychics soon

after she returned home from India. When I was finishing high school, my mom announced to the family that she was going to go to Allahabad for a month to become a certified yoga teacher. She was ahead of her time as far as white America was concerned: long before yoga studios and lululemons were on every corner. We had all been quite shocked when she made the announcement, but even more shocked by the length of time. She would be gone for a month? A whole month?

The first thing I asked was "What's Dad going to do?"

"I really don't care. He'll be fine," she said.

Up until then, I had only seen my mom as a *mom*. That was her identity. And she was good at it. She made dinners in dependable rotation: mashed potatoes and chicken, mashed potatoes and meatloaf, spaghetti with Prego, and chicken fettuccine Alfredo with a side of sliced cucumbers. She dropped us off and picked us up from school every day. Our laundry was always crisply folded. Except for the designated messy drawer, our whole house was organized and tidy. She didn't have needs outside of the family as far as we knew, so when she said she was going to go away for a month to pursue something *she* wanted to do, we were supportive but confused. She hadn't even asked our permission. She just stated her intent.

When she returned, it was clear she was different. Not only because she wore mala beads around her wrists and her shoulders were toned from doing hundreds of chaturangas but also because, even to my teenage eyes, something inside of her had changed. She seemed more self-assured, self-prioritized. She replaced her John Mellencamp CDs with Krishna Das chanting CDs. She stopped dragging us to church on Sundays. She turned a small closet into her meditation room, adding just a single chair and a bookshelf. In that tiny haven, she lit incense, wrote in her journal, meditated, and read books on mindfulness. It was a small place that was hers alone.

That Christmas, she gave each of us a gratitude journal, a book on Buddhism, and an appointment with a psychic named Rebecca, who she'd been talking to herself. My dad gave us very large, framed pictures of ourselves playing sports. "Worst Christmas ever," Brendan said.

Years later I'd ask her what she and Rebecca had talked about.

She paused, debating what to share.

"She said that I have swum across a river and your dad is on the other side waving back at me, telling me he can't swim."

I laughed. That seemed accurate. My dad literally couldn't swim, which was through no fault of his own. He had grown up in a family with five brothers in a tiny home outside Pittsburgh. His dad made ends meet by being a deliveryman for a dairy product company, while his mom had stayed at home, and the cost of paying for swimming lessons was simply not an option. My siblings and I preyed on the fact that our athletic dad couldn't swim and took a sick pleasure in pushing him into the deep end of the pool and watching him panic as he doggy-paddled to the other side.

But the more I thought about the image of my mom on the riverbank, beckoning my dad over, and my dad refusing, the more I realized how symbolic it was. My dad wasn't particularly interested in exploring the depths of a spiritual life the way my mom was. He was undoubtedly kind and generous: calling everyone "my friend," making the repairman a hot cup of coffee while he fixed the AC, and never speaking a bad word about anyone. But when it came to spirituality, beyond kneeling on wooden pews on Sunday morning, he wasn't interested in philosophical or therapeutic ruminations on life, and he certainly wasn't interested in exploring his own feelings. He couldn't reach my mom's metaphorical riverbank.

"He can't swim," my mom said again with a sigh that indicated either resolution or defeat. "He simply can't swim."

A DAY AFTER SUGGESTING I might join Alex and Mike on the road, I took the A train uptown for my appointment with Constantina, a psychic who did readings in her small studio on the Upper West Side.

As I sat across from her in a sheepskin chair, patchouli incense suddenly engulfed my nostrils, and as I closed my eyes, a feather lightly tickled my cheek.

"We invite in Kerry's higher Self and the ancestors who protect her and guide her in this sacred realm," Constantina began, before breaking into a song in a language I couldn't understand.

I wondered if my great-grandma Sarah Boyle would appear. She had emigrated from Ireland and snuck across the Canadian border to Buffalo, keeping the fact that she was undocumented from her entire family for decades (secret!). Or her husband, John Reilly, whose full-time job was shoveling coal into a burning hot furnace at the industrial monstrosity of Bethlehem Steel. I hoped my great-great-grandma Annie Bond would appear, renowned in our family for being a suffragette. My mother had pinned a photo of her on the bulletin board next to our homemade chore calendar. The photograph captured Annie standing stiffly in a white dress and hat with a "Women's Vote" sash around her. Her eyes looked stoic and focused. Maybe even full of rage. Each story I heard about my ancestors helped me piece together the puzzle of myself, as if some of their hardships were encoded in parts of my body, waiting to be excavated, examined, held, and healed.

"Amen?" I said, as Constantina ended her opening invocation.

"May it be so," she said.

I opened my eyes to see Constantina's piercing blue eyes staring back at me. She had creases in her brow and around her mouth, evidence of years of knowing smiles. Yes, she was a psychic, but not just *any* psychic. She was also a feminist scholar, a professor at a well-regarded university, and the author of books on the goddesses.

"Now, what questions would you like answered?" Constantina asked, reaching for my hand and slowly turning my hammered rose gold wedding ring around my finger.

"Well," I said slowly, debating what question to ask first. "How important do you think it is to have a spiritual connection with your husband?"

"How important do you think it is?" she responded gently.

My eyes welled with tears.

"Um . . ." I didn't answer my own question but moved on to the next. "My husband and I just got married. I have a start-up, my husband has a start-up, and I feel like we're living in different worlds with different priorities and . . ." My voice cracked. *Get to the point, Ker. Ask her a practical question.* "I'm wondering if I should keep my own mindfulness business or if I should join his clothing brand."

Despite the hours and hours I'd spent meditating in order to tap into my deep and quiet inner voice of intuition, I had too many voices in my head to know which one to listen to.

There was the feminist: *Do your own thing! Be independent! Don't join your husband's company!*

The wife: *Do what's best for the two of you as a unit! Support his endeavors!*

The people-pleasing daughter: *Make Dad proud! A clothing business is more mainstream and will be more financially successful!*

And the social justice advocate: *Capitalism is extractive! Provide tools for healing!*

All of these voices sounded equally loud, and each one spoke some truth. But which one was right?

"Kerry," she said, holding both my hands together now, as if we were jointly in prayer, "Faherty is a strong-moving river, and you can try and swim against it, but the current will be too strong. Alex would never tell you he needs you, but he needs you. This may not be an either-or. Use the brand as a platform to share all the things you love for a few years. Teach mindfulness to the company. Incorporate your passion for social justice. One's gifts can be used anywhere."

I wanted so much to believe this.

"There will be twists and turns, but all will be well. Faherty will make it. There will be stress, yes, but adventure and joy are coming. I see you with a blond-haired man on a beach, and you are laughing."

"Alex has dark hair," I corrected.

She hesitated.

Closed her eyes.

Then opened them.

"Allow life to flow. The heart will guide you."

~

AS I WALKED HOME from my session with Constantina, I remembered a conversation I had had with my friend Chetan before my college graduation. A second-generation Indian American studying theater at Yale, he would later move to India and become a famous Bollywood actor and an activist focused on a wide range of social justice issues.

When I told him I was going to law school because I was interested in a career in the FBI, he interrupted me. "Here's the thing, dawg. You may be interested in that but . . . what do you *care* about?"

I had never thought about the distinction between *interest* and *care*, but regardless the question offended me. He knew me well enough to know I cared about lots of things: Hadn't my successes in college been a case in point? I was captain of our Ivy League championship lacrosse team, got great grades, was in a renowned secret society, and had a great group of friends. I cared about lots of things. Was he calling these accomplishments self-serving?

Or, wait, was he calling me selfless? Caring so much about other people's expectations of me that I didn't actually know what mattered to *me*?

I shook my head, unclear on how to respond to his question.

"What do you care about?" he asked again. "What's the thing that causes you enough grief to do something about it?"

What caused me grief? What made me want to act?

The questions took my breath away. I scanned my body and my mind for an answer—words and memories and fragile hopes flashing through me like a strobe light without yielding a recognizable silhouette.

"I don't know," I said finally, shame igniting red around my ears.

He hugged me as I approached my dorm room door. I

couldn't tell if he pitied me or if he trusted that one day I'd figure it out.

The question would haunt me for years.

What do I care about?

~

WHEN I WALKED INTO our apartment, I lit a stick of Juniper Ridge incense, letting the familiar scent calm my cortisol levels as I absorbed the information from Constantina's reading. I felt relieved to have some sort of clarity: *Join Faherty.* This was the benefit of psychics: They just told you what to do without having to do the work yourself. I loved a spiritual shortcut.

"Al, you here?" I asked.

I turned the corner to see Alex unloading groceries in the kitchen—truly one of the sexiest acts of service in a marriage. I gave him a big hug, smelling his baking soda deodorant through his slightly sweaty T-shirt.

"I'm gonna join you."

"Like, on the road trip?" His eyes were wide and hopeful.

"Yes, but more than that. I'm going to join you at Faherty full time. I can teach mindfulness on the side."

"I was too afraid to have asked you, Ker," he said, pulling me in for another hug, "but I need you. I really need you."

I would make Faherty the thing I cared about.

Three

I sat in the back middle seat of our pickup truck outside a gas station eating yet another Dairy Queen Oreo Blizzard. "Expense that shit," I had said as we went through the DQ drive-through for the third time that week. It was my go-to joke: Anything that was "expensed" was essentially free. Alex had stopped laughing at it.

"It doesn't work that way, Ker," Alex said, grimacing. He looked at how much money we spent each day, and the diesel fuel and gas station snacks and shared motel rooms for five people were adding up.

Peter, one of Alex's and Mike's friends from childhood, got back in the driver's seat with a bag of slimy carrots. "Need vegetables," he moaned as he adjusted the rearview mirror. In the passenger seat Matt Catalano, also an old friend and a well-known big-wave surf photographer, was looking through photos from the day before. We had convinced him to document the road trip, reality-TV-style. He stopped editing a photo to take a picture of me shoving a carrot in my mouth.

"It's all for the 'gram!" I said, posing, mouth open with shards of carrot on my tongue, and offering up a peace sign. Mike gave a thumbs-up into the camera too. Alex chugged a lukewarm coconut water then dropped the container onto the floor to rest alongside the wrappers of beef jerky, Faherty hangtags, and protein bars.

"I'm living in squalor," I moaned. "How much longer till Dallas?" I was having fun but was tired. We were two weeks into the trip and doing our best to meet as many people on the road as possible. Our marketing strategy was simple: hand-to-hand combat. Make everyone a potential customer. I had become a windup doll, my jaw chattering up and down as I regurgitated our Faherty Brand elevator pitch ninety-seven times a day at restaurants, small boutiques, a country fair, an outdoor bar, a friend's aunt's house. "Hi! Have you heard of the brand? Family business! We're the founders! Clothing for life's great moments! Recycled materials! Try it on!" Some days we didn't have any sales, but so long as someone new learned about the brand, it was worth it.

"Eight more hours," Alex said with his laptop open, forecasting next season's stretch terry pants order. Mike had fallen asleep with his head on the window, a used pair of socks sandwiched between his ear and the glass as a makeshift pillow. An indie folk song about whiskey and mountains and rivers pulsated through the truck's speakers. It made me feel emo. I stared through the windshield at the double yellow line ahead of me, then saw a white cross on the side of the road. Another homemade shrine: someone's name with the date of death handwritten in permanent marker; plastic flowers wrapped around the wooden cross. A public plea to not forget. That the person they loved mattered.

I'd counted forty-four shrines on the trip so far.

Every highway was a graveyard.

THE NEXT MORNING, I sat on the open side of the trailer in the middle of downtown Dallas, my underwear hot and swampy from the humidity. The rest of the team was getting their second iced coffees of the day, and it was only 10:00 A.M. I watched the natural indigo on one of our men's polos slowly drip a trail of blue down the wooden hanging fixture. I was waving a vintage postcard in front of my face to stay cool when, out of the corner of my eye, I saw someone walking toward me on an empty sidewalk.

It was my boyfriend from law school, Abe.

Alex and I had broken up shortly after I settled into Pepperdine law school. We agreed that the distance was a lot: He was working long hours in a finance job in Manhattan, and I was now spending hours studying on the West Coast, focusing on human rights and social justice, after deciding I no longer wanted to pursue a career in the FBI.

Prior to law school, I traveled to Thailand to volunteer in a safe house for girls who had been sexually trafficked, some as young as five. I'd teach them English in the morning, then spend the afternoon making up dances with them, cooking, or sitting cross-legged with them as they engaged in their Buddhist practices. At night, after I hugged them goodbye, I would head to the market for dinner, where I painfully watched well-dressed American men, many who likely had photos of their own daughters in their folded leather wallets, solicit sex from young girls. Like the very young girls I knew and loved.

It unleashed in me unbridled rage.

What causes you enough grief to do something about it?

Growing up, I didn't choose to take a stand on injustice because I didn't have to. I had never been treated different based on the color of my skin (white), my social status (upper class), my sexual identity (straight), or my religion (Catholic); or rather I should say, I *was* treated differently in the sense that American culture prioritized and protected these identities. For much of my life, there was a quiet buffer between myself and other people's pain. That space gave me the illusion of compassion and protected me from feeling too much. But as my world widened, the distance between my suffering and the suffering of others began to dissolve. I began to feel more deeply the pulse of other people's pain, and it inspired me to take action, even if that action was imperfect.

I didn't want to be a lovingly silent bystander anymore. I wanted to *do something*. I spent the rest of my time in law school advocating for those whose basic rights to safety, freedom, and health were not protected: I interned at the Medical Foundation for the Care of Victims of Torture in London, clerked at the ACLU in Los Angeles, investigated religious conflict in northern Nigeria, Armenia, and Azerbaijan, and visited a refugee camp on the Myanmar-Thailand border where ethnic minorities were forcefully displaced from their home.

When California put forward a ballot proposition to ban same-sex marriage, the injustice hit home even harder. My sister, Shannon, was queer, and after leaving Yale and transferring to Occidental College, she fell in love with Herbie, who identified as nonbinary. I was shocked to learn most of my religiously inclined friends in law school did not believe gay people should marry. Yale had been irreligious and liberal and all my friends there believed pretty much the same thing as me, but now I was learning that people I loved did not believe in the rights for other people I loved. How to reconcile such a fact?

"We love Shannon and Herbie," my friends would caveat when I expressed disbelief that they would want to pass legislation that actively harmed my sister's relationship, "but . . ."

But . . . There was always a "but" when justifying the oppression of others.

Everyone was quoting the Bible at Pepperdine so much that I read it cover to cover, treating it like a law school textbook, my studies in contract and tort law quickly sidelined by self-conducted religious studies. I hadn't read Bible verses since CCD class in third grade, and I felt reinspired by the way a brown refugee baby named Jesus adamantly preached what radical love looked like. All that being said, if I had to recite biblical verses back to people in defense of a law that violated the Constitution, wasn't there clearly a violation of church and state?

After discovering gay student organizations were banned on campus, I hosted forums, debated people in the library, and started a chapter of the ACLU at the law school. I don't think I changed many of my friends' minds on the issue, but it felt better to speak my own truth about what I believed to be right than to remain silent.

Abe was by my side throughout most of my social justice pursuits, and we dated seriously despite the differences in our backgrounds: I was a secular, liberal wannabe Buddhist from

Buffalo and he was a politically moderate Christian from Texas who wore a ring around his finger to pay homage to his future wife. Our relationship stood in stark contrast to my college relationship with Alex. Whereas Alex's and my relationship had been ease-filled and almost conflict-free, my relationship with Abe was passionate, argumentative, fiery. He took me to church. And I liked it. I took him to meditation classes. And he liked it. We talked about God. Then we fought about God. We talked about politics, and then we fought about politics. I made Abe promise me, *PROMISE ME,* that he would always vote for a Democrat.

Though I didn't keep in much contact with Alex, during this time he haunted my relationship with Abe, and Abe was convinced I would get back together with Alex after graduation. I didn't agree, but I didn't *not agree.* In my second year of law school, Alex traveled to Thailand and, without telling me ahead of time, visited the girls at the home where I had volunteered. The next week, he sent me a box of cards and drawings that they had made for me. This act of love, both from the girls and from Alex, had made me weep.

Abe thought the care package was manipulative.

The Celine Dion tickets were the final straw that broke Abe's and my relationship. On my twenty-sixth birthday, Alex sent me an email: *Happy Bday Ker. Thought you might love going to this. Take whoever you want.* Attached were two tickets to see Celine Dion in downtown LA in December, six months from now. Seeing Celine was a lifelong dream: All my friends could attest that "It's All Coming Back to Me Now" was one of my most played songs.

Abe, however, did not like the fact that my ex-boyfriend in New York had sent me two Celine Dion tickets. Those damn tickets hovered over my relationship with Abe for months like a dark cloud, symbolizing our growing disconnect. A few weeks before the concert, we broke up.

"I feel like you were the best vacation," I told Abe, "but you weren't home."

"I had a dream of my future wife," he replied, "and I couldn't see her face clearly, but I know it wasn't you."

The day of the concert, my friend Bri and I met at the library at 6:00 A.M. to cram in some last-minute studying before heading downtown.

I hadn't spoken to Alex since his email, but I texted him to share how excited I was.

Hi Al. Today is the day. Thank you.

Um, Ker . . . he texted back. *Pretty sure the concert was yesterday.*

I opened up the envelope where I had stored the printed-out tickets. It said December 6.

Today was December 7.

Oh my god. I had put it in my calendar wrong. I had printed the tickets and never double-checked the date. I had invited my friend, and we had planned our entire exam study schedule around this concert. Alex had spent hundreds of dollars on me and we weren't even dating. I was going to be a lawyer and clearly couldn't read the fine print. I was an idiot.

I'm so sorry, Al . . . I texted. I braced for his response. He would have every right to be mad at me.

Haha, don't worry, Kerbear, he responded, *you don't read good.*

It was the most romantic response I had ever heard. Was there any greater type of love than someone who lovingly laughed at your mistakes?

Maybe we'll see each other someday soon? I texted back.

I'd like that, he said.

The last time I saw Abe was from afar at our law school graduation, his new girlfriend from Texas standing by his side. I texted to see if I could say goodbye to him—I wanted to thank him for the ways he had left an imprint on my life—but he never responded. Now, four years later, here he was walking toward me. His hair was swept to the side, and he wore khaki pants, a crisp button-down shirt, a thick gold ring on his finger, and cowboy boots.

I stood up slowly and then opened up my arms wide, unsure if he would walk into them. He sheepishly smiled and opened up his arms too. As we hugged, the familiarity of his musky deodorant brought me back to an older version of myself that I hadn't accessed in years: of the righteous girl in law school who sometimes listened to Christian rock, who was eager to make the world different than it was, who loved to argue about God.

I had heard that for every choice we make, there is another plane where the unchosen choice still plays out. I imagined myself, in that brief hug, living with Abe in Dallas, practicing civil liberties law, and raising two liberal, church-attending children in mini cowboy boots. How different my life could have been.

We exchanged a few more pleasantries, I watched him walk away, and then I got back on the trailer and rehung some shirts that had fallen off the hangers.

I never saw or talked to him again, but something felt completed in me, as if an energy cord from the past had been wrapped into a neatly crafted bow.

~

A FEW MONTHS AFTER getting back from our trailer tour, I was in the shower washing my hair when I heard an urgent knock on the door.

"Gotta pee!" yelled Sarah, one of our employees.

"Sorry! Coming!" I quickly turned off the faucet, tucked a towel around my naked body, and opened the door for her.

"It's all yours," I said, leaving a trail of water as I walked up the three short stairs to where Alex and I had a bed.

To save money, Alex, Mike, and I had recently moved into the back of our new office in SoHo, which also conveniently served as our first small store. Alex called it the trifecta: a space where we could work, sell, *and* sleep. What could be better?

Mike had a friend from college named Ryan Lawson who was a well-known interior designer, and he decorated the two-hundred-square-foot store space alongside Ninie, who had officially been promoted from warehouse operator to store designer. Together they concepted the Faherty store aesthetic, which was best described as "eccentric surfer beach house chic": A large thatched hut splayed over the cash register, antique taxidermy seagulls lined the shelves, vintage surfboards leaned against the walls, and a large Noguchi lamp hung over a three-tiered vintage red table. Thick wooden hangers on exposed metal pipes prominently displayed our clothes—from women's tie-dye dresses to rainbow-striped sweatshirts.

Behind the store's back wall, a door opened into a strangely configured office and living space with no doors, a big kitchen, one bathroom (which we now shared with all of our employees during the day), and a steep, winding staircase that led down to a windowless basement, where our design team worked. Our other teammates were scattered in narrow open hallways that overlooked the store, one of which also served as Mike's bedroom at night. Alex's and my double bed was in the upper loft space crammed between a desk and the sample closet.

To say the least, the configuration did not benefit our newlywed sex life.

Most nights, after turning off the light, I would feel Alex's fingers drifting past my belly button. I know that culturally some people have sexual fantasies about sleeping with one's boss, but the idea of it in reality was not appealing. I shouldn't say Alex was "technically" my boss, but he *was* the CEO of the business, and he kept track of what Mike and I were doing more than we kept track of what he was doing, and that dynamic was real. Can you imagine waking up next to your boss? Brushing your teeth next to your boss? Eating kale salad with your boss? Doing the dirty laundry for your boss? (And his twin?) It was enough to kill any fantasy.

"We can be quiet," Alex would whisper, as I stared off into the glow of sleep-mode laptops lined with to-do lists scrawled on Post-it notes.

I could hear Mike's mouth breathing across the room.

"For some reason I'm really not in the mood," I would whisper back.

When I told my therapist, Colleen, about our new living situation, she shook her head and sighed: "Boundaries, Kerry. There must be boundaries."

As I walked dripping wet to our "bedroom," I found Alex on the floor doing push-ups, beads of sweat falling onto the blue wall-to-wall carpet.

Alex's phone dinged—the sound of his Shopify app notifying him of a sale. The app registered every purchase, from every customer, from every location, and itemized what we had just sold. I heard that ding at dinner, in the car, while watching football, and often as I kissed Alex good night. It gave him constant dopamine hits: capitalism energizing his bloodstream.

"Yes! Five-hundred-forty-four-dollar sale to start the morning!" he said, pushing himself to a kneel. Our e-commerce business was growing, and it was such a relief to be able to make money before our store even opened for the day. I had flipped through many of Alex's entrepreneurship books, and many of them recited the same goal: *Make money as you sleep!*

So, yes, we were making money as we slept, but that still didn't change how wack our living situation was.

"Tufo, turn around," I called out to our twenty-seven-year-old head of operations, who had a desk with a view of where I was now changing. I was the head of HR, for God's sake: No one needed to see my ass.

"Diverted eyes," he affirmed.

I pulled up my black cotton underwear discreetly under my towel. I had stopped buying the itchy polyester thongs that matched my black bras, though I wondered if I had given up sexy underwear too early in my marriage.

"We need to get our own apartment," I whispered to Alex, pulling an oversize Henley over my head. "I can't live like this."

"We don't have a choice, Ker," he replied. And I knew he was right. It was true that our bank account was in the negative every month, and that Alex's private-equity savings were long gone. We'd done an initial friends-and-family round of investment, hopeful the funds would last a year, but they dissipated into thin air. Or should I say, into outward wire transfers to pay for organic cotton and price tags and zippers. For the cost of a new warehouse that housed our goods and the staff who fulfilled the orders. For the cost of shipping our clothes. For our office/store/apartment rent. For the salaries of our small but mighty team of eight.

Despite the fact that we were growing as a brand, we were always in the red and things were constantly going wrong. Our newest-edition yellow board shorts were see-through, which we only learned after a customer reported on the look on his grandmother's face when he got out of the pool. Our sustainable coconut buttons broke off our shirts after a few washes, and our women's bathing suits' metal clasps got too hot in the sun, then corroded, then snapped in half. The pickup truck that pulled the Mobile Beach House got confiscated at the Mexican border because we didn't have the right paperwork. Mike ordered hundreds of four-dollar handcrafted wooden hangers, but they ended up being too thick to use. One of our signature women's pants arrived from our factory in the wrong color and so our wholesale buyer didn't want them, leading to a fifty-thousand-dollar mistake.

We knew the odds of Faherty making it were slim: 90 percent of start-ups fail, and we were on track to join that statistic as we flailed under our mounting bills. In an urgent need to pay one of our factories, Alex had recently taken on a consulting gig with one of his old employers only to quit two weeks later because of his lack of bandwidth. He had to pay back the initial lump sum, creating even more stress.

Lots of entrepreneurs describe the recipe for their success

as a combination of a great idea, hard work, and persistence. But you know what else largely goes into the mix? Access to capital, aka knowing people with money. Privilege begets privilege.

We still weren't paying ourselves and had approximately six maxed-out credit cards between the three of us, but when we couldn't cover our team's payroll, I called up the only person I knew who could help—my dad—and, through tears, asked him if he could lend us the money.

"Of course," he said kindly. "I'll have to move some things around, but I'll make it work." His consistent generosity to his children always made me want to cry. I thought of him driving seven hours to every lacrosse game to watch me play, even in the freezing sleet, even when I was benched for an injury. I thought of him paying for my entire law school education, and then my angrily refusing his suggestion to get a well-paying, financially stable corporate job. I often felt torn between wanting to please him and make him proud and making my own decisions. But mainly, right now, I felt like a failure.

My mom got on the line.

"Honey, I'm sending you an article I just read about Spanx," she said.

My mom loved sending me articles from *USA Today* or Oprah's magazine about women's entrepreneurial successes. She often underlined passages and wrote notes in the margins, as if to save me the time of reading the full article. I found these gestures to be both annoying and charming.

"Thanks, Mom," I said, before hanging up and sighing in relief.

"We got your dad's money for payroll; now we only need twenty thousand more to pay our sweater factory," Alex said.

"Now, who else do we know who wants to support a start-up clothing brand?"

WE SPENT THE NEXT few months taking many, many meetings with potential investors, sitting in fancy, dark bars ordering medium-rare steaks and fries on their credit cards. We talked about the scalability of the business, our growth plans, our margins.

"I don't invest in family businesses," one investor said. "Too complicated. Especially if it's a husband and wife."

He looked at Alex and me, and I shrugged.

"Good call," I replied, while motioning to the waiter I needed another tequila.

Another investor worked for a venture capital company and wanted to see if he could buy Faherty, flat out. But we'd heard how this story ended time and time again: They would buy us, we would work for them for two years, and then they'd fire us, replace our custom fabrics with cheap unsustainable ones, compromise our mission, spend millions on unnecessary marketing, fire the rest of our company, and then sell it to someone else. Alex knew these guys. He used to be one of them.

"No thanks," Alex said. "We don't want to sell. We want to be doing this for a very long time."

"Give it ten years, and you'll want out," the man in the suit said knowingly. "You can call me then."

Another younger guy took us out for an expensive dinner, downed five vodka sodas immediately, and told us story after story about how rich he was. He didn't once look me in the eye, talking only to Alex and Mike the entire time. I couldn't tell if that meant he wasn't interested in me or if it was simply a man thing to lack curiosity about the emotional landscapes of women. I didn't trust men who didn't ask women questions.

"I kinda liked him," Mike said as we walked out.

"I would have liked him if he didn't hate women," I responded, hailing a yellow taxi on Broadway.

"Ker," Alex said, "we need the money, bad."

"Not that bad," I said.

We'd have to keep bootstrapping it for now.

Four

I woke up in the middle of the night sweating. I'd had the dream again.

I first had it as a child. Then later as a teenager. Then once in law school. It was the same vision: a young woman standing naked at the edge of a rocky shore, long dark brown hair cascading down her back. I could tell by the way she held her head that her eyes stared straight into the sea. I did not see her face. She stood motionless on a boulder and then slowly and intentionally walked into the gray and rough waters. Then she dove into the white-capped waves, and I watched until the arch of her bare back disappeared into the sea.

~

WE MADE IT TO Coachella. Well, we kinda made it to Coachella. We were not at the music festival but were nearby. Four miles down the road at a very bougie five-star hotel, to be precise. For a cut of the sales, the hotel was letting us sell our clothes out of our trailer to their guests who were *actually* going to Coachella. We, of course, did not have tickets.

"How much are they?" Alex had asked when I pitched him on buying day passes to see some of the bands we loved. "Not worth it," he responded when I told him the amount. "Plus, we've got string bikinis to sell."

Alex and I were there with Maggie, our women's designer. After hours of hanging clothes in the desert sun, our shoulders sore and crispy, armpits damp and fragrant, we heard the melody of one of our favorite songs in the distance.

"Is that the radio?" I asked. It sounded stripped down.

"OMG," Maggie said, "I think it's live!" She grabbed my hand, and I grabbed Alex's, and we followed the music to the hotel pool, where, amazingly, we saw one of our favorite bands playing an acoustic set in front of a handful of people on lounge chairs. I gasped at our luck, watching as the lead singer, eyes closed, sang the words we knew so well.

When they finished, we approached. Alex fanboyed the band, telling them how much he loved their music. How we had designed our clothes in a basement office while listening to their first album and blasted their songs on every road trip. We invited them over to our trailer to grab some free gear. They were kind and gracious, and each picked out a couple pieces. Everyone chitchatted and mingled. I watched out of the corner of my eye as the lead singer and saxophone player, who I will hereafter refer to as "Beau," flirted with Maggie.

"You guys should come out with us tonight," Beau said.

Alex told him that he was headed home on a red-eye, but

Maggie was quick to agree to meet up. Alex gave each of the band members a one-armed hug and said he hoped to cross paths soon.

WHEN MAGGIE AND I arrived at the hotel lobby Beau had suggested that evening, he was leaning against the bar and talking with one of his bandmates. He had a slight scowl on his face, and I could feel the energy was tense. Then he caught sight of Maggie, and his expression softened. She ordered an espresso martini, and he had a shot of tequila and a beer, and they started chatting about the festival lineup.

Meanwhile, my fun-assassin tendencies were kicking in. I stood awkwardly at the bar, staring hard at the drink menu, pretending to debate what I wanted while instead making a mental checklist of everything we needed to restock tomorrow on the trailer. We had done almost eight thousand dollars in sales that day, which was huge. But we'd also been getting a lot of constructive feedback: The elastic on our women's pants was too tight, our knit T-shirt dress stretched too much on the hanger, and our men's board shorts stained easily from sunscreen. I had shot Mike a text about all the design issues, and he hadn't responded. He never responded to me these days, which might have been due to his overwhelm or his avoidant communication style, or both.

A few minutes into their conversation, Maggie excused herself to go to the bathroom, and Beau turned to face me.

"Hey," I said to him.

"Hey," he said with a nod. I raised my Old-Fashioned to his tequila for a friendly toast.

"I like your boots," I said, looking down at them. "What type of endangered animals are they?"

He smirked. "Ostrich skin."

"Ah," I said, "I should have known." I scrunched my nose at the memory of an ostrich with a skinny red erection chasing down his mate. Alex and I had witnessed the scene on our honeymoon in Tanzania. When the male ostrich caught up to and mounted the female from behind, her legs buckled beneath her and she collapsed to the ground, swinging her neck side to side in defeat. The visual had made me cry.

"Fake ostrich," Beau added. *Yeah, right,* I thought.

"What's your day like tomorrow?" I said, trying to keep the conversation going, but then interrupted myself. "Let me guess: You'll wake up hungover, want to go for a jog but won't, drink your coffee while writing in your journal about an unrequited love triangle you're in, and then drink lemon ginger tea before getting onstage to perform for a group of people you can't stand."

I was kidding, but as he stared at me, I could tell he didn't think this was funny. That perhaps I had, in fact, perfectly summed him up. He looked away, took a swig of his drink, then looked back up at me, his eyes brimming with tears.

"Do you think my life is a fucking joke?" he asked.

"I . . ."

I felt terrible.

"I'm sorry," I said. "I don't. I don't think your life is a joke . . ." And then my eyes welled with tears too. Something electric and painful ran through my veins: a catastrophic type of energy. I glanced quickly into his eyes, both of us whiplashed by each other's words.

Seconds later, Maggie returned and tapped his arm, and he turned his back to me. I went out and lay on a poolside chaise and stared at the stars. *What the hell just happened?* I wondered.

In the morning, as Maggie and I moved merch around the trailer, I heard her phone buzz.

"Beau says he's sorry for overreacting last night," she said, "and wants to know if we want to come backstage tonight!" She squealed in glee.

"I guess?" I said, refolding some pants into a misshapen stack of blue and white. I thought of my mother folding and folding and folding my laundry as a child. Putting my clothes artfully into my T-shirt drawer, my pants drawer, my sock drawer. How they always smelled like fresh Arm & Hammer baking soda and lavender dryer sheets.

I had a clothing company and still couldn't fold our clothes correctly. I also didn't know how to iron or properly steam a dress without getting a third-degree burn on my wrist, but that was beside the point.

"You're not even trying," Alex had said to me once as he watched me sloppily refold one of our button-down shirts on display.

"Considering I'm the one who does your and Mike's laundry every week," I countered, "you're not one to talk."

"Touché," he had said, laughing with resignation.

Beau's scowl from the night before flashed across my mind. The thought of seeing him again made me feel awkward, but I owed it to Maggie to have some fun. Hadn't she been working long days in the sun, smiling at customer after customer as she sold the garments she herself had helped design? Shouldn't I reward her for that? Shouldn't I be a good boss?

"Absolutely," I said. "Two more hours of selling, then let's close up and celebrate. We'll go out with a bang."

A FEW HOURS LATER, I studied Beau intently from the crowd as his band played their last set: He wore tight pants and aviator sunglasses and strutted around the stage with the mic in hand, his blond hair peeking out of a fedora and blowing in the breeze. As he'd done around the pool, he kept his eyes closed when he sang, as if he were traveling to a place where he was alone and not singing in front of thousands of adoring fans. A few times, he picked up a saxophone, and I could feel the vibrations of its breathy, sensual timbre in the base of my spine, as if it were an animal searching for a call-and-response in the woods.

I closed my eyes too and let the familiar melodies calm my mind. I thought of Alex, likely sitting in our home/office in his Faherty flannel, working at his computer as he put together an investor deck. He would have loved to have been at this concert, and I knew how much leisure and fun he sacrificed on the daily to keep the company afloat.

I sipped an IPA and deeply inhaled the smell of weed wafting up from the crowd. I didn't smoke, but I loved the smell of a cigarette or a blunt outside. It made me feel wild adjacent. I felt relaxed for the first time in weeks.

After the set, I trailed twenty feet behind Maggie and Beau as they weaved through the backstage crowd, mostly women wearing hair wreaths and cowboy boots. I studied Beau from behind. Long and lanky, he had the stride of a star, a powerful presence. But something in the hunch of his shoulders spoke of another side of him, one that might want to hide from the world.

As I battled through the throngs of inebriated, desert-dust-ridden fans, Beau turned around and waited for me to catch up.

"I hate festivals," he said, lighting up a cigarette.

"I know you do," I said, nodding in agreement. "I do too."

He tilted his head to the side, perhaps surprised, perhaps suspicious. Then he smirked and turned his back to me again.

The next morning, Maggie and I packed up the trailer and our commercial driver arrived to take it back East—hundreds of pounds lighter, thanks to the sales we had made. As we finished cramming our suitcases into the back of our Chevy rental car, Maggie got a text from Beau. His ride to LA had bailed. Could we drive him back?

"I guess so?" I said reluctantly. I was surprised he would entertain three more hours in a car with someone who had made him cry forty-eight hours before, but I guess a ride was a ride. Plus, he undoubtedly wanted to make out with Maggie.

When he arrived to join us, he climbed into the front seat, leaving Maggie alone in the back. As we pulled onto the highway, I turned on my Krishna Das playlist and turned up the volume.

"I hope you like chanting," I said, hoping to avoid any small talk. The strategy worked for about half an hour—no chatting, only listening to repetitive *Hare Krishna*s, until Beau broke the chanting trance.

"So, where are you from?" he said, looking over at me behind the steering wheel.

"Buffalo, New York."

Telling people I'm from Buffalo is the ultimate icebreaker, because I've noticed that this fact makes me more likable because people instantly feel bad for me. "*Buffalo?!*" most people respond with a sympathetic but superior smile when I tell them, surely thinking about the city's long, gray, snowy winters, industrial shoreline, and a football team that not only has never won the Super Bowl but lost four consecutive ones (if you know, you know). Beau was no different.

"Buffalo, huh?" he said with a smile. "You don't look like you're from Buffalo."

"I don't know what that means," I said flatly.

He switched gears: "What was your first concert?"

"Ani DiFranco," I said proudly. "'So fuck you and your untouchable face,'" I recited, highlighting one of her most infamous songs.

"Yup, that's a good one."

Over the next few hours we bonded over our taste in music and our affinity for Julia Cameron's *The Artist's Way,* a book that guides people to unlock their creativity.

"I journal every morning," I told him.

"I try to too," he said.

"OMG, we're the saaaaame," I said sarcastically, accentuating the long vowel *a* the way most people from upstate New York did.

"But are we?" he asked, his eyes scanning my profile.

"No," I confirmed.

During the entire four-hour, traffic-ridden drive home, Beau didn't ask a thing about Faherty, which I found liberating.

Instead, we talked a lot about meditation. I told him how I had visited a monastery in Thailand before law school and would wake up at 4:30 A.M. to chant and meditate, and then silently walk with the monks to town to collect alms, usually in the form of food. The monks ate only once a day, and the first time I ate with them, I scarfed the meal down quickly and mindlessly, worrying about how hungry I'd be later in the day (I had low blood sugar! What would I do without snacks?!). When I looked up after finishing my measly meal of the day, all the monks had their bowls still brimming with food. They were chewing every bite, very slowly.

"Like this," I said to Beau as he turned to face me. And

then I dramatically chewed very, very slowly. Lower jaw rotating circularly. Over and over.

"Thirty-two times," I said. "Thirty-two times before swallowing."

"Wow," he said, wide-eyed.

"That's mindfulness for you," I said, picking up my half-diet, half-regular Dr Pepper Big Gulp and taking a swig. "Enlightenment is noticing the taste of the seventh bite of rice."

"Damn," he said.

With my knees momentarily on either side of the steering wheel, I opened a bag of Lay's potato chips and handed him one. "Try it. Chew it thirty-two times."

As he loudly chewed, I regretted giving him a chip.

"I'm bad at this. I lost count after eight."

"I act like I can talk about mindfulness," I admitted, "but I'm pretty much an escape artist wanting to be any other place than the present moment."

"Same," he said. "I get lost in my thoughts and live in my daydreams."

"Well, you're an artist," I affirmed. "And artists need to live in the wilderness of their imagination in order to craft art that benefits us all."

"I hope that's true," Beau said, finally swallowing and putting out his hand for another chip. I gently placed another one in his hand, my fingertip just barely touching his palm.

"I want to get good at meditating," Maggie chimed from the back seat. I had forgotten she was back there.

I too had wanted to get *good* at meditating when I started: sitting for eight minutes a day watching my breath. Then fifteen. Then twenty. Doing body scans and visualizations and reciting mantras. When I first started meditating, I had a future vision of myself, wrinkle-free, with a smile plastered on my face, totally enlightened and free of ego in a long, flowing dress on top of a hill with thousands of followers. *One day, I could be a cult leader,* I had thought. *But, like, a good one.*

"Don't forget," my teacher would remind us at the end of the class, looking at me as if she could read my mind, "we don't practice meditation to get good at meditation; we practice meditation to get better at life."

Fuck.

I told Maggie that story, and she laughed.

I TURNED BACK TO Beau. When I taught meditation to kids, I loved writing short mindfulness poetry that rhymed, but I hadn't written anything new in years. I wondered if it was worth sharing.

"I have some mindfulness poems I can send you," I said to Beau, immediately regretting the offer. Did I really want to share my unserious, shitty poetry with a seasoned and successful artist whose music I loved? You could smell the creativity wafting off him like browned butter and wine. He made art boldly and unapologetically and without caveat, the way I felt like caveating now: *It's not that good, just something small, a little dark, not that serious.*

"Now, that's where I draw the line," Beau said, laughing. "I hate poetry."

"You can't hate poetry," I said, flushed with embarrassment. "You write songs for a living, and songs are poems."

Then we both fell silent.

WHEN WE ARRIVED IN LA, Maggie walked Beau to his friend's front door, and I diverted my eyes as he put his hands on either side of her face and kissed her. A few days later, I emailed Beau and told him to keep in touch and included the poem I had written months before titled "When You Accidentally Kill The Things You Love." It recounted the time I spent in Canada collecting toads in pink plastic buckets and wrapping the top tightly with Saran Wrap.

"Set them free," my mom had said. "You'll suffocate them. They belong in the wild."

"But I found them," I had protested. "And I caught them. And they are mine now."

And in the morning, sure enough, the toads lay limp and still. Dead in the night. In my attempt to love them, hold them, keep them, I had killed them.

I ended the poem:

Some things belong to the wild, running
freely in the sand.

This I learned as a child, I must love
from where I stand.

Beau never responded.

Five

Alex leaned against the bed frame with his computer open on his lap, his eyes entranced by the blue light of his screen. He was working on an investment deck because we were, surprise, surprise, once again running out of money.

We were still financially underwater each month, but business was growing, and fast, and it was thrilling. We constantly met new people. We learned new things every day: from technological solutions to legal loopholes to leadership tips. We celebrated the small wins, cried over the big mistakes, threw great parties, brainstormed new fabrics, new designs, new ways of doing things, and continued to drink copious amounts of cold brew. We were on the road all the time. Mike and I spent Christmas in China visiting our sweater factory outside of Shanghai. We later flew to southern India to visit the factory that made our shirts and stayed for a week at the home of the owner, whom we had grown close to. We did yoga with his kids, swam in the Bay of Bengal, and drank chai with the patternmakers as they helped create new silhouette ideas. We went to Japan for the launch of Faherty in a famous Tokyo department store, and the buyers fêted us with sake and rice bowls and took us surfing and brought us to fashion shows. Still on a tight budget, the three of us shared one hotel room when we were there, alternating head to toe like sardines in a too-short bed in a too-small bedroom that had no door or separation from the bathroom. *Boundaries,* I heard my therapist whisper. *There must be boundaries.*

Faherty wasn't well known yet in America, but we could anecdotally track our success by the number of people we saw in airports wearing our clothes. When I saw not one but two men wearing Faherty shirts one day at the Denver Delta terminal, I stalked them silently for a few moments before chasing them down the escalator, yelling, "Excuse me, excuse me! Are you wearing Faherty?"

"Please don't, Ker," Mike called after me in dismay. Once I caught up to the customers/strangers, I hugged each of them and thanked them for their support. Also a boundary issue, I knew.

While I enjoyed the challenge of building a business and took pride in the clothes we created, I needed a deeper sense of purpose to sustain my motivation. Capitalism is a hungry beast, devouring more of one's time and energy and focus, and without some sort of spiritual reward, it will devour you whole. The things that made me feel most gratified at Faherty were not sales and financial successes, but being connected to inspiring people.

"WHAT DO YOU CARE about?" Chetan had asked.

"Use the brand as a platform to share the things you love," Constantina had advised.

I used these words as guideposts to keep me energized at Faherty. I taught mindfulness to the team and connected with brand ambassadors who were activists and artists. I loved visiting our factories and meeting with the people who worked so hard to make our clothes. I allocated our marketing budget to feature incredible people in our catalogs. And recently, I had arranged for us to shoot our spring catalog in Haiti to showcase the beauty of the surf scene there and made a fifty-thousand-dollar donation to sponsor a classroom serving kids in some of the toughest neighborhoods in Port-au-Prince. After the catalog came out, one of our investors expressed concern that we had written such a large check to a nonprofit when we were still bleeding money every month.

"No one has ever gone bankrupt from donating to important causes," I countered, although I hadn't entirely fact-checked this.

I OFTEN FELT A tension between prioritizing initiatives that were of personal meaning to me and Faherty's profit. I knew Mike and Alex supported me in finding more purpose-driven ways of doing things, and also I felt the stress in Alex's body every day as he managed budgets and debt.

I also knew that what I was about to ask him would add to that stress.

"Al . . . ?" I ventured.

With his back still against the bed frame and his eyes

locked on his screen, he muttered an encouraging acknowledgment that he was listening.

"Mmmm?"

All signs indicated that it was a bad time to bring this up, which was a pattern of mine. I was adept at trying to have important conversations at the least opportune times, like right before a meeting, right before bed, right before he needed to take a shit. But I couldn't hold back any longer.

"Al, I think we should start trying." I cringed at my use of the word "trying." What I really meant, of course, was that I thought it was time we had a baby. Or, more scientifically put, that he start cumming inside of me. How else do you say it? One of my mom's friends had asked me if we were "trying yet?," a question I found to be intrusive, and I responded, straight-faced: "Thus far, Nancy, he has not ejaculated inside of me."

Indeed, we had been doing the ol' "pullout" method since I went off birth control a year after we got married, which had been wholly effective in preventing a pregnancy now that I knew how to track my menstrual cycle. I had recently discovered that there were only a few days a month I could get pregnant, which was shocking to me. For most of my life, I had but a rudimentary understanding of my reproductive anatomy and fertility and how it all worked. When I was growing up, all I learned in health class was that sperm could swim, so never fool around with a boy in a hot tub. In college, my ob-gyn prescribed me birth control, but I never knew the real difference between the blue pills and the white pills or how my actual cycle worked. I only knew that I needed to set a timer at 7:30 A.M. to swallow one a day or I could get pregnant, and I should do ankle circles on flights to ward off a blood clot.

I had spent most of my twenties seemingly inclined to use mindfulness to observe the sensations in my body, but did I even know how my body worked? Most days, I was inherently disconnected from my female organs and flesh, completely detached from the signs my body communicated to me and how the rhythms of my moon cycle shaped my moods, feelings, and desires. The follicular phase is like springtime, when I'm inclined to brainstorm and start new projects. Ovulation is like summer, when my libido and sensuality rise. The luteal phase is when I'm more attuned to my senses. And then menstruation is when I want to hibernate and lie low. I had spent years believing my moods were random and without context, rather than cyclically and hormonally driven. If I had learned to integrate these truths as a teen, it would have spared me a lot of angst as to why I felt certain things and when.

The timing for a baby could work. We—Alex, Mike, and I—had recently moved out of our office/home/store into a tiny two-bedroom apartment in Greenwich Village. Yes, the apartment was above a restaurant that had an HVAC system that kicked in every night at midnight, making it sound like we were sleeping on an airport runway. And yes, the apartment had no natural light, each bedroom facing a brick wall a mere two feet away. And yes, I felt claustrophobic and depressed every time I woke up. But on the bright side, hey, we had actual walls and doors! And the location was prime: a ten-minute walk to the office.

And the best part? We could airbnb it, at least illegally. I activated an account on the app, charging $440 a night, and watched the influx of requests come in. We were traveling all the time to pop-up events and trade shows anyway, so the apartment was often empty. My subletting strategy was the only way we were able to meet rent each month, and I constantly reminded Alex and Mike that I was providing them with a roof over our heads.

"Our friends from Uruguay are coming!" or "My cousins from Wisconsin will be swinging by this weekend," I'd say to the doorman, slipping him a twenty and the keys as I headed out to work. Sometimes, though, I got a little trigger-happy and accepted requests knowing full well that we would be in the city those nights, which meant that Alex, Mike, and I would have to drive an hour and a half to crash at Ninie's house on the Jersey Shore. We always made the best of it, though, blaring country music to try to stay awake with the windows down on the Garden State Parkway as we chewed sunflower seeds and spit them back into a shared used Slurpee cup.

Alex didn't seem enthused by my baby-making pleas. He looked up from his computer, forehead furrowed.

"Ker, I need more time before we have a kid. The business is still too much." He wasn't wrong in this statement: The business was 100 percent too much. But wouldn't it always be? There was no end in sight to the "too muchness." I did want a baby, right? Or did I also want a distraction from my day-to-day life and the hamster wheel of building a brand? Maybe it was both.

"It will take time," I coaxed, laying out all the mathematical probabilities of pregnancy: potentially months or years of trying, then nine, really ten, months of gestating time. Not to mention the probability of miscarriage. Might as well start now.

Alex considered this, then moved to another point.

"Well, what will happen to Mike? We don't have room for a baby in this apartment. We'd have to move again, and we can't afford a three-bedroom apartment. And where would Mike live?"

"Mike will be fine," I assured him.

Alex stared at me, clearly looking for another excuse and taking a beat before finding it.

"We already have a baby," he said. "Faherty is our baby."

He wasn't wrong. Faherty needed our attention fully to stay alive. It sucked every emotional and financial resource we had. It kept us up at night. It took a village to raise. It was a very, very hungry baby.

"But I want a baby who can love us back," I said, shutting his computer and crawling into his lap. He wrapped his arms around me. I could feel his humanness return.

"Al, please. Let's start a family."

He sighed, knowing that when I am righteous, I will not give up on the argument until he concedes defeat.

"I'll do it if you want me to."

This was not the level of enthusiasm anyone wants from their potential baby-making partner, but I heard what I wanted to hear, and in this case, I was hearing an agreement.

"Oh my god, we're having a baby!" I squealed, jumping out of his lap and clapping my hands.

LATER THAT NIGHT, HE pulled out at the last minute, his semen on my stomach.

"Sorry, just a habit," he said.

"Next time," I assured both of us.

IN THE MORNING, I sleepily watched from our bed as Alex got ready for hot yoga. I heard Mike's drawers open in the other room. Yup, he'd be going too.

I wanted less moving these days, not more. Alex and Mike, on the flip side, were still very active. Very, very active. They worked out six days a week, no matter what—hard cardio, hot yoga, weights, deep stretching, surfing, running, whatever. They also intermittently fasted, drinking nothing but black coffee till 12:00 P.M., which punished everyone, particularly our teammates who had to be in meetings with them at 11:30 A.M. as the hanger kicked in.

"Want to come with us?" Alex asked, while pulling his T-shirt over his head. While I was proud of his workout—so disciplined! so healthy!—it also infuriated me. I simply could not bear to work out these days, particularly in the morning. *I feel like a dead person,* I would say to Alex as he placed a cup of coffee by my bed. I didn't know if dead people had feelings, but if they did, I'm sure they could relate to me.

Alex's encouraging requests for me to join him only made it worse. It made me want to rebel. I would not be healthy and strong and energized and productive. I would be chronically tired and weak. I would consume too much tequila at night and cold brew in the morning; refuse to hydrate, swear off salads, push bleach-filled tampons up my vagina, and swear off any workout classes that you had to sign up for days in advance. This was resistance.

I knew it made Alex slightly sad that we didn't work out together the way we used to in college, when we would dead lift together in the weight room and do sprints and circuit training together on the weekends. Pushing our bodies to extremes at the same time had been a form of intimacy in college. But I was over it. On the last day of my lacrosse career, after years of constantly pushing myself to my maximum physical limits, peeing through my spandex, dry heaving on plastic turf, playing through torn muscles and sprained ankles, and watching my teammates waste away into blood and bones due to eating disorders in our pursuit of an Ivy League championship (check) and a slot to play in the NCAA final 16 tournament (check), I was done. My body no longer needed to be a tool for winning.

The day I walked off the lacrosse field after my final game, I wondered, *Why would I ever run again when I can walk?* And now, years later, I thought even more broadly, *Why walk when I can sit?*

I watched from the bed as Alex slipped on his signature Faherty All Day Shorts. He often told customers how great this pair of shorts was: *You can literally wear them all day,* he'd say, *from the beach to bar,* and now, he had proof, to yoga too.

"Ker, please come with us?" he asked again, gently. "It'll make you feel good. You're a mindfulness teacher, an athlete, and the daughter of a yoga teacher. Yoga used to be your thing, remember?"

He was right. I used to do yoga regularly: hatha, Bikram, hot yoga, yin—basically any class I could get into. I could hold a handstand for approximately four seconds, could do a headstand from crow position, and was better than 80 percent of the people in the room, not that I was judging. I even attended a naked yoga studio in San Francisco, where I was living with my college roommates before starting law school.

"Who wants to come to naked yoga with me?" I had asked my friends after I signed up.

"I'm not downward dogging to see a man's swinging, sweaty balls," Carolyn said.

"No way," Emily said. "And someone is definitely going to get a boner in tree pose. Please make sure you bring your own mat."

The thought of sweaty penises in naked yoga class did seem highly unappealing. My friends and I had recently gotten into a discussion around the uptick in the trend of unsolicited dick pics. I found it both endearing and curious that men thought a snapshot of their erect penis in their hand was a gift to a woman who didn't ask for it. The act of serenading a potential romantic partner was an art, and I wondered if that art form was dead. "Not like I'm in the market," I said, "but I'd much prefer a song about a man's emotions."

"I'd rather get a photo of him in dirty overalls while planting vegetables," Emily said.

"I'd rather get a photo of him cooking a homemade Bolognese sauce," Carolyn said. The women had spoken.

Dick peep shows aside, I still wanted to go to the naked yoga class.

WHEN I GOT TO the studio, a young woman with short-cropped bangs, a lob, and tattooed arm sleeves checked me in. She was not naked—at least not yet—sporting a tight black tank and short black spandex shorts.

"I'm Velvet," she said, introducing herself.

"Of course you are," I said. If there was ever to be a naked yoga instructor, her name would be Velvet.

She directed me to the main room, with mirrors on all sides, one dim overhead lamp, and lit candles. I was the first to arrive, and I didn't know the protocol. Was I to strip down now? Or later? I took off my pants but kept on my Hanes tank top and sports bra and my frayed full-coverage, 100 percent cotton underwear and then lay awkwardly and pantlessly on my mat with my eyes closed, listening to Krishna Das. A few minutes later, I heard Velvet walk in, turn off the lights, and say, "Looks like it's just us today."

What.

And then she put down her mat. Directly in front of mine, so we were facing each other. I don't remember much after that except that she guided us through an undressing meditation by candlelight, and then we just stood there doing asanas naked for fifty minutes. I spent the whole time during our prolonged Warrior 2 stances trying not to look her in the eye or watch the beads of sweat drip down her bare breasts across her tattooed stomach onto her thoroughly unmaintained vulva. She looked like a goddess. Naked, empowered, free. She embodied a word that I had never claimed as my own: "sensual." Moving as her body instructed her to, swaying to the melodies, completely unencumbered and free.

"This is intimate, huh?" I joked, trying to break my awkwardness during the triangle pose.

"And exhale," she responded.

I had never made love to a woman. I imagined myself walking off my mat slowly onto hers and delicately placing one hand on her hip, the other on the curve of her back. *Is it time?* I would whisper to her. *It's time,* she would say, pressing her swollen lips against mine.

But I didn't do that. I just stayed in the tree pose, arms open and wide, naked. To this day, I regret not making a move. When I later recounted the story to Alex, I added that before I died I wanted to make love to a woman. "Whatever you gotta do, Ker," he said, shaking his head and smiling.

BUT AS FOR TODAY, I would not be going to yoga with Alex or Mike. Naked or otherwise.

I grabbed my coffee with half-and-half and opened up my journal to write.

"Namaste," Alex said, kissing me on the head before he and Mike walked out.

"Namaste, sucker," I said back.

Yesterday he had said we could start trying to have a baby. I was happy.

Six

Alex and I were back on the leather sofa sitting across from Bruce. We had stormed into his reception area fifteen minutes late, wafting in an odorous sweat from our newly shared natural deodorant. I hated being late, I hated being sweaty, and I hated the ineffectiveness of crystallized charcoal baking soda deodorant.

As we took off our coats in Bruce's office, I could tell he was assessing where and how we chose to sit. I sat with hands under my legs on one side of the couch, whereas Alex sat on the other, legs splayed open. There was construction outside, and the jackhammers increased my irritation. I reminded myself that the noise inside my head was always louder than the noise outside. I surreptitiously did a breathing exercise. Inhale. Hold. Exhale. Hold.

We had resolved the salary issue in our first couples therapy session, which was to say that I would make the same amount as Alex and Mike. Both Mike and Alex, at various times, reminded me that paying me the same amount as them was a generous gesture given that they had the word "chief" in the title (chief creative director and chief executive officer), whereas my self-anointed title was simply "president."

"Is it generous," I countered, "to make the same salary as my two founding business partners, or a baseline standard of fairness and equality?"

Mike and Alex had high standards for working. While I did too, I was admittedly too lenient, too trusting, too complimentary. I couldn't push people to work long hours, instead telling them to go home before me and then leaving myself in a bind to finish the task at hand. I got too intimate with our team members, knew too much about their lives, and was too sympathetic to their stresses. I became the in-house company therapist, taking people to coffee when I could sense they were stressed and buying them cappuccinos as they vented to me about how hard it was to work at such a fast-paced, ever-changing company. I always agreed.

I was often the one who had to let people go, and I *hated* this responsibility. Turnover at Faherty was high. Every six months, heck, every three months, we had an entirely different business—new revenue streams, new production partners, new wholesalers, new legal issues, new designs. Which meant as the business changed, we changed our perception of what type of people we needed: sometimes smart, young, passionate twenty-year-olds and sometimes people with twenty years' experience in retail.

While I knew these changes were good for the business, I would rather run the company into mediocre purgatory than have to fire someone I cared about. It felt like a breakup every time, telling them "It's not you, it's me" or "The business is changing" or "We need to consciously uncouple."

The irony was that, as I got more comfortable having these hard conversations, I also had a deep fear that Mike and Alex would want to fire me one day. I wondered if their vision to grow the business into a globally well-known, profitable brand would eventually be at odds with my vision and my purpose. Maybe I wasn't skilled enough at managing a team, now that the company was doubling in sales. Maybe I wasn't working hard enough to ensure we met our goals of doubling in sales. Maybe their expectations would change. Maybe my idea of success was too different from theirs. Maybe the business would outgrow me too. Maybe I would become a liability to the company: too outspoken, too righteous, too ambivalent, too selfish in my own pursuits.

But I didn't bring that concern up with Bruce today. Alex and I had decided to have a baby, and as such, it was a good time to start focusing on me and him as a family unit.

Bruce asked us where we wanted to begin, and this time Alex gestured to me.

I met my husband's eyes.

"Al, I know we have a lot going on, but I want more time with just us: time without work and without your family and without the constant emotional stress of the business. Even in the rare times that we do get alone time, it's like you're physically next to me but not fully there."

Alex looked down at his hands. His ring finger looked bare without his wedding band. He had lost it a few weeks after our wedding after taking it off to play in a basketball game. When, months later, I finally noticed it was gone, Alex admitted that he didn't want to tell me he had lost it because he thought I'd be angry.

I wondered if that was a good motto for one's marriage: *Don't tell the truth if it'll make your partner mad.*

He had never gotten a new one, which didn't bother me. I had been initially off and on with wearing my wooden engagement ring, which, someone had noted, "may not withstand the elements." "Feels symbolic," I had said back, "because marriage may not either." All that to say, I had transitioned to wearing my rose gold wedding band and I never took it off.

"Sometimes I don't feel like your wife, I feel like your business partner," I added. "Like, I am fifth on your priority list—after the company, your brother, your mom, and your workout routine." I knew the workout routine note was a bit of a stretch, but his obsession with working out made me feel lazy, so I thought I'd weaponize that too.

"When you are completely immersed in work, I don't feel connected to you. Sometimes I feel like we're walking up separate mountains, and when I stop and take a breath or turn to look at the view, I realize you're not standing with me. You're climbing another mountain and I'm waving at you from across the valley, beckoning you back to me."

I thought of my mom. *It's like I swam across the river and am waving to your dad to swim to me, but he can't swim.*

Jesus.

Had I re-created my parents' marriage? And would that be such a bad thing? They were very different but respected each other, they had built a beautiful family together, and they still laughed at each other's flaws. What else was I craving?

Bruce paused. "Kerry, have you shared with Alex that you feel lonely and sad in your marriage?"

"I didn't use the word 'sad,' " I clarified. I hated it when a therapist co-opted any hint of anger into a story about underlying sadness. Anger was easy to handle. Grief was not. "But yes, I'm sad," I said.

"Can you look at Alex and share this with him?"

I turned to face Alex.

"Sometimes it makes me sad because I feel like you're more married to your family and the brand than to me," I said.

Alex nodded slowly. He looked sad too. Crap, I felt guilty. I hated making people sad.

I quickly transitioned my grievances into a declaration of love.

"Al, I love when we spend quality time together, just the two of us. Time to talk about how we're feeling. To explore places beyond just a work trip. To imagine where our lives are going outside the business. To start planning for a baby. It's a testament to how much I love you that all I want to do is spend more intimate time with you."

"I know you want more from me," Alex said, his voice cracking, "but I bear the brunt of making sure this business is financially okay, and my mom and brother are depending on me to keep Faherty afloat."

"That's a lot of pressure on you, to feel like you need to take care of your family of origin," Bruce said, handing Alex a tissue box. Alex grabbed the tissue and blew his nose. I couldn't tell if he was about to cry or not, but deep down I wanted to see a tear come out of him, proof that he had feelings of grief like me.

"And being a CEO of a business can be a very lonely job," Bruce acknowledged.

I eyed Bruce looking sympathetically and almost paternally at Alex. Wait a minute, was he taking Alex's side right now? This session was supposed to be about how Alex was the selfish one, choosing his family and work over me, but the way Bruce was acting made it seem like Alex was the hero.

I was supposed to be the victim here.

But was I? Maybe we both could be the victims. Or maybe both of us weren't the victims or the perpetrators but rather two deeply feeling humans with different needs and wounds.

I had a flashback to the kidney donation.

A FEW YEARS EARLIER, right after we got engaged (an anticlimactic but loving interaction amounting to the following conversation: *I'm almost ready to get married.*

Me too.

Should we do it this summer?

Sure.

Did we just get engaged?

I think so?), Alex had come home from his private-equity job and declared that he was going to donate his kidney to an older co-worker named Art.

"Wow," I had said. "That's really commendable." I couldn't even muster up the strength to donate my very long and perfectly thick hair to Locks of Love. Who was I to say that this was a bad idea? I found the act incredibly selfless and beautiful, and it made me love Alex even more to see such generosity. But also, the timing for the surgery was three months before the wedding, and could it wait?

"Of course it can't wait," Alex said. "Art is dying."

NINIE WAS WORRIED ABOUT Alex's kidney donation idea. Alex's dad had recently died of stage 4 lung cancer, and the thought of her youngest son going under the knife right before he got married was too much.

"Mom, I have two kidneys, and I only need one," Alex said, adding, "Plus, if I ever needed a kidney, Mike could give me his."

"But what if Mike needed one?" Ninie said. "Then what?"

During the lead-up to the surgery—countless psychological tests, blood tests, physicals, and so on—Alex never thought much about the surgery or the gravity of the donation until minutes before his kidney was to be sucked out, put on ice, and inserted into another body.

"This is a big deal, isn't it?" Alex asked, dressed head to toe in a blue gauze hospital gown. A blue hairnet covered his thick brown waves. He looked scared.

"Yes," I said. "Yes, it is." I held his hand as they wheeled him away down the long, sterile hospital corridor.

"Good luck," I called after him down the hall as the nurse made me stay behind. "I'll never forget you!"

He threw up a peace sign as he turned the corner, then leaned his head back onto the metal rolling hospital bed. The drugs had started to hit.

Three days after the surgery, I was in the bath of our four-star hotel near the hospital, crying on the phone to my mom. Ninie and I were taking turns sleeping on the small sofa in his hospital room, and the night before, I had gotten only five hours of sleep. Like my dad, I needed nine to fully function, or else I was a pathetic, self-pitying mess.

"It's just too much, Mom," I said, adding more bubbles to the hot water. "It's three months before our wedding, Alex isn't helping me plan it at all, and now he only has one kidney and is going to spend the next three months physically impaired and emotionally recuperating from donating an organ?"

"It's too much," my mom agreed. She always agreed with my overwhelm, often even encouraging me to be *more* overwhelmed than I initially was, which is perhaps the best type of emotional support.

Amid my cries, I heard the hotel door unlock and the sound of wheels on carpet. He had just been discharged from the hospital, one day later than expected after getting food poisoning from the supermarket salad that I had brought him. Projectile vomiting and diarrhea with a nearly open wound had not been a good or safe combo for a recovering kidney donor.

"Ker?" I heard Alex ask weakly.

"In here!" I said, and hung up the phone, tears still streaming down my face.

"What's wrong?" Alex asked as he wheeled in, hunched over behind his rolling walker and looking confusedly at me, neck high in bubbles. An empty bag of Doritos lay by the tub.

"It's just so hard . . ." I began, before stopping short of recounting all the ways I was currently feeling bad for myself.

He looked at me for a moment. Deciding how to react. He had just had major surgery, donated an organ, gotten food poisoning, slept in a hospital for four days, and I was in a four-star hotel bathtub with expensive bubbles up to my chin, stressed about whether we should have chicken or salmon at the wedding.

I looked at him, bent over and weak in baggy sweats, hair disheveled, and wide-eyed in disbelief that I was centering myself right now. And then he started laughing. Hard. So hard I worried he might burst a stitch.

"Ker," he said, "I'm the victim here, not you."

After I told Bruce this story, all three of us started laughing. Self-deprecating humor was always the best conduit back to one's empathetic reality.

I could indeed acknowledge how lonely Alex felt day in and day out running the company. He rarely saw friends, and even when he did see them, he admitted that he didn't share how stressed he was. He kept so much inside, especially from his mother and brother. I also could acknowledge how good he was at being a CEO. He was a natural leader, a thoughtful coach, a skilled operator, and kind. He rarely got angry when people made mistakes, and even when he was upset, so as not to spread his bad mood. I wondered if what made my husband so good at his job—his laser focus on the business, his never-ending attention to detail, and his endurance in waking up every morning to grow a company—was also the same thing that made me lonely in our marriage.

"Ker, I don't want you to feel lonely," Alex said. "And you are a priority, but I don't have to worry about you like I have to worry about Mike or the business or my mom. Because you're always kinda fine."

I think he was trying to compliment me, this not having to worry about me, but it triggered something deep and broken within me. This was a theme in my childhood: I was the child my parents didn't have to "worry" about, and I knew this came from a random genetic lottery ticket of mental health privilege, but it also trained me at a young age to minimize anything that ignited feelings of *not being fine*. I already minimized my own feelings; I didn't need my husband to minimize them too.

"But sometimes I'm not fine," I said, while folding and refolding my square tissue on my lap, trying not to cry.

"Well, sometimes I'm not fine either," Alex said.

I looked more intently into his eyes, watching his pupils expand and contract as if they too were taking a breath.

"I believe you," I said.

Alex squeezed my hand. I squeezed his back.

Seven

Terminal 5—a concert hall in New York's Hell's Kitchen neighborhood—was packed and loud. Alex, Mike, and I stood in the VIP section of the balcony.

"Do you think we'll be able to go backstage?" Alex asked, straining to be heard over the music. Four Faherty tote bags sat behind me on a folding wooden chair, crammed with free flannels and sun-washed tees for Beau and his band.

Six months had passed since I had met Beau at Coachella. His band's music was the go-to playlist in our office, and Alex loved telling people that we knew them. When we got the Spotify alert that they were coming to town, Alex suggested that I text Beau: "Work your magic and get us some free tickets," he said.

I hated asking people for free things. For one thing, I didn't want to inconvenience anyone or appear needy. But I also knew what it was like to be inundated with requests: My part-time job was dealing with friends and family members whose Faherty discount codes weren't working.

I never reached out to Beau, but lucky for us, the morning of the concert *he* texted *me*.

Hey it's Beau. Do you guys want me to put you on the list to come to the concert tonight?

Would love that, I texted back. I didn't want to admit that I had already bought three general admission tickets—groupie alert! And anyway, I had friends who would eagerly take those tickets. We wanted the VIPs.

Gonna bring free clothes for you all, I added.

Grab me a black shirt, he said. I wasn't sure if he was joking or not. We literally did not carry any black styles in our entire line. Sun-washed reds, yellows, purples, and blues? Yes. Washed charcoal? Yes. Indigo? Yes. Heathered gray? Yes. But black? No. Even *The New York Times* had referenced this fact in the headline of an article about us: "Faherty Is Not for Men in Black." I didn't know Beau well enough to know if he was being sarcastic or actually knew nothing about the brand.

I know what you like, I replied.

~

AFTER THE CONCERT, I was overwhelmingly underwhelmed by the green-room ambiance. I had romanticized backstage life to be all about candlelight and impromptu songwriting and crystal glasses filled with perfectly round-ice-cubed cocktails. But now I was in a room with a tray of half-eaten charcuterie and crusted-over hummus, open Coors Light cans, a few awkward fans, and super fluorescent lighting that didn't do anyone aesthetic favors.

I saw myself in a reflection and smoothed out my white crochet top and rolled the sleeves on the vintage red leather jacket I'd bought at a thrift store in LA. I wondered if Alex and Mike noticed that for once I wasn't wearing Faherty. I reapplied my Maybelline twenty-four-hour lip stain in plum. It often got blotchy during the day as it wore off, and I usually just left it that way. But something about tonight made me want to look fresher, more put together.

I walked over to Alex and Beau as they talked in the corner, cheersing my lukewarm tequila with their lukewarm tequila in our red Solo cups.

"Best concert ever, right, Ker?" Alex said, putting his arm around my back.

"This is your superfan right here," I told Beau, placing my head on top of Alex's left shoulder.

"You know what they say about us Jersey people," Alex said. "We don't pump our gas, we pump our fists."

Beau laughed. It was the first time I had seen him laugh out loud.

"I liked it too but was really hoping for a Celine Dion cover," I deadpanned.

"I can't tell if you're joking or not," Beau said.

"There's Kerry's sense of humor for you," Alex said, laughing.

"It's cool you guys came," Beau said. "We're headed to an after-party downtown if you want to join?"

"We're in!" Alex said immediately.

Minutes later, a group of us gathered outside, waiting for

taxis to take us downtown. Alex and Mike jumped in a yellow van with three of our friends, which left no room for me.

"I'll grab the next one," I said. I was in no rush to get to a bar and already felt slightly buzzy from the cheap tequila.

A few other people I didn't know grabbed the next taxi, so I again hung back. When I looked around again, just Beau and I were left on the sidewalk. The night was damp from a recent rain, and it smelled like fall: decaying leaves in crisp air. Beau leaned up against the side of the brick building and lit a cigarette and inhaled deeply, his polka-dotted blue shirt untucked and hanging loosely over his black jeans. Once again, his boots appeared to be from a skinned endangered animal.

"So," I said, scanning the street for an available cab, "what do you want to talk about?"

I felt strangely nervous, a flip of the stomach in my sacrum. He reminded me of a smoky quartz: captivating, almost transparent, but with a creative darkness I couldn't quite see through. I swallowed hard. I realized I was feeling something I hadn't felt in a very long time: *attraction.* I could count on my fingers the number of people I'd had chemistry with other than Alex over the past ten years: There was Velvet, of course, and there had been a guy named Kofi from law school, whom I approached after Abe and I broke up. I'd eyed Kofi in lectures and in the cafeteria and on the school benches overlooking the ocean, slightly swooning over him from afar, but we had never talked. Two weeks before graduation, and in the middle of finals, I Facebook-messaged him from the Pepperdine law library:

Hey, I know we've literally never had a conversation, but if you wanted to make out later on the third floor, I'm game.

Four minutes later he responded, *Hi Kerry, nice to meet*

you. I'm not sure if this is a joke, but if you're serious, let's meet at ten in the London Room. It's more private. Ten minutes later, we had an epic make-out session. Two weeks later I graduated, and that was it.

I didn't want or need to be attracted to anyone else, of course. I was married and I found Alex to be the handsomest man I knew. He was my life partner; my business partner; my adventure sidekick. I wanted to have his baby. But the energy that passed between me and Beau activated something in me: a strange but familiar pleasure that somewhere in my domesticated body, I still had the capacity to be wild and sensual. I could feel my vulva pulsate.

"Well, since you asked . . ." Beau jumped into a story about a woman named Jessi he was dating. She was a ceramicist and lived in LA and was on a break from her current long-term boyfriend. As he talked, I daydreamed about what she looked like: a woman with dark brown bangs who wore flowered dresses and wrote poetry in Topanga Canyon. I envied that type of woman. I mean, yes, I too could have bangs, but then I'd look like I was seven. And yes, I too could wear flowered dresses, but they made me look like I was playing dress-up. Mainly, I wanted to be the woman who wrote poetry in Topanga and got to date dark and brooding musicians.

"I have this sinking feeling that she'll get back with her ex-boyfriend," he said.

"Yeah, I bet she will," I said. I thought of how Abe always said I would eventually get back together with Alex. He had been right.

Beau's eyebrows rose.

"Sorry," I said, unsure if I was apologizing for my psychic prowess or for the fact that she would break his heart. "It all sounds hard."

"You're a really good listener," he said, looking me in the eyes and tilting his head.

"Thanks," I said, avoiding eye contact.

He handed me his half-smoked cigarette, the ember on the tip glowy and red.

"I would never put that shit in my body," I said, shaking my head and pushing it away. He laughed.

"Okay, well, just a puff," I said, reconsidering his offer.

"You mean a drag?" he clarified.

"Yes, a drag." I grabbed his cigarette with my thumb and index finger, a sure sign of an amateur smoker. Beau laughed again.

"You know, last week we woke up to a dead body in our courtyard," I said, changing the subject as I coughed.

"Jesus," he said.

"She was face up. Brown boots. White top. She owned the restaurant around the corner from us. They think she fell off the fire escape."

Beau's eyes widened.

"In New York City, there's no such thing as an individual. Whether you like it or not, we're all living in each other's lives," I said. To reside in NYC was indeed to join a cluttered petri dish of organisms: Everyone was intricately a part of everyone's lives. Our humanity was porous, our shared energy penetrable—physically and energetically crashing into one another throughout the day: brushed shoulders in the elevator with a neighbor on the way to work, shared eye contact with a person on the street hoping to eat, a held-open door for a woman with a stroller, and the lingering warmth of a stranger's hand on the subway pole. Sometimes it was even more visceral and intimate. Recently, I had watched an old man trip on the sidewalk of Avenue A and crack his head open on the curb. I rushed to him, yelled for someone to call 911, and then gently held his head between my palms as I waited for the ambulance to come, while I whispered to him, "It's okay, it's okay, I'm here."

"His blood was all over me," I said to Beau as I finished the story just as the taxi pulled up.

"What happened to him?" Beau asked.

I shrugged sadly. "I don't know. But after the EMTs put him in the ambulance, I realized he had left his glasses, so I placed them on the bench near where it happened, and no one ever came back for them."

Beau sighed.

We spent the remaining taxi ride in silence as we stared out our respective windows, catching snapshots of strangers' lives block by block down Second Avenue until we got to the Lower East Side.

When we got to the bar, Beau paid for the ride and then opened my taxi door for me.

"Please don't open my door for me again," I said as I stepped out. "Chivalry is basically benevolent sexism."

"What?!" Beau said, laughing. "You're ridiculous. Anyway, I can't help myself. I've got southern blood."

I let him hold open the door for me as I walked into the bar. Then I winked at him and said, "Now I'll buy you a drink. A shot of tequila and a beer?"

A few sips into my first drink, I felt overstimulated and panicky.

"Being a fun assassin," I whispered to Alex, kissing him on the cheek. "I'm going to sneak out home."

"I'm gonna stay a bit longer. I'll see you soon," Alex said.

Headed out, I texted Beau without saying goodbye to him in person. *Keep in touch.*

WHEN I GOT HOME, I started the bath: hot and bubbly. I knew it was not climate responsible to be obsessed with baths, but I needed to take one each night to wash off the residual emotional energy that I accumulated during the day. Sometimes I even took two, taking conference calls from the comfort of my ceramic tub. "Does someone hear water running?" a team member once asked as I desperately pressed mute. Regardless, if I had to be addicted to anything for purposes of self-soothing, baths, in the scheme of things, weren't so bad.

After I got out, I dried off and then slipped naked under the covers. I hated pajamas: I found them both confining and unnecessary and loved the feeling of cool sheets on hot skin. I let out a squeal at having the bed in its entirety to myself. When you share a bed on the nightly with someone, an empty bed feels like a birthday morning: *It's all for me, me, me!* I was surprised Alex was staying out later, but I was also proud of him. He deserved to have more fun.

I opened up my top drawer and grabbed my beige, sleek-looking vibrator and pressed the button.

I didn't have an orgasm until my sophomore year of college. One random Sunday, my roommates and I packed into a car and set out to buy vibrators: bright pink, battery-operated sculptures in the shape of lipstick guaranteed to unleash our suppressed arousal. When we got back to campus, we all rushed into our respective rooms and locked the doors to test their claims. I lay under my thin white comforter, pressed the button, and moved the silicone stick around my vulva, looking for the sensation of pleasure like a metal detector searching for treasure beneath the sand. I found it ever so slightly to the left of my clitoris, and then waited, feeling a wave of sensations swell upward. It took me four minutes and fifteen seconds to achieve my first orgasm. I was both in awe and enraged. I could do this by myself? Why hadn't someone told me this?

How dangerous, how wild, to be able to self-satisfy without needing help from someone else. My roommates and I became obsessed. We respected one another's proclaimed need for a vibrator study break, and we nodded in quiet solidarity when one of us appeared from her bedroom minutes later, cheeks flushed and relieved. Completely and autonomously victorious.

We had discovered pleasure. Which meant that we could also start to articulate which sexual experiences *weren't pleasurable.* We compared experiences and talked about which men avoided foreplay or avoided eye contact. Which men wouldn't return the oral favors. Which men wouldn't stop when we said stop. Which men were sexually selfish. We didn't keep score per se, but we kept track.

As the vibrator, well, vibrated, I thought back to the taxi ride with Beau, his dark eyes brooding and intense, staring back at me. I started to climax just as I heard the apartment door open. Alex was back. I finished quickly, put the vibrator back in my drawer quickly, and closed my eyes before Alex entered the room.

Eight

Alex and I had been "trying" to have a baby for a month or two when he texted me midday at work and said he wanted to take me out to lunch. This was very, very out of character. My husband—and business partner—did not "ask me to lunch." We usually scarfed down chicken tacos at 3:00 P.M. while venting about all the things that we needed to do, we did not do *lunch dates*.

His request worried me. We walked the two blocks to my favorite sushi place in SoHo in near silence and then sat across from each other by the window seat.

"Salmon avocado rolls, right?" the waitress asked me. I smiled and nodded. She remembered my new order. I used to always get two eel avocado rolls, but after my friend Perrin shared with me her recent eel story, I couldn't bear to eat eel again. Perrin's friend had wanted to make sushi at home. Feeling fancy, she bought a fresh eel at a fish market, wrapped it in a plastic bag, walked home, put the bag in her fridge, set the table, and boiled some rice. When she opened the fridge thirty minutes later, the eel flung itself off the shelf, out of the bag, and landed with a thump on her linoleum kitchen floor. It was still *alive*. She screamed and tried to grab the eel with her hands, but it was too slippery, and as it flapped back and forth, its small jaw, lined with tiny, sharp teeth, opened and shut in an attempt to bite her. When her roommate rushed in, they watched the eel slither under the dark and dusty space beneath the refrigerator. She grabbed a grilling fork to try and stab the eel, but the tines bounced off the eel's rubbery, muscular skin, and it escaped farther underneath the fridge. Another roommate heard the commotion, ran in, yelled, "Fuck it," then reached under the fridge to grab the eel's tail with his bare hands, dragged it out from its hiding place, and then began whipping the eel's head against the counter over and over to kill it. Perrin relayed the scene, making loud "Whap! Whap! Whap!" sound effects, describing the eel juice and blood that then covered the floor, counter, and fridge door. When the eel finally lay limp and flaccid, someone dropped it into the pot, and supposedly a monstrous, sour, decomposing smell enveloped the room. Karmic revenge on those who had killed it. Everyone was crying. "Should we order pizza?" Perrin asked.

Drama aside, the story struck me as deeply symbolic of our human capacity to cause harm while trying to meet our simplest, seemingly innocent needs (home-cooked meal! new recipe!).

I hadn't ordered eel since.

Back in the restaurant, Alex ordered salmon rolls too.

We chatted about business for a bit: the design aesthetic for an upcoming pop-up, whether the trailer had passed the most recent Department of Transportation inspection, and whether we were sending too many marketing emails per week (I thought yes, Alex thought no). The more we talked, the more I waited for the ball to drop. Why did Alex want to *take me to lunch*?

When the food arrived, Alex split apart his chopsticks, laid them next to his plate, and then got to his preplanned agenda.

"Ker, I wanted to talk to you because I've been having second thoughts about having a baby."

I split apart my chopsticks, laid them next to my plate, and looked back at him.

"I talked to my family, and they agree with me that you can't have a baby right now. Mike and I need to focus on work. We are building something. A baby will distract us."

"I am building it with you too," I interjected. Sometimes people forgot I was a part of the family business too. Sometimes those people were my husband and brother-in-law.

He continued, "Ker, the business is everything. We need to focus on it. You can't have a baby right now. It'll hurt the family, and it'll hurt the company. It's selfish."

I looked him in the eye and then he looked down, suddenly focused on dipping his salmon avocado roll into his gluten-free soy sauce. I watched his jugular expand the width of his throat. It seemed enticing, that jugular, thick and juicy and bold the way it protruded from his neck. Ripe for strangling.

"Huh?" was all I could muster. We had talked about this. He had agreed it was time to start to grow *our* family. And then he got feedback from *his* family and changed his mind? I thought we were a unit: a team. But there was also another team he was on, and they were playing a different game with a different timeline and different goals.

"We should probably wait a couple years, Ker," he said, putting the final sushi roll in his mouth and chewing with his mouth open, the raw flesh undulating through his teeth, small pieces of chewed-up rice spilling out of his mouth.

For a moment I didn't speak. My chest felt tight. I nicked my bare ankle on the leg of my metal chair and winced. I focused on my breathing: inhale for four counts, hold for four counts, exhale for four counts, hold for the same. My goddamn mindfulness exercise known as *sixteen seconds of calm.* More like sixteen seconds of swimming through fury.

I thought of the woman from my dream standing on the rocks before swimming out to sea. Escaping.

Just as I was about to list all the reasons that I wanted a baby, yet again, I stopped myself. It wouldn't matter. I had recently read a self-help book that explicitly stated, *Never explain or defend your beliefs to another.* Why? Because spiritual choices based on personal desires and values transcended intellectual explanation. Regardless of what I was going to share, I doubted Alex would change his mind based on my justifications. I would save the energy.

I felt like I was in a cobweb and the more I moved and tried to free myself from the sticky silk, the more I became entangled and vulnerable to being consumed.

"You have been heard," I mustered. And then I politely asked for the check.

I expensed the lunch, and Alex went back to the office.

I wanted to go back to our apartment to be alone, but we had airbnbed it to a couple from Argentina. I wanted to call my mom but I was afraid any of her affirmations would only make me more angry. Sure, I could storm back into the office and express my rage to Alex, but then what? Maybe I *was* being selfish, wanting something for myself that inconvenienced the operating manual of the family and put their financial success—our financial success, I supposed—at risk.

I bought a five-dollar frothy cappuccino and a seven-dollar chocolate chip cookie that undoubtedly had a whole stick of butter in it. I thought about taking a walk through SoHo to let my thoughts breathe, but I didn't want to aimlessly wander—my sense of possibility felt dull.

There was only one place to go. I walked back to the office, slathered a smile on my face as I walked past our store manager, past our graphic designer sitting by her desk, and then took the winding staircase into the windowless basement for the scheduled women's pants fitting.

"Do you like the hem more tailored or loose?" the designer asked. Numb all over, I don't remember my response.

~

A NEW DREAM: I'M chewing gum and just as I'm about to say something important to the crowd, the gum starts to dissolve and expand into every corner of my mouth.

"I'm so sorry," I say midsentence, the interior of my mouth full of melting goo. "Let me spit out my gum." But when I reach in to grab the gum and pull it out, it expands again. I pull gum and more gum out, like the never-ending handkerchief-out-of-the-hat magic trick. I keep pulling and apologizing, pulling and apologizing, while grabbing the gum frantically from the roof of my mouth, then from the inside of my cheek, then from the back of my tongue. I can't get it out. I can't talk. Eventually, I give up, turn my back on everyone, and walk away.

"What do you think it means?" I asked my sister-in-law Julia, who was studying to be a therapist. She rolled her eyes, the metaphor so obvious.

"It means you can't speak your truth."

Nine

A few weeks after the sushi incident, I sat across from my new therapist, Liza. I had fired Colleen, telling her I needed to spend more time in meditation, when really it was because of her water bottle slurping.

"You know, how we interact with our therapist is a microcosm for how we interact in our closest relationships," my friend Lindsay noted when I shared why I hadn't told Colleen the truth about needing to part ways. And she was right: Sometimes I just didn't want to go there. What was I supposed to tell Colleen: *I'm sorry that you annoy me*? It was so much easier to just lie and leave, wasn't it?

I had wanted Bruce, our couples therapist, to be my individual therapist, but he refused to do one-on-one sessions with any of his couple clients.

"I don't even need to talk about Alex," I said, trying to convince him to see me alone. "We can just talk about *The Tibetan Book of Living and Dying* and poetry. It can be more philosophical—just, you know, the two of us talking about life." I had a deep desire to make my therapists my friends, which I'm sure they could and did psychoanalyze. I didn't want to be a client. I wanted to be a peer. A friend who they felt safe to confide in. Maybe this was because I too secretly hated boundaries.

"Plus, if you help solve my problems, it solves Alex's problems by default, so it's not a conflict of interest, it's a resolution of interest. It's actually *more* efficient for everyone."

He smiled back at me. Knowingly. "Liza, next door to me, will be great," he said. "And she is a lawyer, like you."

"Fine," I said grudgingly.

I imagined what Bruce had shared with Liza: *Kerry is a slightly repressed and righteous woman with people-pleasing tendencies who has a hard time communicating her needs and minimizes her feelings. Says she wants to be a poet. At risk for self-sabotage and destruction.*

Liza didn't have a leather sofa or acrylic landscape paintings of Ireland or Leonard Cohen books or collections of poetry. She had a color-coordinated bookshelf, a gray Pottery Barn slipcovered couch, and a clear acrylic coffee table that was home to a single box of tissues.

She was so clearly a lawyer.

"I'm cutting to the chase," I said when she asked me why I was there. I debriefed her about the sushi lunch. How Alex had talked with his family, and they agreed he should wait. How they knew what was best for him. How he couldn't look at me when he told me the news.

"Hmmm," she said, eyes closed as if processing the information. Then she opened them. "What's it like having the Faherty family in bed with you?"

~

A MONTH AFTER BEAU'S concert, he texted me a photo of himself rocking a Faherty Henley with two ancient and living tortoises the size of dogs behind him. He had also shaved his head, which made me relieved because he now looked 20 percent less attractive. I loved a man who looked slightly disheveled, scruff on his face, hair wild and unruly like it had been blown in the wind. Werewolf-type vibe. Luckily, Alex rarely shaved anymore.

Nice shirt bro. What's with the turtles? I texted back, inserting two green turtle emojis. Emojis meant I was playing it cool. And also that I was so clearly a millennial.

In LA working on the next album. Tortoises came with the Airbnb, he said.

How's Jessi? I asked.

You were right. She got back with the ex.

Damn. Stick to tortoises from here on out, I said.

Maybe our paths will cross soon? he asked.

It's in God's hands, I responded.

I texted Alex and Mike the photo of Beau wearing the Henley.

Let's repost on Insta, Mike suggested. Social media was still my job.

Yup, yup, I agreed, adding it to the Faherty feed and watching the likes come in.

~

"KER, DON'T BE NEGATIVE," Alex said from his standing desk on the other side of the room. Stacked papers, hundreds of business cards, half-eaten protein bars, and sticky chewed sunflower seeds in empty Gatorade bottles cluttered the surface of his desk. As I heard his accusation, I lit my Juniper Ridge incense stick and started walking around the room with it, watching the smokiness cleanse the room and waiting for my rage to leave with it.

Alex, Mike, and I all shared an office, and unlike Alex's desk, my circular table was nearly empty except for two notebooks (one for my Faherty to-do list and one for feelings), a hardcover book on houseplants someone had recently gifted me, a copy of a lawsuit that someone had just served us relating to a trademark issue, and our employee handbook, which needed to be reviewed. Mike's desk was next to mine, piled high with fabric swatches and styles we had decided were too ugly to make, Pantone color books, and sweaty clothes in plastic bags from midday workouts. We lived amid clothes and dust bunnies and containers of half-eaten takeout, and I often felt claustrophobic amid their cornucopia of clutter.

Minutes before Alex accused me of being negative, we had gotten an email about an opportunity to private label blankets for a huge vendor who sold discounted goods in bulk. The deal would be financially huge. Faherty would make up a new brand name and slap designs on a lower-quality blanket material, which was way cheaper because of the quality and the use of conventional cotton. From a sustainability standpoint, we prioritized organic cotton for our blankets, but this opportunity didn't care about that. The best part of it all? Our customers didn't even need to know we were making the blankets, and we would see a bunch of financial upside.

I had instantly nixed the idea.

Making money was appealing, of course, and the influx of capital would help Alex, in particular, breathe easier. Every dollar we earned poured right back into the business to quell the never-ending cash crunch. Here was the problem of clothing: You had to pay for all the materials months before you ever sold the product, leading the business to need a five-month security blanket of cash to maintain its operational overhead till the next round of product dropped into the market. In sum, we were still always on the verge of going under.

Yes, this opportunity could be lucrative. Except it didn't align with our environmental values, which is what I'd just pointed out.

"Al, I'm not being negative," I said, breathing in the wafts of cedar and pine from the incense. I cringed at the word "negative." Was I? In my mind, I was an eternal optimist. Sometimes to the point of delusion. Sometimes to the point of spiritually bypassing, proclaiming that everything bad that happened might, on the reframe, be for our benefit. I was convinced everything would end up okay, that karmically we were always in the exact place we needed to be to learn the lessons we needed to learn in order to perpetuate our evolutionary and spiritual growth.

I rephrased: "I'm not trying to nix interesting opportunities. I am trying to be discerning: If the deal doesn't align with our commitment to sustainability, we're not doing it."

Alex stared back at his Excel spreadsheet. He had always been a natural capitalist. Ninie once told me that she had found a cardboard shoebox under Alex's bed when he was about six, stacked with money. For months, Alex had been going into her purse after her weekly trips to the bank, sneaking out a single twenty-dollar bill from her white envelope of cash, and tucking it into his box. When I asked Alex about this memory later on, he shrugged and laughed. "What can I say? I like money."

"Ker, if we did the deal, you would be able to support a lot more causes," Alex added, knowing if it related to my part of the business, I might be more enticed. I had recently presented him with a list of the organizations I wanted to support through the brand: environmental organizations, nonprofits focused on LGBTQIA+ issues, mutual aid programs in Native communities, and reentry programs for formerly incarcerated men and women. When our head of marketing looked at it, she said, "These causes are all over the place. We should choose a lane on which organizations to support so our customers understand what we care about."

"Nah," I had responded, "we're a family business, and each one of us cares about different things, so we can do what we want, and if that means a scattered charitable gifting strategy, so be it."

Alex continued to add to his justification of doing the private label blanket deal: "Listen, you and Mike get to do what you want all the time, and then I have to deal with the consequences of your spending. I'm the only one who struggles to sleep each night worrying about the financial decisions of the business." He wasn't wrong about that. Whenever I woke up to pee in the middle of the night, Alex would be up staring into the soft glow of his phone, scrolling, as if consuming information about other successful businesses would somehow make ours successful too. One of Alex's most repeated phrases was *If we don't grow, we die*. But what did he mean by growing? Sure, we needed to grow financially. But what about emotional and spiritual growth?

"Well, I worry all the time too, Al," I countered. "But I worry about different things. I'd rather make a decision that may hurt our bottom line but protects the integrity of the brand's sustainability mission. You and Mike act like you care more about this business than me, but sometimes it seems like I'm more protective about it than you guys."

I knew my final comment would upset Alex. And it did.

"Mike and I have been working fifteen hours a day, every day of the week. Do not say you care more about this brand than we do," Alex said, his voice cracking. "This brand has almost killed me at times."

"If it's killing you so much, then stop trying to grow the business so fast," I said, throwing up my hands. "We don't need to be growing this fast. Don't sacrifice your soul for the growth of the company: That is the curse of capitalism. You're creating your own stress."

"Please don't get emotional and yell at me." This was my pet peeve: When a man called a woman *emotional* when clearly, per his defensiveness, he was the one incapable of handling, containing, or observing his own emotions.

"You think whenever I share frustration that I'm yelling. I'm not yelling, Al. You're the emotional one, not me."

This was our predictable and frustrating pattern. In order to be heard by Alex, I needed to ensure my tone was completely neutral, monotone, and devoid of feeling, because if I raised my voice, I was *accusatory.* If I started crying, I was *overreacting.* If I mentioned that the behavior I was witnessing was ongoing, I was being too *general.* Apparently, I often said things like *You* always *do this.* That phrase never went over well. *Always?!* Alex would counter. *Always?!* And then we'd both be mad, shut down, and leave the room.

In sum, I would communicate how I felt; he would feel attacked and tell me to stop yelling; I would say I wasn't yelling but then get angry at his inability to handle my feelings; and then I would actually start to yell. Then his childhood trauma of having a mom who *frequently* yelled ("always" was off the table) would be activated and he would regress into an eight-year-old who needed to flee the room. Meanwhile, the ten-year-old inside of me who was never allowed to be angry got angrier and louder.

Jayme, our new head of HR, popped her head into our space. "The interns can hear you yelling," she said, putting her finger to her mouth as if to hush us.

I guess I was yelling.

But we didn't do the bulk blanket deal with conventional cotton, so the fight had been worth it.

~

I HATED TO ADMIT it, but Alex was right in some sense: I was saying no a lot. In the past week alone, I had said no to bringing in a fancy consultant who explained things to women like we're idiots (mansplainer); no to a reality TV show (duh); no to opening up a store in a mall (we were trying to prioritize neighborhood locations); and no to many of Mike's marketing ideas (too expensive, too much for the team, too last minute). I had also nixed a couple of styles that Mike had designed that showcased Native-inspired prints.

"I told you to stop doing this," I had said to Mike when he held up a new women's sweater that was objectively beautiful but obviously Native-looking. A few months before, I had held up a sample of a Native-inspired blanket that we made and said, "We shouldn't put Native prints on our products. It's exploitative."

"But if you say it's Native-inspired, doesn't it honor their culture?" Mike asked. I didn't blame him specifically for this assumption; he had been trained at a corporate clothing company notorious for taking Indigenous motifs and co-opting them as their own.

It was certainly better to name and reference that something came from another culture, but if we were the sole people benefiting from their art and lineage, and no resources went back to the community from which the art came, it wasn't honorary, it was exploitative. And here we were, like so many other brands in the fashion industry, slapping Native prints on our clothing because we thought they looked *pretty* and profiting off someone else's culture without giving any resources back to them. And given that members of the Native community were and still are systematically stripped of their land, water rights, and other basic freedoms, any additional exploitation felt like a grave wound.

It made me feel ashamed, and I let Mike know it too.

"We don't have to sell this style, Ker," Mike said, throwing down the print onto my clean desk. "I get it and agree with you. But if preventing appropriation is important to you, then you should do something about it. Don't just complain about it. You're the boss too."

My mom loved saying that after years of marriage, she could blame anything on my dad, even if he had nothing to do with it. I had started to notice a similar pattern in myself that when things were happening at the company, I often made it Mike's or Alex's fault. I didn't like this about myself. It was so much easier to complain and blame others for the brand's shortcomings than to take the personal initiative to change it, but damn it, if I was the one focused on community building and social justice and partnership, I needed to take ownership of it. It was my fault too.

"You know what? You're right," I said, taking the samples out of his hand. "I will do something about it." I went home that night determined to find a way to stop using appropriated patterns and to build actual relationships with artists in the Native community.

Ten

"What's wrong?" Shannon asked me. I had come out to California for both a photo shoot and a trade show and was now sitting on her futon and petting Thunder, her cat. The fact that I was petting something I was allergic to was the sure giveaway something was not right. I could already feel the bottom of my chin itching as the feline allergen hit my skin, but it was worth it. I found Thunder's vibrating purrs to be like a primordial chant that regulated my active nervous system. I kept stroking him.

"I'm feeling rage," I said.

"Good job, Ker! That's growth!" she said.

Shannon was the opposite of Alex. While he didn't like me sharing negative emotions, my sister wanted to hear all of my angst and anger. She was ongoing proof that people who are comfortable with their own suffering are gifted at holding space for others in theirs. She had earned her wisdom, having made decisions over the years that prioritized her own liberation and authenticity despite facing backlash from the people around her.

LIKE ME, SHANNON WAS recruited to play lacrosse at Yale, entering as a freshman when I was a senior. *Following in Kerry's footsteps,* I heard people say time and time again, and I noticed how my sister winced every time they said it.

Early in her freshman year, however, it was clear that she was struggling. Her drinking was increasingly becoming an issue, and I was constantly worried about her, getting phone calls in the middle of the night from her friends when they couldn't find her and once paying for an ambulance to take her to the hospital to get her stomach pumped.

"How is Shannon doing?" my mom would ask in our weekly phone conversations.

"Fine," I would lie.

I thought back to when my siblings and I were in high school, and my mom had written out a family tree and then drawn circle after circle around family members' names.

"What do the circles mean?" I had asked. There were a lot of them.

"Alcoholism," my mom responded. "The odds are not in your favor," she said, intentionally looking into each one of our eyes.

The summer before Shannon's sophomore year, our cover was blown. After one particular incident that resulted in my driving through the streets of Buffalo at 4:00 A.M. to look for her, Shannon admitted she needed help.

"I'm not going back to Yale," Shannon declared. "I can't be healthy there."

My dad was adamant that Shannon shouldn't leave her prestigious Ivy League education. He had worked so hard to make sure his children went to the best school possible: securing SAT tutoring, sending our lacrosse highlight reels to college coaches, getting us volunteering opportunities through his network. And yet, though my dad was determined to set us up for future success, I wondered then how "success" was being measured. What outcome was he hoping for? I had often heard parents claim that they wanted their kids to be happy, but at some point, after watching my peers whittle away their passion, their art, and their queerness to meet their parents' specific set of expectations, I didn't believe the parents anymore. For the many parents I knew, their vision of their children's happiness was shaped more by their own desires than by what their children actually wanted. And I had noticed that a lot of the kids in my mainly white community were groomed in a society where individual accolades and accomplishments were more prioritized than mental health. I rarely heard adults define their children's success through the lens of *resiliency* or *empathy* or *service*. And I certainly never heard the term "success" being tied to how someone helped inspire or uplift the community around them.

"The choice is pretty easy, Jim," my mom countered. "You can have a depressed and alcoholic kid at an Ivy League school or a happy and healthy kid somewhere else."

Sure enough, my sister left Yale, got sober, moved to California, and transferred to Occidental, where she majored in queer theory and wrote her senior thesis titled "Smear It on Your Lips, Rub It on Your Body, It's Time to Have a Menstrual Party." She also fell in love with Herbie. Shannon got free from the institutional and systemic structures that limited her and, to me, this made her one of the most successful people I knew. And now she was the person I trusted most when it came to looking for advice on how to navigate my life in a way that felt most true to me.

"Feel your rage, Ker," Shannon encouraged. "Anger is information and a signal that some things are not working."

A lot of things didn't seem to be working for me right now. I was mad. I was mad at how the Faherty family intruded on my desire for a child. I was mad at how all of Mike's constant new ideas stressed out the team and how he stopped talking to people when they disappointed him. I was mad at Alex's workaholism and sticking up for Mike every time I expressed frustration around Mike's avoidant leadership style. Alex and Mike constantly talked about the importance of *feedback culture,* giving honest critiques on how things could be better, but often when I offered feedback to either of them, somehow it was interpreted as *complaining,* and more often than not, Alex would stick up for Mike. Alex admitted that when I vented about Mike, he took it personally: "You have to remember, Ker, we're twins." The *twin thing.*

And I was also mad at myself. I was spending so much time and energy on building the business that I had lost sight of the basic things that brought me joy: weekends away with friends, attending Middle Church's concerts, reading, cooking, and a more disciplined creative practice. For years I had a blog, enjoying the act of sharing my writing with the world. But now I didn't have the time and energy for much of anything outside of work.

"Remember when you used to cry about human rights abuses and now you cry about models not showing up for photo shoots?" Shannon said as she spread her nutritional yeast and vegan butter over sprouted toast in the kitchen.

I had, indeed, cried yesterday when our model didn't show up for our Zuma Beach surf catalog shoot. I had begged an old friend from law school to fill in.

"Do I have to wear a bikini?" she had asked, wide-eyed and camera shy.

"Yes, yes, you do," I said. "Now smile sexy."

Snot began to dribble down my front lip. Shannon nodded, seemingly in satisfaction. It was probably good I was crying, releasing the built-up pressure of stored emotions out of my nose and eyes, hopefully relieving the strain of a bigger, more major meltdown of emotion. Maybe if I simply let myself cry more, I wouldn't need so much therapy.

Shannon chewed on her toast. "You need to tell Alex and Mike how you're feeling," she said.

"I do tell them!" I said. But had I? Certainly, I was complaining—the lowest level of communication style. I was good at talking about all the things that were going wrong and blaming others for their wrongdoing. But I wasn't owning my own feelings and how I contributed to the problem. And I too was being avoidant. I had gotten increasingly flaky when it came to staying later at the office, sneaking out around dinnertime to catch the sunset from Hudson River Park.

When Alex or Mike pushed back on my truncated work schedule, I made passive-aggressive comments like *I'd be way more productive like you if I stopped feeling things* or *Must be nice having others help make your dreams come true.* These comments shut them both down and prevented us from having meaningful conversations. But couldn't they read between the lines of my sarcasm? I was never more serious than when I was joking.

"Why don't you sit them down in person and tell them honestly how you're feeling?" Shannon pressed.

"Because even if I tell them, nothing will change."

"Maybe it will or maybe it won't. But even if nothing changes externally, you will feel like *you've* changed when you tell your truth," Shannon said. "You need to trust your feelings are worthy of being shared and the act of sharing them is a way of honoring yourself. You matter too, Ker."

She looked at her packed bookshelf, pulled a book out, and threw it at me: *Nonviolent Communication.* "We're writing Alex and Mike an email right now."

Together, Shannon and I spent an hour cocrafting an email per the book's formula on how to communicate with compassion that centered both on "I statements" and expressed specific needs for moving forward. Therapist Liza and I had been working on this "need thing" for months now. I had shared I wanted more time with Alex, but when she asked me what I needed from *myself* to feel whole, I had responded, "I don't really have any needs." She immediately diagnosed me with *pre-enlightenment syndrome,* meaning that I had convinced myself I was *entirely need-free and without desires* under the guise of spirituality.

"You're not enlightened, Kerry, you're repressed," she had said with both compassion and pity.

"Oh, okay" was all I'd said back, because of course enlightened people didn't take things personally.

My email to Alex and Mike was the gold standard for nonviolent communication: It started with positivity. I was direct but poised. I used "I statements." There were no accusations.

No CAPS, no exclamation points, no italics: no indicators of emotionality:

> *Hey Guys, I love how much you love this brand, and I love it too. I'm proud of what we are creating. Currently, I am burned out and feeling like I've lost a part of myself. I am having a hard time prioritizing the workload of start-up life. I need to take a few weeks off from the business to collect my priorities and figure out how I can add the most value to Faherty moving forward. I hope you understand.*

I signed the email *Love you, Ker.*

In the morning, I had two emails back.

From Mike: *Ker, love you but you're a head case*. I think he thought he was being funny?

Alex's response was longer but just as cutting: *Ker—So many people wish they could have a growing company. We get to work with our family and do the things we love. We are building something great. We get to be our own bosses. If you need to take time off, fine, but I wish you were more grateful.*

Clearly my business partners were not burned out. This was their life's work. Their purpose. Their namesake brand. They felt privileged, grateful, and abundant that they got to live their dream every day. And me?

Maybe I was an ungrateful head case.

WHEN I SHARED THEIR responses with Shannon as I was getting ready for the trade show, she shook her head and said, "Sorry, Ker, those responses are really fucked up."

"Thank you for seeing that," I said, relieved by her affirmations of fucked-up-ness.

But what else was there to do now but get back to work?

I put on my bronzer, my twenty-four-hour lip stain, and a Faherty dress and drove to downtown LA for the trade show. Alex and Mike had very much been the face of the men's brand, starring as they did in many of our social media posts, email blasts, and catalogs, but I wasn't always the face of the women's brand, which was growing much more slowly. This was my choice; I oscillated between wanting to be a makeshift reality star who promoted Faherty in consecutive Instagram posts and wanting complete and utter anonymity. Some days I was fine doing a photo shoot, but other days I refused, unable to bear the thought of hair and makeup and the time spent standing around waiting for the right light. I was convinced an entire day's worth of looks could be done in two hours. I can't tell you how many times I'd said, "We got the shot, we got the shot, keep moving," and then, a week later, when our marketing team looked through the selects, they realized we had not actually gotten the shot as they scrolled through photos of me with blotchy lips and one eye squinting significantly smaller than the other as I forced a smile. We had recently had a marketing consultant come in, and his feedback was clear: "Kerry, you make Faherty accessible, which is great. People feel like they can relate to you. But to grow a women's business, it needs to be more aspirational. More stylized. You need this . . ." He opened up Instagram to show me a photo of a blond waif in a field of sunflowers holding a woven basket, her face turning back toward the camera looking demure. "Versus this . . ." He opened the photo of me on Faherty's Instagram wearing a customer service team member's Gen Z oversize glasses and a ridiculous, unflattering sweater down to my knees in a brown and maroon stripe with the caption "Should we make this?"

"Sassy is the new sexy?" I asked rhetorically. But I knew he wasn't wrong. To grow the women's business, we needed some more aspirational photos. I needed to do a better job of making myself more visible as the female founder. Maybe then Alex and Mike would appreciate me more. I would be more visible. I just needed to refocus, push through the burnout, and recommit to the needs of the business.

AFTER SIX HOURS IN a windowless trade show booth showcasing our women's line's new prints and cozy sweatshirts—*Don't you love these color palettes? Isn't the terry cloth so soft? Yes, I'm one of the founders!*—I drove home bleary-eyed and ready to curl into the fetal position on Shannon's futon with the cat I was allergic to. I wanted to call Alex to recap the day, but I remembered I was mad at him from his unsympathetic response to my email. He didn't see me in my pain. I would punish him with my silence.

I opened my phone and scrolled through my contacts. And then I remembered that Beau was in LA. I texted him I was in town.

Wanna hang? I asked.

Totally. Vintage shopping with a friend on Wilshire. Meet me here? The store he named was only a ten-minute walk from Shannon's apartment.

Perfect. Be there soon. I was too tired to change or brush my hair, but I reapplied my essential oil that someone once said smelled as clean as sunshine.

When I arrived at the vintage store on Wilshire, a striking brunette with brown puppy-dog eyes looked up at me. She was wearing a cute, short, flowery black dress with a wide-brimmed brown vintage hat. Beau was wearing jeans, a crisp white tee, and . . . also a black vintage hat. *Wow, nailing the artist look with the fedoras,* I thought. I wondered if I should get a hat. I looked down at my blue jeans, checkered Faherty flannel, and Birkenstocks. I looked like a lumberjack. And not a sexy one. *I should have changed.*

"Hi, I'm Kerry," I said to the woman before addressing Beau. I wondered if they were dating.

"Arum Rae," she said. I brought her in for my signature default hug. I realized it might have been presumptuously intimate, but she hugged me back.

"I've heard a lot about you," she said in my ear with a soft southern drawl. I instantly loved her.

"Really?" I said, glancing at Beau, who was fingering through denim jackets. He looked up at me and our eyes met, which made me suddenly nervous. We hugged briefly.

"Should we get a margarita down the street?" Beau asked.

"Why yes, we should," I said.

Sitting at the dark bar with salt-rimmed margaritas, I quickly warmed up, feeling the Faherty stresses melt away with each minute and asking them to give me all the scoops. No, they weren't dating, they clarified, just friends. Arum was a musician too, and I asked her countless questions about songwriting and getting an album made and how to find a manager and the business model of being a musician.

"The world of music is so fascinating to me," I said. She laughed and said talking about music was boring; she would rather talk about fashion.

"Also boring," I said. "Literally every season we have the same three problems: what to make, how to make it, how to sell it." She laughed.

Beau watched us, smiling to himself as we talked in circles around him. A few hours later, we went back to their Airbnb, made tacos, and sipped more tequila while listening to music. I couldn't believe how much tequila I had consumed, but I still felt good. I felt better than good. I felt alive. Near midnight, we made a fire, and sat in silence for a while, all of us entranced by the flickering of the orange and red flames.

"Creepy story time?" I offered, taking a twig out of the fire and watching it burn slowly closer to my hand before throwing it back in.

"Here we go again," Beau said, rolling his eyes.

I shared with them the ongoing dream I had about the naked woman standing on a rocky coast who swam deliberately out to sea.

"Oh my god," Arum said. "So tragic and dark."

Then I told them about how I used to be obsessed with criminal profiling, reading and rereading Dr. Henry Lee's crime scene analysis on murder sites as a kid. How in college I wrote my senior thesis on assessing the credibility of psychopaths.

"I've gotten really good at assessing how someone is feeling by noticing when and how their jugular expands when they swallow," I told them, leaning in close to Beau and stroking one finger down his neck as his esophagus expanded. "Like, just now, I can tell I'm making you anxious by talking about this."

"Jesus," Beau said, swatting my finger away and laughing at me with wide eyes. "You look basic, but deep down you're a sick fuck."

"Thank you for seeing me," I said dramatically while putting my hand to my chest.

Beau grabbed his guitar and started to sing one of his

songs, and Arum joined in, her voice a blend of Patsy Cline and Amy Winehouse. Their harmonies hit me right in the heart, activating a sort of longing for something I couldn't quite name.

"Damn," I said, feeling the remnants of salt on my cheek as my tears dried as they finished. I hadn't even realized I had been crying as they sang their melodies. "You all should do this for a living." And we all laughed. I felt a strange knowing that these two people would be in my life for a very long time. I also knew I was very, very drunk. The tequila had hit.

I leaned back in a lawn chair and stared at the glow of light emanating from downtown LA, the scent of jasmine and gasoline in the night air. I felt like I was witnessing myself from an eagle-eye view decades and decades from now with these same two people around a different fire, laughing about how much time had passed. How much unknown impending grief and heartache would each of us live through in the coming years? How much more wisdom would we have one day? I imagined we would reminisce about this night. *Remember when?* Beau would ask. *I remember everything,* I would say.

In the early hours of the morning, as we stared at the stars in silence as the fire slowly dimmed, two large tortoises walked toward us, lured by the lettuce Beau had put out for them hours before. Their slowness and sturdiness made me want to weep. These days, the whole world felt like it was spinning faster and faster, and here were these turtles, who had likely been alive since the early 1900s, doing laps around a chlorinated swimming pool, completely oblivious to humanity's spiral toward the apocalypse. Usually I found the noise of an animal chewing to be abhorrent, but watching them chew a bite of lettuce slowly before they swallowed seemed the pinnacle of mindfulness and presence. I thought of the monks chewing thirty-two times.

Around 2:00 A.M., I curled up in the fetal position on a couch and fell asleep, clutching my own body to stay warm. When I woke up in the morning, I had a blanket wrapped tightly around me. Years later, Beau would admit it was he who had wrapped me in the blanket as he watched me sleep.

~

I'M NOT COMING HOME YET, I emailed Alex that morning, hungover and bleary-eyed. Why rush home when my business partner and husband thought I was a head case?

The trade show was over. I needed solitude. Nature. Time to feel.

I drove two hours north to Ojai and booked myself a small, minimalist room at the Krishnamurti Center, a retreat center named after the twentieth-century Indian philosopher known for books on self-inquiry, including *Think on These Things.* I had a lot of thinking to do. I spent hours walking around the surrounding land, inhaling the orange blossoms until I was intoxicated and woozy with the sweetness of the scents of living things. I found myself a shady spot on a patch of grass and opened my journal to start writing. I hadn't written poetry in ages, but something about spending the evening before with two singer-songwriters inspired me to write. "Off Track," I titled the poem, before writing: *If only my to-do list had been poems.* I wrote another one below it: *We huddled round the flame/singed our brows on flying embers/now smoke spells out your name/what was real I can't remember.*

I closed my eyes and noticed the sound of the birds in the

distance: melodies I recognized but could never place correctly to the species of bird. I felt an overwhelming gratitude for my solitude, a stillness that helped me access the lush wilderness of my imagination that often lay unaccessed. I felt a strange and unsolicited sense of love flowing back to myself from a source I couldn't determine, as if the earth, if I let it, had an infinite amount of love to offer back to me.

As I wandered back to the Krishnamurti Center, I grabbed an orange from the base of one of the trees, even though a sign clearly said not to. It had fallen off a branch, ripe and ready. I slowly peeled it and sucked on each slice until my hands, my chin, my neck, and my wrists were sticky and sweet. I could hear the slow and satisfying crunch of the sole of my foot hitting the gravel path. It felt wildly rebellious to be meandering with no agenda or need but to be present.

I thought about myself as a child, walking the shores of Lake Erie slowly in search of sea glass. How if I walked too fast, I would miss them. Sea glass was my form of treasure growing up: not money or gold or anything that could be traded in for any value, but rather broken, beautiful pieces of things discarded. Things that had washed up that I could proclaim as my own before they washed back away. To find these treasures, I needed to walk unhurried. I missed that little girl.

When I got back to the center, I lay down on the crisp white bed and cried.

Eleven

I prepped the wildflowers around the tables at a newly opened restaurant in Nashville. I checked the clock. Beau was going to be here any minute for a sound check, and a hundred friends and Faherty customers would be arriving soon thereafter.

Upon returning from California, I hadn't taken the break I needed. I didn't want to be deemed an ungrateful head case. Instead, I pushed through and tried to cultivate purpose at Faherty in other ways. The night with Beau and Arum had activated something in me. I wanted to re-create that feeling of being enmeshed in music and mindfulness and creativity.

I started hosting small gatherings in our small apartment, building evenings around community, connection, and conversation. These gatherings often began with a short meditation and then segued into a musical performance by one of our friends, including Beau and Arum when they came through town. More and more people kept showing up, and Alex suggested that, given how big these nights were becoming, I should build a more formal seasonal event series through Faherty.

I agreed and soon started hosting events across the country: an open-mic night at an empty loft space; an album launch at our recently opened Malibu store; a talk on sex and psychics in our Prince Street store in NYC; a holiday soirée with a gospel choir in a Brooklyn warehouse; and a "waste-free" dinner at a farm in Williamsburg where no trash was generated and all the extra food was composted.

People always thanked me for inviting them to these events, but the truth was I needed them; they were as much for me as for anyone who came. Being an adult could be lonely; living in the city could be lonely, and starting a company could be isolating. In bringing people together, I found joy in widening my circle of friends, and I found that the people who showed up matched my eagerness for a shared community; who wanted things to be different; who had an imagination for creation; who poured their creativity and passion into art and entrepreneurship.

EVEN THOUGH BEAU HAD already sung at the last three out of five Faherty gatherings, he happily agreed to do the one in Nashville. When he arrived, he had his saxophone in one hand and was holding a college-lined notebook filled with newly written songs he wanted to test in the other.

"Where's Alex?" he asked, looking around.

"Alex couldn't come," I said, tapping the mic to make sure it was working. "Too much work. Gotta divide and conquer."

Beau raised his eyebrows. Thinking.

"Is he getting jealous at how much time we're spending together?" he asked, unlatching his saxophone case.

"Should he be?" I asked, eyebrows raised as well. Beau and I had indeed been spending a lot of time together, our travel schedules syncing up often, and we regularly talked on the phone and via text.

"He would be if he knew how much I had a crush on you," he said. It was the first time he admitted that our friendship might be entering nonplatonic territory. I hadn't been sure if I was making it up on my end. The eye contact. The giggles. His vague song lyrics.

I looked him in the eye, and he smiled.

My stomach dropped. I looked away.

"Crush? More like *crutch*," I deflected. Most of our chats these days were about the various girls he was pining over and asking me for advice. I had become his built-in therapist, encouraging him to meditate more, drink less, read spiritual texts, and get reusable mugs for his tour bus. "You're just using me until you fall in love with another unavailable woman."

"So true," he said, and burst out laughing.

"Asshole," I said, slapping his leather sleeve. "Twenty-minute warning till you're onstage."

~

AT OUR FINAL THERAPY session with Bruce, I asked if I could hug him. He said yes.

"Thanks for saving our marriage," I said.

"Is it saved?" Alex asked. And we all started laughing.

"We're at least good for another year," I said, referencing the joke we had shared with Bruce that Alex's and my marriage was a year-to-year contract—one that needed to be renewed and renegotiated every year. As I always affirmed, every lawyer knew that any contract that aims to be binding forever—e.g., a wedding vow—could be considered *substantively unconscionable,* even when entered into voluntarily.

Alex and I both admitted that while Bruce was a marital magician, he was too expensive for us to keep seeing, and besides, we had made some good progress. Couples therapy wasn't a competition per se, but it kinda was, and both of us had come out winning. Because we were former athletes, this made us feel good, knowing neither one of us had to stomach a loss. I had won in the sense that Alex had agreed to pay me the same salary as him and Mike. Alex had won in the sense that I outwardly recognized that his obsession with the brand was a gift—so many people never found their true purpose in life. And we both won in the sense that we were actually talking about how we were feeling.

This meant we were fighting more, but Bruce assured us this was healthy. For years, I had prided myself on being in a relationship with someone I never fought with, as if it was a badge of honor. I only later realized that the reason we never fought was because neither of us felt safe enough to share how we *actually* felt: I was worried about being minimized, and he was worried about being yelled at. Sharing more of ourselves with each other was vulnerable at times, but it was also deepening our emotional intimacy, something I had long been craving. None of our problems had been solved, but we had expanded our tools to deal with them.

After we said goodbye to Bruce, we stopped for a cheeseburger at Rosemary's, a candlelit farm-to-table restaurant in the West Village. The room was filled with tables intimately placed next to each other, and I could hear the couple next to us brainstorming a new business idea: a coffee shop, greenhouse, and an arts and crafts studio in one. I shouldn't have been eavesdropping, but I had to interject: "Sorry, I'm a voyeur, but I fully support this." They smiled back at me, and it infused me with imagination.

"What would you do if we didn't have Faherty anymore?" I asked Alex, putting the palm of my hand out to reach his—an invitation for connection. I thought he'd be excited to daydream.

"Ker," Alex said with defensiveness in his eyes, as if it was a trap. "Please don't ask me that. There is nothing else I'd rather do than work at this company."

"Okay, I wasn't trying to . . ." I removed my hand and smoothed the napkin on my lap. I wondered if he saw the question as a form of betrayal, insinuating that his identity could be unlinked from Faherty when it was obviously so tied to the brand. I changed the subject quickly, not wanting to regress the progress we had just made in therapy.

"Anyway, Tyler and Abby are pregnant," I said, welcoming the distraction of our food arriving and cutting my burger in half. Abby was one of my closest friends in Brooklyn, and she had just shared the news with me the night before when we went out for Negronis and she had a . . . virgin one.

"That's awesome," Alex said, taking a bite of his salad.

"I know we've put the baby thing on hold," I said, "but what are you thinking in terms of timing?" In the past, I would have made a snide comment on how the Faherty family was my birth control, but I was trying to employ Bruce's communication techniques to curiously ask open-ended questions. This was growth.

"I'm definitely more open now that we got some funding," Alex said. By luck or grace or God or white privilege, a person we had never met had recently written an email to info@fahertybrand.com asking us if we needed an investor. *Why yes, we do,* we had responded. We now had a six-month cushion of money in the bank, which up till then had been unheard of.

"Like it's almost game time for real?" I asked, hopefully.

"Almost game time," he said, smiling, putting his hands back in mine.

Twelve

The assault happened on a warm evening in May.

I had just spent three hours chanting to Krishna Das in a fancy event space in Union Square that was lined with Thich Nhat Hanh's hand-calligraphed prints of Zen Buddhist mantras like "Peace in every step" and "Are you sure?" I wasn't sure of many things, but I knew I wanted to buy one of those prints one day, whenever I had enough money; spiritual consumerism was my vice.

As I slowly walked the five blocks back to my apartment, I could still feel the echoes of the chants in my body like a Tibetan singing bowl pulsating in my veins. As I neared Ninth Street and Fifth Avenue, something made me want to stop. I looked up into a townhouse and paused. There was always something Little Match Girl–esque about walking through the city at night, peering in windows from the sidewalk, imagining how another person's life was unfolding within wallpapered rooms. Maybe one day Alex and I could afford a brownstone like this. Maybe one day we would have a baby and have a high chair that overlooked cherry blossoms on a New York City street. Maybe one day, I'd sit in that brownstone and write a book.

Maybe, maybe, maybe.

A beautiful Japanese lantern hung from the apartment dweller's second-floor ceiling, and I took out my phone to take a photo of it to add to my "One Day" album. I tucked my phone back into my pocket, walked a few more steps, and that's when it happened: a single blow to the right side of my head. It was so hard, so shocking, so fast, my brain couldn't compute what had just occurred. I cupped my temple in delayed protection and turned around to see where the hit had come from, looking straight into the face of a very tall stranger.

Our eyes locked and I watched as a look of confusion spread through them: his pupils dilating. I hadn't fallen, and this seemed to shock him even more than me.

I had only one thought: *You don't even want my wallet, do you?*

He didn't. It wasn't a mugging. He sprinted away diagonally across the street, back into the shadows of a dimly lit Ninth Street.

That's when I started yelling: "I think someone just hit me in the face?" but was drowned out by the traffic that now seemed to pass in slow motion. A man in a suit approached me ten seconds later, and I asked if he saw what had just happened. He hadn't seen the punch, but he had seen someone running. When I asked him if he would walk me home—my apartment was only a block away—he politely declined, noting "he was dating someone."

Um, *what?*

I walked the final two blocks back to my apartment alone in a daze, opened up the freezer, put a pint of peanut butter chocolate chip ice cream to my right temple, and then texted Alex, who was out to dinner with friends: *SOS, I just got punched in the face. This is not a prank. I repeat, this is not a prank.*

Coming! he texted back. *Call the police!*

I didn't want to call the police, but the thought of the guy hiding behind a car and slugging someone else made me reconsider. After the cops arrived and I recounted what happened, they looked at each other knowingly. "Knock Out's back," one said to the other.

"What's that?" I asked.

"It's a gang initiation. Google it," one of the cops said. Sure enough, a simple "knock out" search featured video after video of unsuspecting pedestrians getting clocked in the temple, instantly knocked unconscious as they fell to the pavement.

I supposed I'd won. I hadn't fallen down.

"If my body hadn't been so relaxed after chanting hundreds of *Hare Krishna*s, I definitely would have hit the concrete," I told the police.

They looked at each other, and then one of them handed me a copy of the police report.

"Good luck, lady."

The next morning, after Alex went to work, I started projectile vomiting and hailed a cab to the nearest emergency room. The scans confirmed I had a concussion.

Days later, I noticed there were cameras hanging on the apartment building overlooking the scene of the crime. Now was the time for my forgotten FBI dreams to come true. I asked the doorman if I could look at the security camera footage, and once I explained why, he agreed. We replayed the black-and-white footage from the night in question until we found the exact moment that the stranger sprinted from behind a car and clocked me as hard as he could.

"Play it again, play it again," I directed, as we watched it together over and over.

"DAMN!" the doorman kept saying every time we saw the punch.

I know it sounds strange, but I found the Knock Out incident exciting. This was a new story to tell when people asked me how I was doing. Now I didn't need to answer people's standardized questions on our clothing company; now I could talk about something shocking! True American crime! And I had the video to prove it! The doorman sent me a digital copy, and I replayed the video at dinner parties and at team meetings, earnestly watching faces grimace at the point of contact.

"Oh God," they'd say, turning their head.

"Bad, right?" I'd exclaim in glee.

My mom was worried I wasn't processing it appropriately.

"Mom, please," I interrupted, waving my hand.

"Don't minimize, Kerry," she responded. "You always minimize. You were assaulted and have a brain injury."

"I'm fine, Mom," I rebutted. "I'm *fine.*"

~

"THIS IS A BIG deal with possible long-term health effects," Liza said, head tilted, after I showed her the video. She listed the side effects of postconcussive syndrome: fogginess, depression, fatigue, trouble concentrating.

"Check, check, check," I said. "Or . . . it could be burnout." I could always blame Faherty for my problems. "Or maybe this was a literal cosmic punch from the universe indicating that I needed to make some life changes?"

What I didn't admit was the panic I felt every time I walked down the street and heard footsteps behind me. How I tensed my body and inhaled sharply. How I looked over my shoulder over and over and over again as I walked to work, to get coffee, to meet friends for dinner, waiting for someone to run up behind me and hurt me again. I didn't tell Liza or Alex or really anyone about the fear, because what was the point? Nothing they could say could change my body's fight-or-flight response.

I changed the subject. "Don't you think it's strange I texted Beau that I was hit in the head by a stranger and it took him two days to respond?"

Liza looked at me: listening, critiquing, judging.

"Like, I know he's in the studio, but if a friend told me they were punched in the *face,* I would be like, *Oh, are you okay?*"

"Is Beau a normal friend?" Liza asked.

I paused, letting the question linger in the air for a moment. If questions had a form, this would be a tangled fishing net.

"I know it's confusing," I said, "but yes, Beau is a friend. And in some weird way, I feel like my relationship with Beau is helping my relationship with Alex. Like the other day, Alex told me how grateful he was that I had Beau in my life now, because he could tell the relationship made me happy. And it has. I feel like a sensual woman again. Which means my libido is back. Which means I want to have more sex with Alex. And we are. We're ready to have a baby. I feel like I have my *life force* back." I emphasized the words "life force," placing one hand over my heart and the other over my ovaries. "So it's a win-win for everyone. Everyone is happier."

She paused.

"Okay," she said slowly. "Though in the past few sessions, you've seemed increasingly preoccupied with Beau, sharing how much you talk to him and how concerned you are with his life and his problems. I'm wondering if it's a coping mechanism you've had since childhood that you focus on tending to other people's needs—like Beau's—to distract yourself from processing your own feelings."

Here I was talking about creative life force energy, and Liza was talking about childhood patterns (boring). I noted I might need to fire her.

"Beau isn't a distraction," I said, annoyed. "He's an expansion." I believed this. Beau had been sending me demos of his songs, which I listened to over and over: a straight shot of iron to my anemic creativity that I drank down in desperate, thirsty gulps. I had been writing poetry regularly for the first time in years. Something about the structure of a poem created space for me to articulate how I was feeling: finding the smallest number of words to tell the biggest story, letting the gaps between the lines fill in the sentiments of all that must remain unsaid.

Liza pressed her lips thinly together. I could tell she was about to tell me how she actually felt.

"Kerry, I believe you are having an affair and Alex is in denial and Beau is chasing an unavailable woman."

Yup, knew it.

"This isn't an affair, Liza," I pressed back. "Nothing physical has ever happened. It's not even emotional. It's a spiritual connection."

I shared with her my recent psychic reading (way wiser and more efficient than an hour-long therapy session) that detailed what was *actually* happening: Beau, Alex, and I all had soul contracts with each other. My soul contract with Alex was clear—one that centered on long-term commitment and respect and love and the cocreation of something beautiful, be it family or brand. But Beau and I had a soul contract to awaken a part of each other that lay dormant.

Maybe this relationship was meant to wake me back up to something within me. I had started reading more books on quantum entanglement and past lives to make sense of the connection. I recently sent Beau a book titled *Many Lives, Many Masters* about a mainstream psychiatrist who, after working with one particular patient, became convinced that souls travel across many lifetimes together in various roles and relations, karmically intertwining and contracting to help each other spiritually evolve. Inside the book, I had inscribed a poem: *I called you here with me/arranged for us to meet/needing a reminding presence/that life is mysterious and sweet.*

Did you get the book? I texted.

Yes, he said.

Did you read it? I asked.

Not yet, he said.

Did you read the poem? I asked.

Yes, he texted back, *I hate poetry but it expressed my exact sentiments.*

I was glad Beau liked the poem. Recently I had asked Alex if he wanted to hear a poem I had been working on about yellow butterflies, and he had responded with a laugh, "Lame." I made the mental note to never share my writing with him again.

"What I'm trying to say," I said to Liza, "is that it's nice to feel a spiritual connection to people who indulge in their creativity. Arum is one of these new friends too. I've been sending her poems too. Don't I deserve to have a community of people around me who understand this part of me?"

"Kerry, spiritualizing away your grief through the guise of past soul contracts won't prevent you from feeling unprocessed pain in your current life."

"Okay fine," I conceded. "Listen, I know Alex is my life partner. I want to start a family with him. And also, sometimes I have a longing for Beau. Can't two things exist at once? Can't a married woman sometimes feel desire for someone or something outside the confines of her home?"

"Let's discuss more next month," she said, opening up her calendar. "Perhaps we should book a longer session?"

~

WHAT I DIDN'T TELL Liza about, however, was the conversation I had with Alex a few days before my session. Al and I were just about to walk through the door of our apartment after another late night at work when Alex stopped me in the stairway.

"You know, Ker, I think there's a thirty percent chance you'll have an affair one day."

This caught me off guard. I took a moment before responding.

"Thank you for sharing that. If I were to potentially have

an affair, would you want me to tell you before or after it happened?"

"Before," Alex said. "Because you don't know how an affair can ruin a family." His big blue eyes stared at me, filled with pain. I pictured him at twelve years old hiding in his bedroom in his New York City apartment, crying as he overheard another fight around something he did not yet understand. Alex had shared this story not once but twice during our sessions with Bruce.

"You're right," I said. "I don't know how an affair could ruin a family."

I thought of my childhood home, free of yelling. But I also thought about my mom swimming across the river, waiting for my dad—who couldn't swim—to cross.

"I don't want to ruin our family, Al," I said. "I want to begin *our* family, remember?"

He sighed. "I know, Ker." He pulled me in for a hug. His arms were home to me, comforting, sturdy, and kind.

"Love you," I whispered. I needed to remind myself that this was home. Alex was my home.

"Love you," he whispered back.

I turned the key in the door and slowly exhaled.

Thirteen

I found out I was pregnant the day we buried my grandpa Bob. The week before, we knew he was at death's door: He could no longer get up, his skin was becoming more and more translucent, and he slept most of the day. My mom was enthusiastic in ensuring her dad had a great death, drawing on her earlier experiences as a nurse and weaving in her yoga training teachings. She played Enya 24/7. She burned incense. She lit candles. When the priest walked in to deliver his last rites and said, "You're looking good, Bob," my grandpa's eyes shot open.

"I better look good," he responded to the priest, as he glanced up to either the ceiling or the heavens. "I got a date."

We kept wondering what his last words would be. I thought of the reports of Steve Jobs uttering "Oh wow. Oh wow. Oh wow" before he passed. And the story of a Hindu swami who asked his family as they gathered around his deathbed, "Why are you all crying? I've done this a thousand times before."

I don't recall my grandpa's last words, but one of his final conversations was scorched into my memory. As my mother told me, shortly before he died, my grandma Tootie asked everyone to leave the room so she could be with her husband. In her hand, she held a small shot glass of vodka, which served both as a form of my grandpa's pain medication and to quell any withdrawal from the absence of his nightly cocktail. Tootie sat on the right side of her husband's bed, put the vodka in front of him on his pullout tray, and grabbed his hand. My grandpa opened his eyes and turned his head ever so slightly to his wife of sixty years. Tootie raised the glass up to his mouth, but before giving him a sip, she paused.

"Bob," she said. He blinked a few times. He was alert.

"Tell me I'm wonderful, Bob," she said, leaning into him so their faces were close together. She had raised five of his children in the house he was born in. They had gotten married young. She was an artist and an art teacher, and he owned his own small business. Every morning he brought her coffee in bed—truly one of the greatest acts of love. Certainly, as for all couples, there had been sacrifices. Things unsaid. Maybe there had been secrets.

"Tell me I'm wonderful, Bob," my grandma repeated.

My grandpa nodded, as if in agreement. But it wasn't enough for her.

"Tell me I'm wonderful," she said more sternly.

He was silent for a moment or two. Perhaps letting his tongue moisten. Perhaps to muster up enough energy to speak the three words. Perhaps understanding the importance of this moment: that on his deathbed, his wife wanted, *needed,* to hear this affirmation after all these years that she had mattered, that she had done good.

"You are wonderful," Grandpa Bob whispered faintly back to her.

"Thank you," she said, bringing the vodka to his lips and letting him take a sip. She walked out of the room smiling. Shoulders lifted and wide. Satisfied.

Tell me I'm wonderful, Bob.

On my grandpa's deathbed, my grandmother had only one main need: She wanted to be seen.

~

MY GRANDPA DIED TWO days later in the middle of the night. My mom had hoped there would be an otherworldly sign when it happened. When my dad's mother passed years before, our oven timer went off randomly at 4:44 A.M. Hours later, we got the call from the nursing home. She passed at 4:41 A.M. Three minutes for her soul to fly from Pittsburgh to our house in Buffalo to kiss her sleeping son—my dad—on the forehead one final time.

My grandpa set off no oven timers to signal his transition.

My mom's youngest brother had been sleeping on a cot next to the hospice bed in the living room and, upon hearing a rattle in his dad's lungs, grabbed his dad's hand, before feeling the life force drain out through clasped fingers as my grandpa took his final breath.

"Do you want to see the body before they take it away?" my mom asked. I did. As I stood beside his bed—the very bed where he had, a mere few hours before, been breathing—I touched my grandpa's hand. It felt rubbery and flaccid. Tibetan Buddhists believe that a soul can linger in a transitory realm between death and rebirth called the Bardo, a gap in which you are neither here nor gone. *Where are you?* I asked him in my head. I looked around the room: at the photo of him and Tootie on a sailboat on a cloudy summer day, wind in their hair. I stared into his eyes in the photo, which now looked like he was trying to communicate to me from somewhere neither past nor future. *Still here,* I swore I heard him say, *still here.* I strangely felt closer to him in that moment than I had when he was alive.

A few days later, in typical South Buffalo Irish Catholic style, we huddled around a sticky folding table gnawing on beef on weck and chicken wings. Had there not been prayer cards with my grandpa's face on them, I would have believed we were about to watch a Buffalo Bills preseason game. My mom and her sisters quietly rustled around telling my grandma where to go and what to eat.

"Grandma," I asked as I watched my mom take away Tootie's second glass of red wine, "how does it feel to be told what to do all the time?"

"Oh," she said, "I just smile in agreement and then do whatever the hell I want."

I made myself a note to make this my new mantra.

How are you feeling? Alex texted. He hadn't come with me to the funeral. There was a lot going on at the office. And I was fine with his decision. I'd rather he was consumed by work at work than consumed by work at my grandpa's funeral. Stress was contagious, and I didn't want any of its residue on my skin.

Okay, I texted back. But that wasn't entirely true. I didn't feel okay.

"I feel nauseous," I whispered to Shannon, dropping my chicken wing and pushing away my Labatt Blue beer bottle, which suddenly tasted like a dirty quarter. "I think it's the concussion," I said.

"Or . . ." Shannon made a circular motion around her stomach. She knew we were trying.

On the way home from the funeral parlor, I told my parents I had a headache and needed to stop at a CVS for Advil, then ran in to buy a pregnancy test, which the cashier put in a nondescript paper bag at the checkout.

As soon as we were back at my parents' house, I straddled the toilet, feeling my warm, dehydrated piss all over my fingers as I tried to ensure the plastic stick was saturated enough to determine the fate of the rest of my life. Thirty seconds later, the results appeared in bright blue lettering: *pregnant*. I tried to think of an appropriate way to tell my mom, considering her dad was only seventy-two hours dead.

"Maybe, like, wrap up the stick in a box?" Shannon suggested.

I thought that was a good idea. Right before dinner, I announced to everyone I had a gift for Mom. We sat in a circle, and as she slowly unwrapped the crumpled newspaper to reveal the urine-saturated stick, my dad gasped in glee.

"I've been praying for this moment!" he said with tears in his eyes. My mom was confused. She was on her third glass of Cabernet and her dad was dead.

"Circle of life, Mom?" I said as I got up to give her a hug as she tried to process the information.

She squeezed me back. "Circle of life," she said knowingly, and I could almost feel my grandpa in the corner chair nodding in agreement.

I waited to tell Alex I was pregnant until I got back to the city. The pregnancy announcement was the perfect anniversary present: We had been married for three years almost to the day. The morning I told him, I sandwiched the stick in wrapping paper with a bow on top, and handed it to him, watching his face closely as he opened it. He began crying instantly, tears of joy. I felt relief pulsate up and down my body. Maybe there could finally be an "us." Maybe we would finally be our own family.

"I know it's a girl," I whispered, hugging his neck. "I just know it."

We ran to show Mike. Given that he and Alex were identical twins, technically Mike was having a baby too—half his DNA would be in it. He was asleep in his bed but I shook him awake. "Guess what?" I said as I shoved the stick in his face.

He blinked a few times, confused. Then he registered the news. "Isn't it too early to be telling people that?" he asked, before rolling over to go back to sleep.

Despite Mike's drowsy concern, I think he was happy for us. And it didn't matter anyway. Alex and I were starting our own family.

~

WHEN I TOLD BEAU I was pregnant, he was silent on the phone for a full minute.

"Congrats, Ker," he finally said. "I'm really excited for you guys. You'll be a great mom."

"Thanks," I said, swallowing hard.

Fourteen

Another dream: I sat on a bench in front of a baby grand piano in the backyard of my childhood home, trying to play "Clair de Lune." My sister sat by my side, her chin resting on my shoulder. "You can do it, Ker," she encouraged me.

"I can't remember the notes," I kept saying over and over again, tears falling down my face and splattering on the black and white keys. I had played this song a hundred times. Why couldn't I play it now? I plopped my forehead onto the keys in a Stravinsky chord of despair.

"I can't remember the notes," I said again in defeat.

~

BEAU INVITED ME TO visit him in Asheville for a weekend. For purposes of transparency, I asked Alex if it was okay. While Alex never appeared outwardly threatened by the relationship, I still felt inclined to ask his permission. Alex was driving when I made the request and I watched his hands tighten around the steering wheel. He stared ahead through the smeared windshield as he asked back: "Do you think it's okay?"

I rubbed my expanding stomach, avoided eye contact, and looked out the window. It was okay, right? I was just going to visit a friend. My whole life was focused on supporting Alex's and Mike's dream. I'd come back feeling refreshed and inspired. Surely I could do something for myself? Nothing would happen, right?

"I'm okay with it if you're okay with it," I said.

"Whatever you got to do, Ker."

I couldn't tell if Alex was being repressed or if he was using reverse psychology on me to show me how much he trusted me, in order to manipulate me into not wanting to break his trust. Or if he was actually the Buddha, giving me full agency to make my own decisions in a loving and nonattached way.

On the way to the airport, I watched a single red balloon swirling in the sky over the Brooklyn Bridge. It was the most beautiful thing I'd ever seen. I knew it had slipped out of a child's tightly clasped hand. I knew it would ascend and then burst and plummet into the East River. I knew a seagull would pick through its rubbery remains and maybe even choke on it. But at the time, I only whispered as it soared—*You're free, you're free, you're free.*

As I was about to board my plane, my mom called me in a frenzy. She had heard only vaguely about Beau—piecemeal vignettes of his concerts or his visits—but a mother often knows things.

"Do you have to go to Asheville? We're worried about you," she said. "Between the concussion and the pregnancy, you're just not yourself."

I could hear my dad whispering in the background. Quiet, frantic whispers. As I assured them of my clearheadedness and *fineness,* it occurred to me that I wasn't used to being the subject of their concern: They were always worried if Shannon was safe, sober, and financially secure or if Brendan's depression had seeped back into his brain. But me? They never had to worry about me, except, of course, when they'd had to wire me thousands of dollars to keep the company afloat. But that was an investment. That was capitalism.

When I landed in Asheville, I walked out to the arrivals curb and waited for a glimpse of Beau's vintage blue 1969 convertible. When he pulled up, the top was down and I could see his blond curls blowing in the wind. He was wearing aviator Ray-Bans and had a mustache, his white T-shirt cuffed around his slender biceps, which showcased a tattoo of a wolf's head. I suddenly had a hard time breathing, unsure if I was having an existential crisis or if my jeans were too tight because my uterus was expanding. I had already gained eleven pounds from my daily anti–morning sickness diet of sausage, egg, and cheese. I made a note to buy spandex maternity jeans when I got home.

"Hello, Beau," I said, throwing my duffel into his back seat.

"Hello, Kerry," he said, smirking, eyeing my baby bump before turning his gaze to my now much larger breasts. We stopped for brunch on the way to his apartment, and I told him about driving past the Queens Calvary Cemetery on my way to the airport, where four hundred thousand people were buried in perfectly divided plots. How cemeteries were basically just superfund sites: Millions of gallons of formaldehyde were pumped into now nondecomposable flesh, which in turn were stuffed inside chemically impregnated mahogany boxes and buried beneath concrete slabs, pesticide-treated grass, and plastic flower arrangements.

"Like, what if all those graves had been seeds? Queens could have had a forest. A big one," I said.

I told him about an ecologically better and ancient alternative: natural burial. I had a friend named John Christian, a mortician who ran the largest natural burial ground east of the Mississippi: a cemetery that actually conserves and protects the land. All humans are buried free of embalming and wrapped in shrouds that will decompose or caskets made from handwoven birch branches. The family themselves bury their loved ones with shovels of fertile soil ripe for anchoring the roots of wildflowers. As the bodies decompose they literally remove carbon from the air and serve as nourishment for worms.

"Now, that's the real circle of life right there," I said, "us humans becoming soil and seeds."

Beau's eyebrows rose.

"You're such a good storyteller. Should we go back to my apartment for a quick nap?"

"You weren't even listening, were you?" I said, rolling my eyes.

"Sorry, I'm a bit distracted," he said, grinning, and then stood up and grabbed his keys.

WHEN WE GOT TO his apartment, he stripped down to his boxers and jumped into bed, and I got into bed wearing my Faherty tee and jeans.

"Jeans in bed?" he asked.

I looked down awkwardly at my unbuttoned vintage Lee's.

"Jeans in bed," I said unsurely as I took off my shoes and felt the weight of my body sink onto his mattress. I thought of the naked yoga class in San Francisco before Velvet walked in: me, lying down on a padded mat, unsure of what would unfold, feeling a blend of arousal and angst.

Beau and I lay next to each other on our backs, a thin white sheet over the silhouettes of our bodies as if we were in a morgue. There was music playing on the record player, faint and soft, in the other room. It might have been Sam Cooke.

"Beau?" I asked in a whisper in the lull between one song and the start of another. Like a sigh between conversations.

"Yes, Ker?" I could feel the warmth from his torso generating heat under the sheet. I started to sweat.

"What do you want from me?"

"I need an anchor," he said, turning his cheek on his pillow to look at me.

"I know you do," I said. We both knew I wasn't that anchor. How could I be?

"Will you look at me?" he asked.

I stared at the ceiling hard, imagining that I could sear a hole through it and then through the roof, forming an imaginary portal that could catapult me out into the sky like that red balloon soaring free, flying high above any worldly attachments and obligations for only a moment in time.

"No," I said, shaking my head as I continued to stare at the ceiling. "If I look at you, bad things will happen."

"I don't really know what to do here," he said.

"I don't know either," I said.

What was there to do?

He stared at the ceiling too.

"I'm not sure this relationship belongs to this life," I said.

I heard him exhale slowly.

"Like maybe I was your mom in a past life? Or, like, your sister? And that's why . . ." I paused.

"You were not my mother," he said, laughing and inching sideways a little closer to me. I could almost feel his arm hair against mine, two split-open circuits trying to fuse for a cohesive flow of electricity.

"I spiritualize you, and you sexualize me," I said, thinking of how so many of our conversations centered on my sending him cuckoo-la-la writings on astral travel and astrology and soul contracts, while he always made vague sexual references about "trying polygamy."

"Truth," he said. And then he sighed again. "I didn't believe in any of that past lives shit before," he said, "but I think I'm starting to."

I smiled slightly and nodded. I had so many books in my head that could compartmentalize and place this relationship neatly in a safe box. If I named it, diagnosed it, rationalized it, spiritualized it—it would keep me safe. I would know the game I was playing with clear instructions on how to move forward. This was a past-life relationship, that's all, both of us reminding each other of the unawakened part of ourselves: I brought him lightness and security and peace, a feeling like he was loved in the world, and he reminded me of playing in the shadows of darkness and the ability to translate pain through art. He reminded me that I was worthy of being an artist too.

We lay there in silence for minutes, maybe even an hour, with our breath rising and falling, sometimes in unison, sometimes alternating. In that silence, five different versions of me pursuing five different decisions all unfolded like a black-and-white film highlight reel one watches at a funeral. I watched all the possible plotlines, feeling all the loss, all the betrayal, all the pleasure, all the grief, all the joy, all the humanness that could have unfolded. To this day, the image of me lying there makes me want to cry: a girl wanting so much to be good, to be loyal, to be wild, to be committed, to be free.

If Beau fell asleep lying next to me, I don't know. If I fell asleep, I don't know either. But at some point, Maverick, Beau's bandmate, burst through the door and sat at the edge of the bed and started talking about how he and his girlfriend had broken up, and how his insomnia was back, and how he was drinking too much. I finally interrupted him.

"I know you think your life is fucked up right now, Mav, but I'm pregnant and married and lying in bed next to a man who is not my husband."

"You're right," he said. "You're right. That's really fucked up too."

~

ON THE FLIGHT BACK, I sat next to a woman and watched as she opened up her tray table to write a letter in black ink in her notebook. *Dear Ben,* she wrote. I glanced away when I saw that she was crying, her tears dimpling the paper. I wanted to say something comforting to her or whisper, *I know, sweet-pea.* But instead, I looked out the window, listened to music, and counted the tiny baseball fields scattered across Mary-land.

When we landed, I smiled at my seatmate slightly. I wanted to grab her hand as she stood up and tell her that I knew that she felt lonely in her despair, but that even strangers like me saw her in her silent pain. That she wasn't alone. But instead I said, "Excuse me," as I grabbed my baggage. I did not tell her that I whispered his name, *Ben,* in solidarity on her behalf, a hundred times from thirty-four thousand feet above.

WHEN I LANDED BACK in New York, I took an Uber to meet Alex at our friend's house for dinner. He didn't ask me how Asheville was, and I didn't share anything. Maybe we were proving Bruce wrong after all: Maybe talking about your feelings and fears didn't make things better. Maybe oversharing just hurt the other person. Maybe the best couples were those that simply kept the truth to themselves and weren't handcuffed into the dark corners of their partner's expectations. Maybe the soul deserved privacy and could live in multiple worlds at once: like the Bardo.

A couple of hours later, we returned to our apartment, and when I opened the door, our tiny living room glowed. Tea lights were everywhere: sitting on the edge of the bookshelf, the windowsill, and the IKEA table, their flames flickering and their shadows dancing across the walls.

Alex brought me in for a hug. He had lit the candles for me, hoping I would be moved by his act of romance. And I was. But it was also a major fire hazard.

"How long have these been lit?" I asked, trying to smile.

"A couple hours," he said. "I know how much you love candles, and I wanted you to walk in and have it look nice."

I almost said, *You could have burned the house down,* but I caught myself.

I could have burned the house down, I heard echo in my mind.

Fifteen

When I walked into the spiritual bookstore in Los Angeles, a few doors down from where we were hosting yet another Faherty event, a pale woman with huge eyes asked me in a British accent if I wanted to do a psychic reading.

"Of course I do," I said, putting down my bag as she escorted me to the back. She said her name was The Owl. Murmuring to herself, she pulled out tarot cards and started to turn them over on a small folding table lined with a printed tapestry of moons and planets.

"You're having a baby," she said. I was four months in but had on a flowy Faherty poncho that covered my stomach. There was no way she could have known that.

"Yes," I said.

"The picket fence or the open road?" she asked. I knew what she meant, or rather how she referred to them.

"Picket fence," I said slowly. She nodded and then closed her eyes. Then her body contorted as though she had chills.

"Someone is here," she said. "Big stature. Stoic. Recently deceased. It's your grandfather?"

I nodded.

"He's saying he left a watch."

I shook my head. No watch.

"He is whispering to you, 'Everything in time.' Do you know what this means?" I closed my eyes. Put my hands on my belly.

I was married to Alex. I loved him. We were having a baby. I envisioned our future home: a small garden in the back with tomatoes and flowers and a small wooden fence around it to keep out the bunnies. I thought of my future children swimming in the ocean while we watched them on striped towels with books on our laps. I thought of Alex and me in our old age, weathered and wrinkly and sitting in rocking chairs laughing about the painful chapters of our lives. How we had still made it. I thought of quantum entanglement and everything being connected and unfolding at once in different places on different planes. Of the hundreds of lives that we live or leave in every decision we make. Pieces of ourselves left behind and pieces of ourselves still undiscovered. I imagined thousands of invisible strings wrapped through all of our loved ones' hearts like cords that kept us tethered together through centuries. Soul families that chose to come back lifetime after lifetime in different roles.

I wanted this life, as it was unfolding now.

"I think so," I said, my eyes welling with tears. "I think so."

A few hours later, my mom called. She was cleaning out my grandpa's closet. "There's a watch here if you want it?"

Everything in time.

~

THREE MONTHS BEFORE AVA was due, Alex and I finally moved into our own apartment in Brooklyn Heights, a small two-bedroom on top of a bodega that had cheap, delicious cold brew. Mike was now living alone in our once shared rent-controlled two-bedroom in the West Village. "I suppose it's time," he admitted.

"Aren't you proud?" I asked Liza in our next session.

"Big step for your and Alex's autonomy as an individuated couple," she said, grinning. "To finally live together alone."

"Well . . ." I hesitated. "Arum moved into the other bedroom for a few months. She's been in transition since moving to New York City."

Liza's eyebrows rose.

"It's just until Ava is born," I added. "And it's been so good for me."

It really had been. After long days at the office, I loved coming home to Arum's calm and gentle energy and brainstorming together about her creative pursuits. Without her company in the evening, I would have been alone; Alex still worked late at the office nearly every night. Arum and I spent hours on kitchen stools talking about her lyrics, marketing ideas, and her new record contract. My inner lawyer loved the nitty-gritty of legal clauses. I wanted to know all the details: the promises, the rights, the percentages.

Then I had a great idea: I could be her manager while I was on my maternity leave! Anyone I mentioned this to who already had children scoffed at the idea, but I was convinced I'd have the time: I heard new babies slept a lot, and it'd be nice to have a reprieve from thinking about Faherty all the time. Working with Arum felt like a form of creative adjacency: I wasn't an artist, but I could surround myself with friends who were. Watching her work on her album lubricated my imagination. Maybe one day, I too could take all my poems and journal entries and birth them into something to be shared with the world.

One night, Alex came home to find Arum and me working on a marketing deck for her album launch. When I joined him in bed, he turned on his side and said quietly, "I wish you would spend some of the time you're spending on building Arum's career back at Faherty."

The comment annoyed me. I'd spent every waking minute the past three years making Faherty better, pouring all of my energy into it. Couldn't I do something for myself?

"I like spending my time on music," I said. "I can't think about Faherty day in and day out. And Arum really appreciates the value I add. She wishes I could be her business partner."

Alex sighed. "She's lucky to have you, Ker. And you should do whatever makes you happy. I'm supportive. I guess what I'm trying to say is I miss you when you're not in the office."

"I miss you even when I am in the office," I said, putting my head on his chest, trying to locate his heartbeat. "Sometimes even when we're physically together, I still can't find you."

~

I KEPT ADDING MORE plants to our Brooklyn apartment. I heard they cleaned the air, but that's not why I wanted them. Something about their presence soothed me; seeing something alive helped remind me that I too was alive. Plants had needs that must be tended to. Simple ones, but needs nonetheless: healthy soil, an occasional brown-leaf plucking, and sometimes a spritz of water for my new orange tree.

My new motto was *plant seeds, watch what grows.* I started planting my leftover vegetables from my fridge in terracotta pots filled with soil. I peeled off the skin of an avocado pit, wrapped it in a paper towel, put it in the cupboard for two weeks, and waited until roots started to sprout from it, then stuck it in dirt. I propagated broken-off cactus limbs and planted them in empty yogurt cups. I put two lettuce seeds in a pot, and one of them grew bright and green. I invited a friend over and we ate the lettuce leaves with our hands, chewing in silence to appreciate the miracle of a nutritious and wild thing growing inside a Brooklyn apartment. I wondered what happened to the other seed: If seeds don't grow, are they considered dead? Or are they simply waiting for the right conditions to become?

And me too. I had a seed within me: a baby who was now the size of a watermelon.

At the Red Hook garden center, I picked up stacks of seed packets, silently mispronouncing their native names. Perennials were easiest, of course. Plant them once. They disappear in winter, then miraculously grow back in the spring. Their dependability shocked me; the endurance of dying off and then sprouting back again with no physical intervention was a miracle. Could it be that easy to sprout back to life after dying, year after year? I threw a few packets in my cart.

Then I walked to the annuals section: the ones you have to

replant each year. Begonias. Petunias. Most herbs. They were generic but pretty. Come winter, they'd be 100 percent dead, which was its own kind of predictability. I added a bunch of them to my cart too.

Alex liked to tell our houseguests that I was cultivating an indoor garden. I didn't correct him, but I didn't just want a garden. I wanted a jungle. I wanted towering plants and vines to crawl up the windowsill looking for something to strangle. I wanted thick, oxygenated air, and soil to spill out and stain our rugs, making my bare feet muddy and wet. One day, I wanted to walk into my living room to find that crows had made a nest in my Norfolk pine and hear their cacophony of caws warning of danger ahead. I didn't want domesticity. I wanted messiness. Heat. Humidity. Supple soil. I wanted the wilderness.

Between all my propagation and seed planting, weeds also started to grow around my carefully seeded flowers and ferns. How did they get there? How could an unnamed, unknown, unplanned plant be growing as if from the stardust of soil?

I asked a friend who is a much better gardener than me what to do with the weeds, and she corrected me. "There are no weeds, Kerry," she said sagely.

She clarified that weeds were not a blanket *type* of plant: They each had a scientific name with a story of origin. We simply labeled them weeds when they appeared in places we didn't want them to appear.

"Take dandelions, for example. When they're on a manicured lawn, they're weeds. But anywhere else, they're yellow *flowers,* offering pollen to the bees or herbal remedies. Their value is determined based on the beholder's decision: Are they a threat and a nuisance? Or beautiful and healing?"

I watched as the weeds grew around my basil plant, bravely and boldly demanding that they had a right to thrive too inside the corners of my small Brooklyn apartment. I would let them grow. They too had a right to fight for survival. To exist.

There were no weeds.

Sixteen

Three A.M. and I was up again. Time to pump. The lactation consultant I'd talked to recommended I take a few days off from breastfeeding. My nipples were completely bloodied and chapped, skin flaking off my swollen areolas. The consultant told me that to get the right latch I needed to pretend I was holding a football. I thought of my dad completing a punt return in college: *like a leprechaun running through a field of clover,* a coach had said about him. I thought of Alex running with the football under his arm at Yale to score the winning touchdown. Why was a lactation consultant giving a new mother a football analogy while my father and my husband were quite literally on the other couch *watching* football with their pink and peppy male nipples perfectly intact? I hated when people told me what to do, even when I had paid them to tell me what to do. But I had moved my newborn into my arms like a football—laces out—during my feedings and it had indeed felt less excruciating, more like a vacuum than a chopping board. I supposed this was progress.

So far, nothing about this whole mothering thing had gone as planned. Prior to my due date, I had done hours and hours of orgasmic birthing meditations and chanting techniques, convinced that my birthing process would be a simple squat and "pop!" Instead, a stomach flu activated my labor, and I vomited for sixteen hours straight. At the hospital, while I alternated between licking ice chips and throwing up in a bucket, Alex got the stomach flu too and curled up in the fetal position, shivering, on the small, scratchy love seat in the hospital, while my mom brought him coconut water and placed her hand on his forehead, declaring *he felt warm*.

"Can I have *one* day about me?" I moaned, bloated with meds and contractions. "One day." The only positive memory of the entire experience—besides having a child, of course—was that the final episode of *The Bachelor* was on, and I was so relieved Ben chose Lauren B., because I still believed in love!

After my dilation stopped progressing, my doctor wheeled me into the C-section operating room, where I continued to throw up: dark green bile dribbling down my chin while my stomach muscles were, quite literally, outside of my body. Eventually our beautiful baby girl was pulled out of my uterus, and the doctors placed her on Alex's chest while I tried to come back to lucidity. We named her Ava James. And I instantly loved her.

I loved the warmth of her newborn skin against mine, and

while sometimes she co-slept with us, tonight she was in a bassinet in the room next door. There was nothing more lonely or depressing to me than being up alone in the middle of the night breathing to the sound of a breast pump machine as the rest of my family slept soundly without me. The only thing that made it more depressing was doomscrolling. Which I also was currently doing. I googled all the ways my child could die. Guns came up as the number one cause of death in America for children. Not cancer, not drowning, not cars. Guns.

I typed "roller coaster reels" into my Instagram search bar. My friends thought my roller-coaster watching was strange, albeit endearing: a personal quirk that made people simply respond *huh* when I shared it with them at parties. Often in idle moments during the day, I would pull up a video of someone livestreaming on a roller coaster, hold the phone two inches from my eyes, and then silently scream, mouth open as the track plunged downward, feeling the slight flip in my stomach as the secondhand gravity overtook me. I was terrified of roller coasters, crying every time I went on one in real life. Watching roller-coaster reels now was a form of exposure therapy, much like eating pickles. I wanted to like pickles so badly. Every time I ordered a sandwich at the deli, I'd lick one, hoping—just hoping—today would be the day I enjoyed it. But every time I tried it, my taste buds turned up in disgust. Not yet. Still, I had hope. People could change, you know?

After six minutes of watching people plunge down steep drops, I started to feel motion sick. I couldn't look at my phone any longer. What else was there to do? I thought about meditating, but that sounded boring. I thought about texting a friend. But who was up at this hour? I thought of Beau. He had texted me on my due date, two days after I actually gave birth: *Are you a mom yet?* I had sent him back a photo of me, wrapped in a warm Faherty blanket on the hospital bed, holding Ava. He sent a pink emoji heart back.

I considered what to write to him, considering that I was now a lonely, isolated milking cow whose child could one day get shot in school. The opposite of sex appeal. He didn't know *Kerry the mom* yet. Would he even want to know this version of me? Did I even know this version of me yet? What would we talk about now? I thought of how the day before I gave birth, I had hugged my friends, telling them it had been a good life together and wishing them the best of luck. *Ker,* they responded, *you're giving birth, you're not dying.*

A part of me may be, I had responded. *But time will tell.*

Maybe I shouldn't text Beau. I should exercise restraint. I put my phone back on the dresser. Back to the pumping sound.

Oh, hell, what was the point of anything anyway? The hormones, or maybe life itself, were making me a nihilist. I would text him, albeit something *helpful.*

Hey B, just a reminder to stop doing drugs.

He immediately texted back. *How did you know I was up, and how did you know I was doing drugs?*

Because I know things, I said.

Whoosh whoosh whoosh went the pump on my bloody nipples. *Whoosh whoosh whoosh.*

Ugh, he texted back, *the ghost of Kerry always haunts me.*

~

I FOUND THE REQUIREMENTS of raising a healthy human depleting and claustrophobic: the sleep schedule (barely had one), the sleep training (couldn't do it), the lack of extra breast milk (supplemented with formula). I found neediness to be a repulsive trait, and Ava's understandable needs were never-ending: the feeding, the changing, the wiping, the putting to bed. Every time she cried when I put her in the car seat, a little of my life force evaporated.

Other parents gave me unsolicited feedback constantly. Everywhere I turned I was fed conflicting information that convinced me I was doing everything wrong and somehow endangering my child. The wrong bottle. Wrong diaper. Wrong lotion. Plastic everywhere. Chemicals everywhere. I was desperately trying to keep my child alive while also unintentionally slowly killing her. This was America.

I didn't take a maternity leave. Instead, I took Ava to the office, pumped in front of the interns, breastfed in the dressing room, and passed her around like an emotional support dog. So much was happening at work: We were in the process of opening three new stores, needed to restructure our marketing department, had recently hired a new women's designer, and were about to shoot our fall catalog in Puerto Rico but didn't have the proper samples due to production delays. In the afternoons, after dealing with Faherty issues, I chugged my second cold brew of the day, put Ava in the stroller, then met Arum at her weekly meeting with her record label to chat through her distribution strategy.

Ava was not an *easy baby.* She cried all the time, refused to go to sleep, and got carsick, throwing up in taxis and Ubers and airplanes. I started traveling with gallon-sized Ziploc bags wherever I went.

At night, I made my friends come over and take turns bouncing with Ava on a blue medicine ball to quell her exhausted cries. While I made dinner, I listened to my friends' stories about their recent dates and tried to imagine what it would be like to have sex with someone who was not my husband. I had lost my virginity to Alex and then had seriously dated Abe. The math was simple: My count was two.

After my friends left, I would draw a bath, and I'd spend an hour in a too-small Brooklyn bathtub, my head tilted on the tile wall with a sleepy Ava perched on my knees, just breathing, breathing, breathing while soaking in the hot water. Then I'd put her to bed, fall asleep alone, and murmur a "good night, love you," when I heard Alex creep into bed.

And in the morning, I'd do the whole routine all over again.

Months and months passed. Painstakingly slow months.

FOUR MONTHS AFTER HAVING Ava, we hired a full-time nanny. Almost all the childcare options seemed underwhelming and unbearable: Pay someone to watch your kid (the cost of which might be equal to or greater than your own salary), give up your career to stay at home, or try to piecemeal it all together.

The day Pam started, she showed up thirty minutes early and walked around the apartment pointing out how nothing was childproof. "And this," she said, opening the cabinet under the sink. "You cannot have liquid detergent here." I took notes on my phone titled "how to be a good mom."

"Got it," I said, frantically typing, as she showed me the exposed cord from the TV. "She'll chew on this like a puppy." *Or a bunny,* I wanted to add. Decades before, my mom had brought home a miniature gray bunny named Sam in a small, cozy cage. But in her empathetic pet-pleasing way, my mom felt bad for poor little Sam and his small living quarters. So she bought Sam a bigger cage. And then replaced it with an even bigger one. But she still felt bad. So she decided to let Sam out of the cage to hop around the room, only to find that Sam peed all over our wall-to-wall carpet, pooped on the treadmill, and chewed through computer cords. This enraged my mom: How dare Sam shit on, quite literally, the freedom she had given him?

One day, I walked home from a playdate and Sam was gone.

"Where is Sam?" I asked my mom.

"Sam is in a better place," she said. To this day, she *swears*, she absolutely swears, that she dropped him off at a "bunny farm," but I never saw proof of this fact.

"This was your fault," I said to my mom. "You were the one who wanted to give Sam more freedom to move around, and then you punished him for it." She didn't disagree.

I tucked the TV cords into a drawer, then ran into the nursery, where Pam was changing Ava. "You're not wiping her vagina properly," she scolded, undoing Ava's diaper to show me clumps of hardened diaper cream in the crevice of her private parts. And she noticed that there was a bottle in the crib: "Never give the bottle in bed, honeyboo. It rots the teeth." Her affectionate "honeyboo" nickname made me want to cry in relief, as if she saw me too as a child that needed tending to.

"Got it," I said, nodding.

The next morning, before Pam walked in, I raced to the crib to get rid of the bottle in bed, but she caught me and scolded me again. "Not my first rodeo," she said, laughing while shaking her finger at me.

I handed her coffee, gave her a big hug, and said, "I have a feeling you're going to save my life."

And day after day, she did.

~

EACH MORNING, I WOKE up tired and defeated and strangely lonely despite now having a child, a full-time nanny, a husband next to me, and a fantasy lover. I had all the privileges in the world and still felt I was failing at everything: bad mom, bad wife, bad entrepreneur. Time moved slowly, and I could not handle one more person tilting their head at me sympathetically while cooing at my child and saying, *Doesn't time just fly by?* No, it didn't. I felt like I had aged by decades, and I couldn't believe it would be two more years until my child could speak to me in a full sentence.

I wore my exhaustion on my face. I had recently heard of "slugging," a term to describe slathering petroleum jelly on your face at night to keep the moisture in, so in an attempt to keep up with the times, I began slathering fossil fuels on my skin. I thought of growing up and seeing my mom's medicine cabinet with Vaseline jars: Maybe she had been ahead of the beauty curve after all.

Besides the slugging, my most trusted beauty secret was still compulsively wearing Maybelline twenty-four-hour lip stain. It was always too bright and too bold against my pale skin, and though it got increasingly blotchy throughout the day, I'd rather have blotchy color than no color. Perhaps then, I reasoned, no one would notice the bags under my eyes and the weariness in my gaze and how I was clinging to my fragile identity as a walking zombie/repressed working mom. They would only think: *Wow, that's bright red lipstick.*

~

IT WAS SATURDAY AND we were at the park again. I hated the park: It smelled like hot metal, the trees were malnourished, and the squirrels were on the verge of rabidity. As I pushed Ava on the swing, I thought about the news article I had recently read about a mother who had a psychotic break and for seven hours straight pushed her daughter on a swing in a daze. When she finally snapped out of it, she realized her child was dead.

How long had I been pushing?

Ava turned her head to smile back at me. I kissed the side of her cheek, *mwahmwahmwah,* and transmuted my restlessness into a Nelly Furtado song, yelling, "I'M LIKE A BIRD! I'LL ONLY FLY AWAY!" over and over. The more I sang the song, the better I felt, imagining myself with wings flying up and above the city out into an open sky, feeling free, free, free.

Ava squealed and giggled. I relaxed when she smiled.

On the way back home, I walked by the Brooklyn Promenade, overlooking where the Hudson River and East River met below the Manhattan skyline. I saw a small bouquet of dried flowers pushed between two wooden slats on a bench. Pushing Ava in the stroller in front of me, I walked closer to see a metallic plaque cemented below the flowers that read: *For Karl, the cutest little baby in the world. March 10, 2015–July 13, 2015.*

Proof of Karl's aliveness. He had existed. He was loved.

I was not Karl's mother. But I was not *not* Karl's mother. I exhaled slowly, feeling tears brim in my eyes. Ava was now six months old, two months older than Karl had been when he died. I pictured myself having to bury my child. A tiny coffin. A tiny dress. A tiny shovel to bury her in a field of wildflowers at a natural burial ground.

My heart broke into a million pieces for every mother everywhere who bore the devastation of burying a child. Here I was spiraling at how hard it was for me to be a mom, while Karl's mom would undoubtedly give anything to hold her child again. I did a Tonglen meditation: breathing in the pain of mothers everywhere who had lost a child, letting myself feel their grief, then breathing out comfort and peace and love to them. Inhale the pain. Exhale love. Alchemizing collective grief into love in every breath.

I love you, I whispered to baby Karl.

I love you, I whispered to baby Karl's mom.

I love you, I whispered to Ava.

I love you, I even whispered to myself.

Seventeen

I once found a sperm whale on the beach in South Carolina. It had washed up the night before and was lying on its side, bloated, tail stiff, eyes cloudy. Strands of blubber hung loosely from the small holes that seagulls had pecked into the flesh.

"Plastic bags," the marine biologist murmured when he examined the whale on the beach. The news was full of similar scenes—malnourished whales washing up dead on shores across the country—and the autopsies were often the same: mounds of plastic lining their stomachs. He didn't say what gender the whale was, but I knew it was a she. She had been hungry and the very thing that she thought would nourish her, killed her. I touched the tip of her tail before they strapped her to the bed of a pickup truck. Her skin felt cold and rubbery, not unlike my grandpa's hand after he died. I wondered if the whale's soul entered the Bardo too—if maybe, somewhere, she was still frolicking in the sea, plastic-free, with a baby calf beside her.

~

"THERE IS NO AWAY," Dr. Chad Nelsen said as he gave me a tour of his Surfrider office lined with surfboards and photos of Jack Johnson and prestigious environmental awards. Surfrider was one of the organizations Faherty supported yearly, and we were interviewing Chad, its CEO, for an upcoming catalog feature.

"I cannot be in one more fake family photo shoot for our catalog," I had told our head of marketing when she asked for content ideas for our spring campaign. Mike, Alex, and I weren't fighting per se, but our narratives about one another were becoming increasingly laced with annoyance. And anytime we had a family shoot, these grievances reared their heads. *Why are there so many people on the production team?* Alex would ask me, doing the math of their salaries in his head. *Why is the fit of this sweater too tight?* I'd ask Mike, trying to stretch the yarn out. *Why did you skip the design meeting where we discussed sweater silhouettes?* Mike would ask back, while refusing to look me in the eye. And then we'd be sitting in thick wool sweaters in the middle of July trying to pretend it was the holidays, just sweating, sweating, sweating in our frustrations while trying to get the cover shot. Yes, sometimes we still laughed together, but mainly we just sweated.

"Understood," our marketing director had confirmed, which

was why I had flown out to SoCal to chat with Chad: Inspiring environmental activism was what the people needed, not fake family photo shoots. I admired Surfrider's mission, utilizing grassroots volunteerism and legal advocacy to push plastic reduction, ocean protection, and clean-water policy both locally and nationally.

"There is no away," I repeated back to Chad. I let this idea permeate deeper in my mind. I thought about this in terms of plastic. Of clothing. Of where we store repressed emotions.

"Everything we have ever made, bought, received, and thrown out still exists somewhere in the world," Chad continued. "There is nowhere we can make things disappear."

I knew this truth all too well. I said I cared about the environment, and yet I was a walking hypocrite. I ordered take-out often, and everyone knows that even when you put those plastic containers in recycling, ain't nothing being recycled. I traveled all the time for work, both via my gas-powered vehicle and my flights (usually middle row 16D given that I still hadn't figured out how to get frequent flier miles). I ate meat, a lot: cheeseburgers, roasted chicken, medium-rare steaks. I took too many baths and used up a lot of digital energy via cloud storage. And that was just in my individual life, not to mention that my full-time job was in one of the dirtiest industries in the world: clothing. We worked hard to make ourselves a "sustainable" clothing brand, but how could any clothing brand truly be sustainable? Every day I woke up and helped make and sell things that people didn't really need. Indeed, I'd recently read an article that cited an exasperating statistic: There are enough clothes in the world *right now* to clothe the next six generations. And here we were, day in and day out, designing and selling new ones.

Were we singlehandedly contributing to the climate crisis? Was it better to just quit? Or was it better to enter a flawed and dirty industry and try to do things better? Could capitalism be done more consciously or was it a lost cause? Could I be both a part of the problem and part of the solution at the same time? I didn't know the answer. I still don't. But I do know, Faherty was my job and I cared about it, and I was committed to making the best decisions at work that caused the least amount of harm. And the team around us shared the same commitment.

So much of Faherty's commitment to sustainability was and is tied to the small, daily, unsexy decisions we make about our supply chain: the farms and mills from which our materials come, the operating ethics of the factories, and the overall quality of craftsmanship. We are anti–fast fashion, meaning we want to make clothes that can last a long time. The most sustainable item in your closet is, after all, the one that you wear time and time again. We prioritize low-impact materials like organic cotton and recycled yarn and try to ensure our stores are fueled by renewable energy. Every decision has a cost-benefit analysis, sometimes resulting in higher prices, production delays, or more work for our team.

I brought up our Faherty poly bag conundrum to Chad. I had recently made our team stop using poly bags to ship our clothing in. Almost every garment manufactured by a clothing company was shipped in a poly bag derived from fossil fuels. Billions and *billions* of those plastic bags then end up in a landfill each year or the ocean. I thought of the sperm whale on the beach, starved to death by a stomach lined in plastic. I was not living in an ecosystem separate from that whale: My choices affected her life. Feeling the weight of this truth, I had our team start sourcing and shipping our clothing in paper bags. But the new packaging was the bane of our store team's existence.

"We can't use these," Alex said one evening in the back of our SoHo store, holding up a ripped white paper bag with the words *THIS IS NOT PLASTIC* on it. "It's burdensome to our store team. The packaging is not see-through, so every time they need to find a different size for a customer, they have to rip it open to see what's inside. And last month, Ker," Alex added, "our Boston store flooded and all the clothes got wet. If they were encased in plastic, they wouldn't have been ruined. Don't forget we could use *recycled* poly bags, Ker, which would solve the sustainability issue *and* help our store team."

These were all very fair points. And he wasn't wrong. Besides, I had heard arguments that recycled plastic packaging was way less energy intensive than paper packaging made from trees. But then again, paper didn't cause whales to starve to death. I didn't know what decision was more right or more wrong, but I did know it felt better to me, in *my* stomach, to use paper.

"We're using paper," I said determinedly in a tone that Alex knew meant not to fight me on it.

"Do what you gotta do, Ker," Alex finally acquiesced.

ON MY WAY HOME from interviewing Chad, I stopped at a coffee shop to get another cold brew. I had forgotten my reusable mug at home. I considered skipping the coffee, knowing a plastic cup would take something like 450 years to decompose. I had a sudden vision of my personal landfill filled with toothbrushes, floss, tampons, product jars, to-go containers, bodega bags, coconut water bottles, and to-go cups. So many coffee cups: the sins of every sip.

I ordered the coffee. "No lid or straw!" I requested. After the barista handed it to me in a plastic cup, I took a sip and it tasted smooth and cold, but with a slight aftertaste of moral failure. Once again, I had chosen convenience over sustainability.

There was no away.

Eighteen

Beau was in town for a few days for press meetings and asked if he could crash on our pullout couch. *Of course,* I had said. On his last night, a group of us migrated to our dimly lit New York City rooftop and, with a view of downtown Brooklyn, karaoked to our favorite emo nineties hits. I sang Ace of Base, belting out the lyrics to "The Sign" while making up an impromptu dance.

"Look at those moves," Beau said, laughing. Alex reminded everyone that what I lacked in skill I made up for in confidence, sharing how back in college I had boldly tried out for the hip-hop team despite having absolutely no hip-hop experience except for watching *Save the Last Dance* twenty-five times. Needless to say, I didn't get a callback.

As everyone's karaoke got louder and everyone but me got

drunker, I snuck off to bed, not only because I was, obviously, the fun assassin but also because I was six months pregnant.

The pregnancy had not been a surprise, but I don't remember it being intentional either. Alex and I had an unspoken understanding that if we didn't have our second—and likely final—kid now, we would lose the stamina to endure through the daily toddler routine all over again. Most days, we were on autopilot, undulating between routine and rushing. Alex woke up with Ava and did Magna-Tiles. I packed the snacks. We both persisted through the painstaking saga of putting on her socks and shoes. We clutched Ava's hand each morning as we rushed down the street to her preschool. Then Alex and I rushed to work. Then Zoom meetings, emails, in-person meetings, more emails. I crossed off task after task in my notebook. After leaving the office, another routine ensued: bath, pajamas, teeth brushing, a bedtime story.

If our days were filled with a mundanity, why not at least add another human being to the mix that was bursting with love? We were privileged to be able to afford Pam to help babysit the kids, and Faherty seemed slightly more under control: We had secured a good loan to help with cash flow, recently hired a new head of people who could take a lot off my plate, and had a new office downtown that felt spacious. Nordstrom had now picked up the men's line. With the current timing, the new baby would be twenty-two months younger than Ava.

I woke the next morning to the sound of a coffee cup being gently placed by my bedside. I opened my eyes and massaged out the pillow lines creased across my cheeks. Alex looked fresh, his thick hair wet and tucked behind his ears. He had, as per usual, woken up before dawn, run three miles, crushed a push-up and burpee routine, stretched, showered, and then taken Ava out for a walk, bringing home lattes for me and Pam, and undoubtedly Beau too.

I took a sip of the creamy coffee and sighed deeply. "Thank you for being my angel," I said to Alex.

"Thanks for the quickie last night," he said, grinning. When he had crawled into bed the night before, I stirred awake as he spooned me from behind, rubbing his leg—our sign that physical intimacy was an option. He availed himself of my unspoken invitation.

"Proud of us," I had said when we finished, my head on his chest, feeling the fast postcoital heartbeat through his ribs.

And I was. Trying to maintain an active sex life while pregnant and raising a toddler was a feat, and whenever we did it, it felt strangely productive. "Sex helps to keep your second chakra lubricated," one psychic told me, "which is the source of Creator energy—not just in the form of creating a child, but also in the creation of artistic expression." I liked the idea that sexual intimacy could also serve as life force energy for the creation of art. I had recently started a new Instagram account under another name and anonymously posted poems there despite having no followers. The act of sharing my words with no regard for how others would respond made me feel wild and mysterious. Maybe one day I'd post them from my own account, unafraid of attaching my name to my deepest, darkest thoughts.

"I'm heading into the office, Ker," Al said, packing up his Faherty tote bag. "Don't forget we have a catalog review at ten thirty."

"Yup, I'll be there."

Alex then paused and looked at me curiously for a moment. As if he wanted to say something else. Perhaps he questioned if I would make it to the meeting. A few days before, I hadn't shown up to the office at all, instead going to a matinee of a new independent film highlighting human rights violations in the cotton industry. Or perhaps something more disturbing crossed his mind. Perhaps he was thinking of Beau sleeping alone on the sleeper sofa in the next room. Perhaps he recognized that the two of us would soon be alone together with only a toddler enthralled in *Moana* as a chaperone. Perhaps he wondered if Beau's and my friendship wasn't just a friendship. Or perhaps he didn't think any of these things at all, and it was simply me, lying in bed, who wondered.

Whatever Alex was thinking, he left me with a directive. Or a plea.

"Be good, Ker," Al said, kissing my forehead.

"I will," I assured him.

~

I WAS SO BORED with myself. Week after week, month after month, I sat on Liza's couch and complained about the same three problems: (1) Faherty work dynamics, (2) Faherty family dynamics, and (3) Beau.

"This continues to be a very intense triangle," Liza said as we unpacked the "be good" story. For example, she noted that when Beau came to town, Alex encouraged me to spend solo time with Beau. And then Alex would listen to Beau's music, and he'd tell Beau that he was his superfan. And then Beau would tell Alex what a role model he was for him. And then all three of us might be at the dinner table, and Alex would go to the bathroom, and Beau would say, "I wish I had you to myself." And then Alex and I would crawl into bed that night and have sex with Beau sleeping in the other room.

Certainly it was better to get some of my needs met outside

of the marriage instead of spiraling in discontent and resentment in my marriage, right? When I was with Beau, I felt like an old version of myself: one whose identity belonged solely to me, unencumbered by the demands of business, motherhood, and marriage. His world of travel and music and creativity was intoxicating. He loved feelings and shared them honestly, which in turn helped *me* feel too: So many of my emotions had been locked away over the years, as if they were unwanted visitors who I couldn't entertain due to the busyness of life and the business at hand. I had avoided them for good reason. If I felt the depth of my feelings and excavated what made me feel certain ways and why, then certainly the next step would be having to be accountable to them? Which meant if I wanted to feel better, things would need to change. I would need to change. But how? And what would be the consequences?

I thought I had escaped my Irish genetic proclivity for addiction, but deep down, I wondered if I too was an addict: self-medicating with fantasy to avoid feeling my discontent. Beau was my drug of choice: I thought about him whenever I wanted to escape my life. On Instagram I tracked what songs he was singing in concerts and how they'd changed from the demos he sent me. I listened to his songs compulsively, dissecting the lines to figure out who he had written them about and tracked the chronology of his life via his Spotify song releases. I googled him, youtubed him, texted him, then wished I hadn't texted. He often talked in radio interviews about how he loved poetry, and I whispered, "Son of a bitch" under my breath.

The unhappier I was in my own life, the more I needed to drink from him, even if it was from the confines of my own imagination. There were only so many types of thinking the brain could do: Wasn't it better to use the mind to create an imaginary fantasy world than to swirl in anxious and discontented thought patterns?

"Kerry," Liza repeated.

I blinked hard a few times, trying to return to my surroundings: the gray-and-white room with the fake orchid in the corner. I made a note to bring her a pot of soil with a real flower in it. Proof of life beyond humanness should be a requirement in every therapist's office to remind us that we're not the only species on earth right now trying to survive.

"Can I ask you a question?" she asked.

"Yes," I said.

"What does it feel like to be abandoned?"

See, I knew Liza saw me. She heard me. She understood the marital dynamics I was dealing with. That I was abandoned by my husband in his obsession with Faherty and I deserved a refuge, even if it was a fantasy.

"I feel grief that Alex abandoned me," I said.

She shook her head.

"No," Liza said. "How does it feel to have abandoned *yourself*?"

"I haven't abandoned myself," I said indignantly.

And then I started to sob.

Nineteen

When Doug Good Feather walked into our Faherty office, the first thing he observed was that there was a ghost that walked the halls. "And one of your team members has encountered him," he added.

Since my conversation with Mike around Native-inspired prints, I had spent months connecting and brainstorming with Native artists on collaboration ideas with Faherty. A mutual friend had connected me to Doug, who was an artist, veteran, and teacher from the Standing Rock Lakota and Dakota Nation. He also ran a nonprofit that offered Indigenous healing practices to those struggling with addiction and post-traumatic stress disorder.

After months of phone calls getting to know each other, Doug came to visit our team in New York City. He spent hours sketching out designs for artwork he later named the Spirit Horse, a silhouette of a horse surrounded by a medicine wheel. After lunch, Doug shared his life story with our team and reminded us that the longest journey a human could make is not one of geographic distance, nor up the rungs of the ladder of success, but rather *from the head to the heart.* He explained that so much of the epidemic of loneliness in our current society was due to our human tendency to be caught up in our own thoughts and fears and not see the interconnectedness between the human and more-than-human world. "To live more consciously," he said, "we need to return to our heart and to listen to the earth."

He also shared the parable of two wolves, which is commonly attributed to the Cherokee tribe. In the tale, an elder tells his grandson that inside every person there is a battle between two wolves. One wolf represents qualities like anger, envy, regret, greed, guilt, resentment, and ego. The other wolf stands for qualities like joy, peace, love, hope, humility, truth, and compassion.

"Which wolf will win?" the grandson asks his grandpa.

"The one you feed," the elder replies.

I thought of my Gemini nature: one side that was the committed, entrepreneurial, lawyerly wife and mother, and the other the bohemian, wild creative who dreamed of a life untethered to others. Two different parts of myself at battle at all times. Both wolves hungry. Maybe both wolves could be fed and cared for, but I was beginning to wonder if only one of them was sufficient to lead the pack. The other one would need to be tamed.

After Doug left for the day, one of my teammates pulled me aside.

"Doug was right," he whispered. "There's a ghost in the office."

This particular team member had come in to work on a Sunday a few weeks before, and while he was in a bathroom stall someone had knocked on the bathroom door. The knock scared him: No one else had been in the office that day. He quickly zipped up his pants and opened the bathroom door, only to find that no one was there. And then, two seconds later, the ceiling above the bathroom stall where he had just been standing *collapsed.*

Had he not answered the knock, the large chunks of plaster and ceiling would have fallen hard on his head. I wondered, did this mean it was a *good* ghost? That it saved him from getting a concussion or something worse? Together we did a simple Google search and learned that there had been several deaths in the building. A man had fallen down the elevator shaft in 1904 and another died there in 1908.

When I texted Doug to tell him what had happened, he said: *The spirit world and real world overlap. The spirits walk among us and protect us.*

Months later, we launched the Doug Good Feather Spirit Horse blanket collaboration and it became a bestseller. As our relationship deepened over the years from collaborators to family, I would later help Doug buy a house from which he could run his nonprofit, Lakota Way Healing Center.

We also began collaborating with a renowned designer named Bethany Yellowtail of the Northern Cheyenne Nation. Bethany admitted that one of the main reasons she was open to working with Faherty was that she had studied how thoughtfully we handled the partnership with Doug and appreciated that on our website we had outwardly apologized for past appropriation.

"Most white-run brands don't apologize when they commit harm. They try to throw money at a problem, but they don't apologize or change their ways of doing things," she said. "It's hard to trust people when they fail to acknowledge past harm."

Trust. That was the cornerstone of these partnerships. Not marketing and not profit but building a mutually reciprocal relationship based on care, love, and the consistent act of *showing up*. We were committed at Faherty to getting better, even when we made mistakes. And we did make mistakes. For example, in the initial months of working with Bethany, she designed a sweater with a beautiful motif for our women's line. Our men's design team liked it so much, they made a version in men's. When we showed Bethany a final sample, she stopped us: "The motif I gave you symbolizes fertility and can't be placed on a male garment," she explained.

It was a learning curve for us to understand that highlighting Native art was not the simple act of putting a print or pattern on a garment; rather, each motif and symbol had a meaning—one that was an important part of the artist's lineage and culture, sometimes even requiring approval from their elders.

These collaborations turned into deep friendships, and in these relationships I found purpose at Faherty again. I was moved by how Bethany, Doug, and, later, our other partners like Lehi Thunder Voice Eagle, Steven Paul Judd, and Jennifer Berg used their art and business to give back to their own communities. Each of them had more expansive ideas of success, beyond the mere act of making money. Instead, they qualified success through the lens in which their work uplifted and supported their community. The idea of measuring success based on the *well-being of the collective* was far more inspiring than quantifying success based on the money of a few, which was the obvious and primary tenet of Western capitalism.

Given what I was focusing my time on, I announced to the team that I was switching my title from president to chief impact officer. Though my day-to-day tasks didn't change that much, something about declaring that I had a new title made clear my priorities. If I wanted things to be different both in my life and the fashion industry, then I needed to take agency over what I could control. I would focus on sustainability, partnerships, culture, and philanthropy. I cared about this brand and its impact on the world. Faherty was Alex's and my first baby, after all, and I wanted to raise it well.

~

"SOMETIMES I WISH . . ." ALEX said, staring at me from his side of the bed.

I awaited in suspicious suspense to hear what work problem urgently needed to be solved at 11:30 P.M.

Some couples watched murder documentaries as their foreplay into a good night's sleep—true American marital masochism—but Alex's and my masochism was talking about the business. Our bed was often where our most honest and intense Faherty meetings occurred: facing each other in the dark, brainstorming ways to increase sales, rehashing the typos in our catalog, and sharing insights on interpersonal dynamics between team members. Nothing like a heavy dose of work stress to work its magic on your melatonin levels.

"Yes, bug?" I encouraged.

It wasn't about the business.

"Well, I've just been noticing a lot of my friends' wives, like, *do things* for their husbands . . ." Alex chose his words very carefully.

"Oh?" I responded with a hint of surprise.

He continued. "Like they make them dinner after a long day of work. Or put away the laundry. Or bake them their favorite desserts . . ." Mike had a new girlfriend, and she had, not once but twice, baked gluten-free treats for him to bring into work.

I knew where this was headed. I kept listening.

"And you do lots of nice things, but not for me." Alex had recently admitted to me that he felt like I cared about other people more than him: helping them move and decorate their apartments, inviting them over for elaborate meals, brainstorming their business plans, loaning money, and gifting them therapy and psychic sessions from my Rolodex of self-help teachers.

"Ker, instead of putting money in savings, you're literally spending thousands of dollars a year on other people's therapy," he'd remarked recently.

"There is nothing more valuable in the world than healed people," I'd responded. "It's worth every penny. We all benefit from raised consciousness." I had offered to pay for his therapy too. And Mike's. But neither took me up on it.

"I just wish you cared for me more. Well, not cared, but, like . . ." He tried to find the word.

I knew the word.

"Serve you?" I suggested with eyebrows raised.

"Yeah, like serve me," he said sheepishly, laughing at hearing the word aloud. "I wish you served me."

From a mere statistical perspective, I did a large majority

of the household duties, the hosting duties, the childcare scheduling, and the social calendar duties. Every day I woke up to support his and his brother's dream. I gave him emotional and physical affection and words of affirmation. What was I missing?

"Maybe you don't want a wife," I suggested. "Maybe you want a mother."

He paused, considering what I'd just said, neither defensive nor in agreement.

"I'll have to think about that," he said.

~

MY PHONE BUZZED IN the middle of a marketing meeting to review our email blasts template. I looked down: It was from Beau.

Hey, there's something I want to tell you.

I already knew what he was going to say. His texts and outreach had been quiet for the past couple months, and I had recently had a dream of a woman with a short blond bob at one of his concerts who came up to me and said, "Please let him go. It's my turn now." I knew what she meant.

So happy for you, I texted back. *You deserve someone who can be your anchor.*

How did you know that's what I was going to tell you?

Dream world. Sorry.

Ugh, fuck this lack of psychic boundaries, he said. *But yeah, I'm really happy.*

I was happy for him too. He deserved to have someone available, someone he could start a family with. No one should want a life they can't have.

Twenty

If Ava's birth was difficult, Riggs's was worse.

After Ava, I wanted to try for a VBAC, also known as a vaginal birth after cesarean—but when my dilation stopped progressing, they wheeled me in for another C-section. When my ob-gyn made the small incision to reopen my scar to pull Riggs out, I watched a spray of red blood—my blood—splatter and saturate the blue paper sheet that separated my chest from my pelvis. They had lacerated my uterine artery, I later learned. I heard my doctor yell, "Fuck!" and then I heard someone yell, "Get him out, get him out!" Someone grabbed Alex and pushed him outside the operating room into the hallway, where he stayed for the next two hours, his face pressed against the small window, waiting for a glimpse of his newborn son and signs of life from his wife.

In the chaos, I had no idea what was happening, except that the nurses and doctors were frantic. I heard my doctor yell that she needed another doctor. And that's when I began to feel very, very foggy.

I heard Riggs crying in the corner, alone.

"Will someone hold my baby?" I begged, fighting for lucidity through the anesthesia, the primal demand for my baby to get skin-to-skin contact rising through my throat. "Will someone hold my baby?" I begged again.

Minutes went by, maybe five, maybe twenty, and then another surgeon rushed in, took one look at my vitals, and yelled, "Where's the blood?! She needs blood transfusions! She's fucking hemorrhaging to death!"

"I can hear you," I whispered from the table, feeling fainter by the moment.

When telling people my birth story after, I would often mention the laceration and the transfusions, but what I didn't share was that lying there on the operating table, I began to believe that I might not make it. And that, in the moment, despite hearing my newborn child crying somewhere in the room, I didn't even care that my life was slipping away.

A calm blanket of ambivalence about living or dying engulfed me, an overwhelming feeling of peace all around. Suddenly, I felt a profound knowing that it didn't matter if I lived or died because ultimately, I wasn't going anywhere. I understood at that moment that I was simply transitioning from one state to another—understanding, for the first time truly, that energy could be neither created nor destroyed. I had read so many books on dying and near-death experiences, and whatever I was experiencing was exactly as most of them recounted: a warm and loving energy enveloping every inch of my veins. It felt like home.

I didn't die, of course. And I didn't get to stay in that state of golden love. Instead, at some point, I woke up in the recovery room and looked down at Riggs sucking on my nipple.

I was okay. He was okay. We were okay, right?

For months, I replayed the scene over and over, telling people how bad the birth was. I studied Riggs closely, wondering if he carried the trauma of those first few moments of his life somewhere in the body, afraid that my sweet, sensitive Pisces child's first moments were of isolation, confusion, and chaos. And that somehow it was my fault.

~

AFTER REPLAYING THE BIRTH scene to Liza, she opened up one of her desk drawers.

"I think you should see a friend of mine," she said, slipping me a business card. "Cassie's a natural health practitioner who does bodywork."

I didn't know exactly what *bodywork* entailed, but I knew that I probably needed to get in better touch with my own. I remembered James Joyce's description of one of his emotionally detached characters: "Mr. Duffy lived a short distance from his body." Sometimes I too felt a short distance from my body, or maybe even a long distance from my body: floating two miles above earth most days, watching the tiny version of myself go about my day, an ant scurrying in and out of cracks in the sidewalk.

"And she works on children too," Liza added, "and can help them integrate traumatic birth processes."

"Thank you," I said, overwhelmed with gratitude. She saw me. "Thank you."

I SAT ON THE edge of a massage table in a small, sunlit Brooklyn office filled with crystals, essential oil bottles, and loose herbs; the room smelled faintly of patchouli and jasmine.

Cassie worked tenderly to smooth and flatten the hardened, fibrous rope of purple skin around my C-section. She did it so gently, it tickled, and I almost started laughing, but then a wave of nausea and exhaustion suddenly came over me. As she continued to work on the scar, I felt myself slipping deeper and deeper into a trance, as if the blood around my uterus were coagulating into thick, brown sludge. Eventually, I passed out completely.

"I think I just went to the underworld," I said slowly as she shook me awake to let me know the session was over. I could barely move. "What the hell just happened?"

She smiled knowingly. "That's the anesthesia leaving the body," she said. "I could smell and taste it: thick and metallic."

"Anesthesia leaving the body?" I gasped. I had never heard of such a thing, not even on goop, and Gwyneth knew all the alternative, controversial wellness tips.

"Sometimes the drugs get stuck in the sutures of the scars," she affirmed. "For your next session, bring Riggs along."

A month later, I was back on the table. Riggs sat on my lap squirming.

"Can I let him watch *CoComelon* clips?" I asked sheepishly. I knew that *CoComelon*'s creepy AI music would likely dampen the sanctitude of the session, but desperate times called for desperate measures.

Cassie smiled, free of judgment.

"Of course," she said. "Now let's relive your birth," she said, placing one hand on my back and one hand on Riggs. "Tell me what happened, step by step."

"It was really bad," I began. I told her how my uterus had been accidentally cut after they pulled Riggs out and how Alex had been escorted outside. She nodded, then with one hand firmly on my back and the other on Riggs's back, she reframed.

"Riggs came out healthy and Alex waited outside, watching over you lovingly."

I paused. *Okay.*

"And Riggs was crying alone in the corner," I continued.

"And a nurse picked him up and held him tightly, rocking him," she reframed.

"And a doctor came in yelling that I needed blood transfusions, and I thought I was going to die."

"A well-skilled surgeon rushed in to help. And strangers had willingly donated their blood to save the lives of others, and there was lots of fresh blood available to replenish you. And you lived."

I nodded.

"And soon you were safely out of the operating room, and Riggs was in your arms, and Alex was by your side, and everyone was okay."

I nodded again. Yes, her version of the events was true as well.

"Never again say you had a terrible birth," she said. "With all that love and skill and support every step of the way? Everything was perfect."

My cheeks were wet with tears. I had been carrying the

weight of how terrible it had been. How Riggs had been traumatized. And now someone was telling me that maybe, in all of that suffering, it was still somehow perfect?

I didn't quite believe it yet, but I almost did.

Everything was perfect.

Twenty-one

Another dream: I stood in front of a red door holding a huge bouquet of flowers. A line of people waiting to receive a flower from me stretched down the sidewalk. Alex walked toward me. I tilted my head to him, gesturing to the long line, motioning for him to take his place at the back. That's what would be fair, of course. Because all these people had been patiently waiting in line for so long. But he didn't want to wait.

"Can I cut?" he whispered to me with an eager, hopeful smile. In the dream I nodded, though somewhat grudgingly, and then I reached into my large bouquet and pulled out a single flower for him. Bright and yellow.

He paused. Looked down at it. Looked back up at me, still eager. He wanted another flower. I shook my head.

"One flower each," I said.

These were the rules. Whose rules? I do not know. But I think they were mine. My rules.

"Ker," he countered, tinged with desperation, "I'm your husband . . ."

"One flower each," I repeated, and I watched as his face fell. Wanting, just wanting, more love. He was my *husband,* and I knew he deserved more flowers, but in order for my energetic bounty to last, it had to be allocated appropriately across my family, my friends, my kids, the business, partners in need, and myself. There was something communistic about my love—evenly rationed. I knew it wasn't fair to the people I loved most to give such evenly proportional doses of attention and time. Ava had recently had a friend over and eyed me suspiciously as I knelt down beside her friend to chat. "You love her more than me," Ava had accused after her friend went home.

"Of course not," I said. But I suspected she wasn't the only one in my family who wondered if I loved someone more than them.

Sometimes I felt like a salt lick, gratifying on the tongue initially but leaving people thirsty. One lick and they wanted more. Everyone wanted more.

"I already gave you one," I responded to Alex's second request for another flower.

And then I turned my back on him.

~

ONE MORNING ON THE way to school, Ava asked about a building we passed every day.

"What is that for?"

"It's an old folks' home," I told her. And then, because I

wanted to be a good mom who taught her children empathy and the harsh reality that many people die alone in the world, I added, "It can be really lonely for people who live there."

Ava stared at the building for a minute. "I think you'd like it there," she said matter-of-factly.

"Really?" I asked, unsure where this was headed.

"Yes," she said. "Because you love being alone."

I wasn't sure if I felt seen or offended.

LATER THAT DAY, I went out for a walk. Alone.

"Be back soon," I said to Alex, pressing the button on the elevator and watching our apartment door slowly shut behind me, the mess of the day remaining on the other side. I took a right out of my apartment and started to walk slowly down the slope from Cobble Hill to Brooklyn Bridge Park, where pier after pier had been remodeled into mini ecological enclaves up and down the waterfront. I opened up my phone and selected one of Beau's songs, inhaling it for a quick fix to remember a part of myself that was neither a business owner, a wife, nor a mom. When the song ended, I switched to Enya: music that was just as emo, but less masochistic to my psyche.

I read an article once about how Enya lives alone in a castle with her cats in Ireland, but that she admittedly doesn't feel lonely because her love affairs with beautiful melodies and words nourish her so completely. That moved something in me.

As I walked, Enya's celestial chants activated a dull ache in my sacrum: I felt a yearning for something I couldn't place—a longing for some place, some life that was just beyond the scope of my fingertips. A homesickness for something I couldn't quite name: a returning to something that would make me feel safe and assured that everything was okay. It was a homesickness for *myself:* for the person I used to be, the person I might become, or the present me, who still seemed somehow out of reach.

Ava was right. I did love being alone. My hunger for solitude was insatiable, which was almost laughable given the life I'd chosen to lead, which was a life in which I was never alone. I commuted to work on a crowded subway. I worked in an office filled to the brim with people and clothing. I shared an office with my husband. I came home to children with needs. I worked with Alex's family during the week, and then, on the weekends, went to our shared family house that Alex had helped Ninie buy years ago. Recently, I had burst into tears when we arrived to the house and there were six other family members crashing there for the weekend.

"Al," I said, "I told you I really wanted alone time for us and the kids to regroup and rest."

"Sometimes you have to make sacrifices," Alex said, not unkindly but not sympathetically, as I went upstairs to hide in our room. I wasn't a victim. I knew what I signed up for: entering into a big, entangled family that wanted to build a big, successful brand. I had willingly signed up for it. And I loved so many parts of the family and the business. And yet, sometimes I didn't feel like it was *my* world. That I didn't have space to exist fully in it. That my needs and desires mattered too.

"Meaning I need to sacrifice what for what?" I asked.

He didn't answer.

ALONE TIME WAS AS important for my soul as sleep. Like an oyster turning a piece of sand into a pearl, I needed solitude to alchemize my irritability and my nihilism into something valuable and beautiful. And in order to have that time alone, I needed to steal moments like a thief: A solo car ride. A bath. Another walk. Choosing solitude was writing a love letter to myself, where I could wrap my arms around my heart and ask, *How are you doing?* and then wait long enough to hear the answer. Was it self-absorbed and a flaw to yearn for so much *me-time*? Or a sign of beauty and self-love that I loved tending to the garden of my messy mind?

I STOPPED AT PIER 6 to sit for a few minutes in front of a sunflower garden overrun with long, tangled weeds. I looked at my watch: I had already been gone thirty minutes. My time of freedom was ticking down slowly and I felt a desperation to elongate it: *If you want more time, move more slowly through,* I repeated to myself, a mindfulness mantra I had heard years ago. I found a bench and sat down on it. In a world organized around productivity, sitting midwalk *because I wanted to* was a form of resistance.

An older man sat next to me on the bench.

"Did you know this park has over 150 species of birds?" he asked me while pulling up a pair of binoculars to his eyes.

I wanted to tell him how I had recently heard the fact that 2.9 billion birds have gone missing in North America since 1970. Gone missing, meaning dead when they should have been alive—eradicated because of lost habitats, changes of climate, pesticides, and house cats. But I didn't tell him that because he looked content, and that type of fact makes one feel discontent.

Instead, I said, "Wow, incredible." And I meant it. So many birds in Brooklyn!

He quietly pointed out a flash of red between the sunflowers.

"Hi, Grandpa," I whispered to the cardinal. I had heard cardinals were our dead loved ones coming back for a visit. Soon after my grandpa's death, he appeared to me in a dream, sitting in a lawn chair by the lake drinking a can of Molson beer. "Is it true every time I see a cardinal it's you?" I had asked him.

"One outta every four," he said, before taking another sip.

When I lost sight of the cardinal, I said goodbye to my new birding friend, and kept walking until I felt my phone vibrate in my pocket. I hoped it was from Beau. Did he still think about me?

For someone who extolled the virtues of mindfulness and being present, I was an escape artist, fantasizing about all the other lives I could live someplace else. Deep down, I wondered if I was a runner, constantly formulating an if-then plan to cope with disaster. If the company went under, then . . . If Alex died, then . . . If something happened to one of my kids, then . . . If I got sick, then, then. Then.

Return, Ker, I whispered to myself, picking up the phone to read the text.

It was from Alex: *You back soon?*

I had been gone too long. I didn't need any plan Bs; I was living in plan A. I thought of Pema Chödrön's teachings of "the wisdom of no escape." There was nowhere to go but here, my life now.

En route, I texted back, quickening my pace.

A block away from home, I picked up a seven-dollar mocha with whipped cream, fuel to get me through the rest of the afternoon: the cleaning of the apartment, the making of dinner, the bedtime routine. I took my first sip, foamy and sweet, and breathed deeply, the sugar and caffeine jolting the body back to reality.

When I walked back into our apartment with chocolate around my lips, I saw Alex's eyes dart to the clock on the wall. I had been gone too long. But I had returned with fistfuls of gifts: I was more at ease, more patient, more relaxed, more present. More love-soaked.

"I didn't think you'd come back," he said lightly.

I looked around the messy apartment: chicken nuggets on a tray, a deconstructed fort of blankets covering the couches, half-finished kombuchas on the bookshelf. My Norfolk pine needed watering, but I could get to that. Alex's laptop was open on the kitchen table, which was a clue to the fact that he had spent the last hour working on spreadsheets. I suppose he went missing too.

"I almost didn't," I said jokingly. Then I wrapped my arms around him and let myself sigh into his chest, drinking in his slightly salty smell—a mixture of gluten-free pancake mix and my Everyday Oil, which he now slathered on his skin daily.

"Sometimes I worry you'll fly away," Alex said into my ear.

I wondered if he was talking about today's long walk or referencing something bigger. I thought about the northern wheatear, a bird the size of a sparrow that migrates from Uganda to Alaska every year. From Alaska to *Uganda*—nine thousand miles. Did any of them plummet into the Bering Strait, exhausted, not knowing they were almost home? Surely they could have found a closer place to migrate for berries and bugs, but something in their adaptive evolution must have proved that they'd be rewarded for the long journey, returning months later, plump and full.

"And if I do fly away?" I tested.

"I'd find you and bring you back," he said.

Twenty-two

I hadn't talked to Beau in months, but I tracked him, watching his Instagram Lives, zooming in on his puffy eyes, assessing whether he was drinking too much again. I imagined years from now he'd be a mala bead–wearing, meditating, sober musician, but he wasn't there yet. It worried me.

"Should I reach out?" I asked my friend Kathryn.

"Nah," she said. "You can't save him."

"I don't want to save him," I said, rolling my eyes. "I want to help him. I have *really* good advice." I once sent him one of the guided mindfulness albums I had recorded years before, and he texted back, *You always know what I need.*

But I also knew that trying to help never helped. It was a Docherty family joke we shared that every time we tried to help someone in the way *we* thought was best, it proved straight up *unhelpful* to the person. I had learned by now that anytime one of the women in my family offered unsolicited advice that started with the phrase "Do you know what you should do?," it was just a sneaky attempt to control and shape-shift the other person. Not only that, but I had personally begun to see a correlation between me trying to save someone from their own intrinsic harmful patterns and trying to avoid my own. Why work on acknowledging and meeting my own needs when I could just tell someone else how to meet theirs? It had become clearer and clearer to me that the most content, healed people rarely give advice, whereas the most dissatisfied people spew unasked-for feedback. Which one did I want to be?

"Don't say anything, Ker," Kathryn said again. "It's not your place. Just write down what you want to tell him, and he'll hear the message energetically. Telepathy is real." I did believe telepathy was real, often getting a text from someone right before I was about to call or having vivid dreams about how someone was doing before they told me. Sometimes, I could walk into a family setting and *hear* if someone was annoyed at me without them opening their mouth. *I can hear you,* I would want to say, their unspoken judgments zinging into my consciousness, as I tried to smile and pretend everything was fine.

The next morning, in my journal, I wrote Beau a letter.

> *Sometimes in the middle of the night I wake up thirsty and walk barefoot to the kitchen for a cup of cool water and sip it slowly in the dark. Then I tiptoe into my children's room and sit on the edge of their beds and gently stroke their hair away from their closed eyes as I whisper quietly, I love you. They can't hear me, of course. They're asleep.*

But I trust my words to land like seeds on soft and fertile grounds. I have no stake in your journey, but I hope you get sober one day.

I didn't send it.

Weeks later, I woke up to a text from Beau: *Hey, catch up soon? I'm thinking of getting sober.*

~

I SAT ON THE toilet in the back of our San Francisco store hearing blood clots the size of golf balls plop out of me. Since Riggs's birth, my period was ferociously and debilitatingly heavy. It was also formulaic, which was to say I hemorrhaged on the second day of my period from the exact hours of 2:00 P.M. to 8:00 P.M. eastern time. Sometimes, when I wanted my friends to feel bad for me, I would scoop out a clot the size of a pig's heart from the toilet, hold it in the palm of my hand, and send them a photo. I always felt relieved when they affirmed how *fucking insane* this was: my own personal monthly menstrual blood bath.

I had spent hours googling what was happening medically, diagnosing myself with a heavy-period condition called menorrhagia: *Do you go through two supersized tampons in an hour? Do you feel lightheaded? Are your blood clots bigger than a quarter? Do you sleep on towels at night so as not to wake up in your bed to a murder scene? Check. Check. Check. Then call your doctor and go to the ER.*

Oh, okay. Clearly I could not go to the ER whenever it was that time of the month.

All the blood loss made me queasy. I had also become strangely addicted to carrots. They were the first thing I wanted when I woke up: a long, orange, barely washed, organic carrot with my cup of coffee. And then the craving endured throughout the day. Midmorning snack, carrot. After lunch, carrot. After dessert, carrot. It drove Alex crazy. "Ker, this is disgusting," he said time and time again, while holding up a flaccid, rotting carrot half he had found on the dresser, behind a cushion, in the bathroom sink, or in the car cup holder.

"Well, you leave your used contacts everywhere," I rebuked, "and they become shriveled, dried shards of glass that cut my feet when I walk on them unsuspectingly at night."

"No," he said. "They evaporate."

But I knew he was wrong, because I had been tossing my used daily contacts down the bathroom sink for months, and when I told our landlord that our bathroom sink was clogged, he came over to fix it and found hundreds of them stuck together in a congealed plastic slime.

"What the fuck?" he said.

"Sorry, I thought they just disappeared," I said.

"Nothing disappears," he said, pouring more Drano down the pipe.

"NOTHING DISAPPEARS" SEEMED LIKE an appropriate statement for my emotions too: all my resentments and fears and hopes buried in my uterine lining. A psychic told me that the cause of my bleeding was that I was energetically hemorrhaging, giving my life force to everyone else—my kids, my husband, my work, my friends, and even strangers. This happened in a hundred ways every day as I opened up my email, my Instagram, my text messages, saying yes to other people's needs even when I didn't want to—donation requests, informational interview requests, job requests, free clothes requests, advice requests. I tried to answer each communication, no matter what, even when I felt depleted. Everyone gets a flower! I felt grateful that I, both as an individual and through our company, had resources we could share, but in doing so, my field of energetic wildflowers was becoming increasingly sparse. Why did I feel like I owed my valuable time and attention to other people whenever they asked for it? Why did I feel like my self-worth was tied to ensuring others got their needs met to the detriment of my sacred and limited energy? Why couldn't I say, *I'm sorry, I can't*? One step further, why did I even need to apologize? Why couldn't I just state, *I can't*? Or, more succinctly, *No*.

"If you don't start saying no, be prepared to keep bleeding," the psychic said at the end of that session.

Despite the fact that my mom loved psychics, she encouraged me to make another appointment with an actual doctor.

"Something isn't right," she suggested gently, watching me organize Legos while gnawing on a carrot.

"I'll go to a doctor when I have time," I said.

"Don't minimize, Kerry," she said. "You always minimize."

Twenty-three

I was sitting cross-legged on the gray sofa when Liza remarked that she thought it was "interesting" that I rarely shared how I felt about being a mom.

"Motherhood is boring." I shrugged. "What am I supposed to tell you? How much I wipe? Wiping butts. Wiping high chairs. Wiping counters. Wiping coconut butter over my C-section scar. Very meditative, all this wiping."

Liza smiled knowingly. I couldn't hear her thoughts, but I couldn't *not* hear her thoughts around my pre-enlightenment syndrome.

"I am obsessed with my kids, but they're inconvenient," I added. I loved my children, but I didn't love mothering. I loved being with them, cuddling with them, walking with them, talking with them, but I didn't like *doing things* for them. Meeting my children's constant needs hijacked the other parts of myself that made me feel alive: my time, my independence, my creativity, my sensuality.

Liza was right: I didn't talk about mothering that much. But again, what was there to say? I found conversations around child rearing to be boring: details about whether the kids ate *adult* food, whether they were potty-trained, whether the parents were raising their child like a French *bébé*. I often felt like most of us moms were bleary-eyed windup dolls in a déjà vu matrix: the sleepless nights, the prepping of breakfast no one would eat, lost socks, temper tantrums around the string cheese not being taken out of its wrapper properly. I didn't want to talk about these things with anyone. I wanted to talk to people about what they fantasized about, whether they were satisfied or discontent, what made them feel ashamed, and what made them feel alive. I wanted to talk about sex and death and madness and past lives and longing and art and plants and poetry. I wanted to talk about *creating*.

I wondered how often therapists encouraged their male clients to talk about *fathering*.

"I told you the other day how Ava made me stop reading *The Giving Tree*," I reminded Liza, as Ava had started crying mid-book. "Stop, Mom, just stop," she had said, tears streaming down her face as I described the tree as a stump. "It's just too sad." I wanted to tell her it made me sad too, watching this tree give and give and give away everything she had till there was nothing left.

Liza kept prying. "I'm more interested in how you're handling the identity of being a mom. How are you *feeling*?" She emphasized "feeling," as she always did.

"I know what you're trying to do," I said, staring her down. I believed most therapists proclaimed an internal victory whenever they got one of their emotionally repressed clients to cry, and I suspected Liza was trying to make me cry again, to get to that vagus nerve or whatever it was called where my entangled grief and sorrow was stored. To get to the root of the molten-lava truthiness of who I was and who I wanted to be. I hated when she did this. Once, she asked me what would happen if I went there—to that place of grief—and I responded: "You think I can just wake up this happy and optimistic? If I waded into the well of sadness that all humans everywhere have to endure through, I might never come back."

She looked back at me.

I tried to change the subject and mentioned that Beau had a concert in New York soon and I was wondering whether I should go and make small talk with Beau's new girlfriend, but Liza brought it back to the kids. "How does it feel engaging with Beau now as a mother of two?"

I tried to talk about how Mike had stopped asking me for advice on what we should design for the women's line. "Why would my male cofounder not ask his female cofounder what women's clothes she wanted to wear?" I asked.

"How does motherhood affect how you think about the business?" she asked.

I told her how Alex recently scolded me because I hadn't signed up Ava for the soccer team we had agreed on, missing the deadline for her to play.

"How has your marital relationship changed now that you're a mom?" she pressed.

It felt fragmenting. I was fragmented. All my old identities had dissolved. The lawyer who focused on human rights? Gone. Mindfulness teacher. Gone. Entrepreneur? Half-assed.

Friend? Dwindling. Creative? Never prioritized. Mother? Subpar.

"I'm bad at everything," I said, crying.

I HAD ASKED MY own mom recently what she thought of my parenting skills. She had offered to babysit for a weekend while Alex and I visited our West Coast stores. The moment she arrived, she went into full domestic overdrive, bleaching the stains out of my white tops and organizing the toiletry basket under the sink and my Tupperware drawer. She spent hours *goo-goo-ga*-ing with Riggs, reading Ava stories, and baking homemade chocolate chip cookies for them. She was a natural mother and homemaker, gratified by caregiving.

"Do you think I'm a bad mom?" I asked, watching her on her hands and knees while she held up a rag filled with dust bunnies, a dried contact, a yellow square Lego piece, and what looked to be a white dog hair from my neighbor downstairs: all of our New York humanity converging through a metal HVAC grate.

"Riggs is breathing this in, Ker. He has childhood asthma. You have to clean the vents."

"Noted," I said. "But do you think I'm a bad mom?" I asked again, enunciating each word slowly so she could understand the gravity of my question.

Before having kids, I had dreamed that one day I'd be the type of mom who made homemade dinners each night, food that satiated my children's diverse palates. I imagined bringing them to museums and hosting DIY birthday parties with no plastic toys; I'd read them chapter book trilogies; I'd teach them another language; and I'd never give them a screen.

But I wasn't that type of mom. I was never home early enough to make a home-cooked meal, and dinner often amounted to three chicken nuggets, four grapes, two slices of a cucumber, and half of an unwashed, gnawed-on carrot—my own teeth cutting it in half.

I didn't like going to museums or playdates, declining every birthday party my kids were invited to because I couldn't stand the thought of small talk. Despite hating plastic, I had bins and bins filled with emaciated blond Barbies and PFA-ridden dinosaurs because they helped entertain the kids for hours so they wouldn't bother me. More often than not, despite having worked all day, I turned on the TV for them when I got home so I could have a minute of time to myself to doomscroll through Instagram or call a friend before the bedtime ritual.

"Sometimes you have to do things you don't want to do," Alex had said to me recently after I politely RSVPed no to a Little Gym birthday party at 2:00 P.M. the next Saturday. Instead I had planned to take the kids to the garden center to pick up a cactus and then dawdle into some vintage stores.

"Believe me, I know," I said. "Everyone's life is doing things we don't want to do. But sometimes it's okay to do what I want."

"All the other moms will be there," Alex added.

"Pretty sure they don't want to be there, either, Al," I said. "But good for the self-sacrificing, martyring moms who show up. I'm not going."

"Do what you gotta do, Ker," he said, shaking his head. I swore I could hear some sadness in his voice while noting that he didn't volunteer to take the kids to the party in my place.

"I don't think you're a bad mom," my mom finally responded. "I just think you have a lot of other priorities, so the kids don't always come first." I wondered if she was reflecting back on how, a few weeks before, she had watched me spend hours in a pop-up store setting up racks and racks for a Faherty sample sale while the kids played with hangers and toilet paper in the ADA-compliant bathroom. They should have been in bed. "We're hungry," Ava had complained as I realized it was 8:30 P.M. I had forgotten the snacks, yet again.

"Okay, fine. But do you think I'm a *good* mom?" I asked, slightly reframing the question.

I watched her now put her dusty rag in the bucket of baking soda, vinegar, and soap. Too much silence lingered between my question and her answer.

"Oh my god, Mom, you don't think I'm a good mom."

"I didn't say that. I didn't say that! The question caught me off guard. I think you're a great mom in all the ways you know how to be great."

I didn't know what she meant, but I kind of knew what she meant. I wasn't good at the logistics of parenting, but I hoped I was satisfactory in providing my children with spiritual and emotional tools? Ava knew what mindfulness was, could visualize a peaceful place when she was upset, and knew the names of approximately thirty-two different feelings, even noting, *Sometimes you can feel two things at the same time.* She said, *My body, my choice,* in the bathtub when Riggs tried to wash her hair, and she thought a good president should be one who shared (*because a lot of people didn't share*). Meanwhile, Riggs knew about past lives, made up dramatic dances to pop music that reflected his current mood, and said when he was angry his "heart felt like a rock."

"Me too," I had agreed.

When I told Alex later about the conversation with my mom, I asked him if he asked himself a hundred times a day if he was a good dad or a bad dad. If, at night, he ranked himself like a mathematical equation: adding up all the good things he had done and then subtracting all the ways he had failed, in the hopes of getting to a number above zero. If he tied his worthiness to how well he cared for others? If he wondered if he was doing enough?

"Nah," he said, "I don't really think about things like that."

"That must be nice," I said. "That must be really nice."

~

BEDTIME WAS ONE OF the few parts of the day when I felt like I was a good mom, because not only was I really good at taking baths, but I was also really good at lying in bed and making up stories. The nighttime ritual always began the same way: I'd draw a bath, get in myself, declare that the bath water was still too hot, and then send Ava and Riggs on a quest to find plastic toys that needed cleaning. When they returned with their chosen, dirty toy, they'd find me in the tub, surrounded by bubbles, head against the cool ceramic, eyes closed, sighing deeply through a slightly open mouth. This was how I won four minutes of alone time.

Then I'd get out, they'd get in, Riggs would splash too much water out of the tub, Ava would pretend she wasn't peeing in the bath, and I would mentally drift away, thinking of the unanswered emails. The poem, unfinished. The laundry, undone. Beau in the studio. The monks in Thailand, chewing thirty-two times.

Return, Ker.

I knew presence was not preferential. If I wanted to practice what it meant to be right here, right now, it meant accepting that in this moment, there was nowhere else to be. I often daydreamed about what it would be like to pursue an unencumbered life of solitude and spirituality, but I realized I was already living in an ashram. My own ashram of motherhood: sitting cross-legged next to lukewarm water full of pee and soap and plastic hippos amid squeals and temper tantrums and clenched teeth, worried sighs, and giggles. I was exactly where I needed to be. I could evoke gratitude: My kids were alive and healthy and fed and safe. I thought of other children in both my own city and in homes across the world, who were not healthy and fed and safe. I breathed in their pain for a moment, feeling tears come to my eyes. They were not my kids, but they were not *not* my kids. I could feel the invisible thread of pain from their small hearts to mine.

"Why are you crying, Mom?" Ava asked.

"Because we're lucky," I said. "Now let's get in bed for a story."

Lately, I had discovered the perfect one-minute song to sing at bedtime, and the kids loved it. When the kids begged Alex to sing it a few days later, he discovered that I had been singing the theme song to *The Fresh Prince of Bel-Air.*

"Wow, Ker," he later said to me, laughing. "You really should start giving more parenting tips."

"Sometimes I'm a genius," I responded. "It's a modern-day lullaby and hits all the marks: It's about a prince, it rhymes, and it has a beginning, a middle, and an end. And it's exactly fifty-eight seconds."

Tonight, however, the kids didn't want the *Fresh Prince*.

"Tell me a story about someone who wins a lot," Ava said.

"You mean *swims* a lot?" I asked in an attempt to change the subject. Ava was currently a competitive child, obsessed with being the best at things. I didn't want to dim her innate desire for healthy competition, but sometimes it was too much. Time and time again, I'd have to tell her, "This is not a race," as she tried to see who could brush their teeth faster, get dressed faster, bike faster. When we did race, sometimes I purposely made her lose and then flaunted it, obnoxiously yelling, "Yes, yes, yes!" in glee. Losing made her cry, but for God's sake, the kid needed to know life disappoints at times. And besides, even when you think you're winning, you may be losing. I'd spent the first half of my life wanting to win at everything and pushing myself to be the best, and that mentality had f-ed me up: equating my worthiness to what I accomplished, not how I did it or how I felt.

"No, Mom," Ava clarified, sitting up in her bed. "Tell us a story about someone who *wins* a lot."

"Okay." I sighed. Time for a life lesson. I closed my eyes and thought about the Four Noble Truths of Buddhism, two of which are that life has suffering and that the cause of suffering is attachment. *Here we go.*

"Well," I began, "there once was a little girl named Fiona the First, and she always wanted to be first: first in line, first to eat, first to lose her teeth, first to go to school. First to finish her homework."

"First to climb a tree?" Ava asked.

"Yes," I said.

"First to fly on an airplane?"

"Mmm-hmm," I said. Ava squealed.

"First to poop?" Riggs asked, unsurprisingly. I had forgotten he was awake.

"Yes, Riggs," I said grudgingly. Not to stereotype, but boy humor had a consistent theme to it.

I continued. "Fiona was also the first to graduate. First to get a job. First to get married. And you know what else she was first in?"

"What?" Ava asked. Her eyes were glued to mine, her warm breath near my ear on the pillow. The suspense was killing her.

"Fiona the First was the first to *die*."

Ava's eyes widened and her lips puckered into a frown. She looked away, then stared at me again, something resonating inside of her. Then her lips turned up into a smirk. I smirked back.

"Good one, Mommy," she said, nodding her head in approval.

Sometimes we really saw each other.

Twenty-four

There was a ghost in Ninie's house.

There had been signs from the start. Lucy—Ninie's ten-year-old goldendoodle, who I never petted because I claimed to be allergic even though she supposedly didn't have dander—hated being alone in the house, pacing for hours until we came home, and barking into the back corner of the first floor.

Alex refused to admit that Lucy's anxiety stemmed from the presence of a spirit. "Lucy is just anxious and depressed, with feelings of abandonment," he said. But I disagreed. There was Lucy's sixth sense, but then there was another incident. Our friend Natalie had been downstairs during her son Caleb's naptime when she heard the pitter-patter of tiny feet scurrying across the floor above her.

"Caleb," she yelled up, "back in bed!" Silence. Natalie grabbed her trusty baby monitor, only to see that Caleb was asleep in his crib while she heard the sound of another young child's feet running up and down the second-floor hallway: the ghost of a little child.

"Dahlia," I declared when Natalie recounted the incident. "Let's name the ghost Dahlia." I don't know why I knew it was a girl, but I did. I recommended we buy a Ouija board.

"No way," Alex said. "Those things are fake and are designed knowing that someone will always move the weird wooden planchette to spell a creepy message." He looked at me knowingly, and I was reminded of my twelve-year-old self yelling, "It's spelling 'HELP ME'!" as my friends gasped in fear. It was true that there was always one person moving it . . . and, admittedly, I was always that person.

I loved having a ghost in the house, and I loved being spooked. As a kid, I watched endless episodes of Nickelodeon's *Are You Afraid of the Dark?* and chanted "Light as a feather, stiff as a board" in séance-type settings to see if my friends would float off the ground. I was infamous among my friends for telling horror stories around a fire, and my bookshelf was filled with books on the supernatural, including one of my favorites: *Do Dead People Watch You Shower?* (spoiler alert: They do).

I wondered if one day Dahlia would visit me.

A few months after the Natalie incident, I walked into our local liquor store to buy Ninie her favorite chardonnay.

"Address on the account?" the woman behind the register asked so I could claim the neighborhood discount.

"Ninety-two South Street," I said.

"Ninety-two South Street!" she exclaimed. "I lived there for years!"

"What a coincidence!" I said, laughing as I pulled out my debit card. "So you know about the ghost?"

Her voice dropped and she put her hand on my fingers midswipe. "The little girl, right? She died in the back room of the first floor. It used to be a doctor's office. We used to hear her running down the halls."

We locked eyes.

"Us too," I whispered back.

~

WE FOUND THE BABY robins on a warm and haze-filled summer day at the end of August. We were at the pool and Ava was running between the diving board and the snack bar when she heard the chirping. She flung off her goggles and started crawling on her knees looking under lockers for the source of the sound.

"I found a bird!" she yelled. A baby robin had fallen from the corner of a wooden doorframe, where clearly a mother bird had made her nest. "And here's another! There's three!"

I knelt down and saw the chicks, their tongues vibrating as they chirped in desperation for their mom. My friend Kathryn, who claimed she was a bird in a past life, who bought my children bird-watching books, who always spotted owls while driving, told us with determination to build a new nest. One by one I picked up their pink, fragile, and featherless bodies with a sun-warmed pool towel while the other kids at the pool made a makeshift home filled with flower stems and twigs. Suzanne, who worked in the snack bar, came over, looking annoyed.

"If you touch a baby bird, the mother won't return," she scolded. Ava's eyes widened as she looked at me. I looked around for the mother bird, seeing her perched on a telephone wire a few yards away. She was still calling out in guttural chirps. There was nothing she could do to save them. What was she communicating to her babies? Was she trying to soothe them? Or externalizing her own helpless grief? Wasn't I just like her? Trying so hard to protect my kids, but knowing once they fell from or flew out of the metaphorical nest there was so little that I could do to determine their fate?

"The mother will come back," I said to Ava firmly, as I gripped the shaking birds in the towel. "The mother always comes back."

THAT NIGHT, I LAY awake in our attic bedroom. It was hot, and I worried about the baby birds and wondered whether Faherty would make it and when Alex would stop working so much and if I was a good mom, and how everyone I loved would someday be dead. Sometimes, I rehearsed the funerals of the family members who were still alive, as if practicing their losses could protect my heart from future pain. I thought for a moment about what would happen if Beau died. How life on the surface wouldn't even change, because he had his life, and I had mine.

I don't remember falling asleep, but I remember waking up feeling that someone was next to me. I can tell you with certainty that a mother can always sense when a child is standing by her side.

And then I heard a voice whisper, soft and aching, "Open your eyes."

She was next to me. Dahlia. I could feel her breath on my eyebrow. I kept my eyes closed.

"I can't," I whispered back. I had been waiting for her to

come to me, but now that she was here, I was too afraid to look at her.

She whispered again, this time more urgently.

"Open your eyes."

"I'm sorry," I said again, clenching them shut. "I can't."

I could hear my heartbeat. The inside of my mouth was dry like cobwebs. I turned my back to her and pulled the sticky sheets over my head, desperately scanning my mind to think about anything other than little Dahlia next to me. *No one's there. No one's there,* I murmured to the pattern of Alex's rising and falling breath. I eventually fell asleep.

In the morning, I told Alex what happened.

"Weird," Alex said. "Let's go to the pool."

The second we arrived, Ava ran to check on the birds. All was quiet and still. No chirping. I scanned the snack bar and saw Suzanne across the way, watching us. She met my gaze, shook her head, and then walked away. I knew then that the birds were gone.

"Where are my birds?" Ava wailed, running up to me. I knelt down to her eye level.

"They're gone," I said. "But they were not abandoned." I visualized someone scooping up the ravenously chirping babies in the dark and then discarding them into a black plastic garbage bag without a prayer or funeral. "The mother would have come back."

I thought of the woman in my recurring dream swimming out to sea. I wondered if she had children at home. I shook my head to get the image out of my mind.

"The mother always comes back," I repeated determinedly.

I HAVE FEW REGRETS, but one thing still haunts me: that in the middle of that hot summer night, I did not open my eyes to see that translucent little girl, surely wrapped in a gauzy nightgown, standing barefoot by my bed. She'd been searching for a mother in the night. I had betrayed her. I should have done what was right. I should have looked her in the eye and told her that she wasn't alone forever. I should have walked her back to bed and told her that the mother always comes back.

NO ONE EVER SAW or heard from Dahlia again.

Twenty-five

I walked around my parents' retirement home noting which cheesy antiques we could sell if Faherty went bankrupt. Surely some of my dad's leather-bound books were worth something? My mom used to joke that when my dad died, she would cram as many leather books in his casket as possible. "And just when everyone says no more will fit, I'll cram in one more," she would say. I had a feeling these books represented something undiscussed in their marriage: my father flaunting unread books while my mom stored her beloved and torn spiritual books in her closet. Did most spouses have one last resentment they wanted to cram in their loved one's coffin before burying them six feet deep?

Alex, the kids, and I had recently driven fifteen hours straight to my parents' house in South Carolina. It was spring

2020, and as everyone was dying, we were bleaching our groceries, fighting with family members as to whether their health protocols were good enough, and trying to make sure Faherty didn't go under. The initial financial outlook of the business was grim: All of our stores were shut down, wholesalers had canceled their orders, our manufacturing partners' health and livelihood were at risk, and we had furloughed a large number of our team members.

As Alex and I went into business triage, we put my parents in charge of the kids. My dad took the morning shift, playing hours of Magna-Tiles before falling asleep on a chair due to a heart condition that he would not—true to family form per his past cancer secret—mention until months later.

My mom took the afternoon babysitting shift, which she often did with headphones on.

"I guess she goes MIA too," I commented to Alex as I watched the kids argue among themselves as she listened to her second Zoom meeting of the day. It was forty-five days into lockdown, and as alcohol consumption spiked across the country, my mom decided she wanted to quit drinking. She'd joined a recovery group called The Luckiest Club, which offered daily meetings encouraging sobriety. While these meetings were highly inconvenient from a babysitting perspective, I was deeply inspired by my mom's commitment to give up alcohol.

"Do you feel different?" I asked her a few weeks into her abstinence.

"Yes, in that I've never felt more myself," she said. I made a note to myself that one day when I pulled out the family tree to show Ava and Riggs our genetic proclivities toward addiction, I should circle my mom's name as well. I also noticed in myself the feeling of *wanting* more every time I finished one glass of wine and considered another: a taunting reminder of what likely lingered in me too.

Most days, Alex worked downstairs and I worked upstairs, fluctuating between being in full HR mode with the team, forcing my kids to memorize sight words, and watching all of the world's suffering through my phone. I will never forget the images: lonely hospital bed goodbyes, a Black father named George Floyd calling out for his mom as he was suffocated by a policeman, the scenes of overflowing morgues, and Native families on reservations pleading for basic resources.

As I sat on my bed watching the coverage, I felt grief coiled into a snake of rage in my stomach, and my first thought was: *Will anything change?* The second one was: *Will I?*

As I sat watching the newsfeed, I noticed two different versions of myself hashing out next steps: one of inertia, withdrawal, and complacency; and one of outspokenness, accountability, and action.

Wolves, begging to be fed.

The therapist Prentis Hemphill states, "The self is not an individual": None of us exists as a separate identity. Each of us is a silk thread woven together in a complex spiderweb of humanity, and what happens to one person affects the health of all of us. For God's sake, we quite literally inhale and exhale one another's breaths, whether we want to or not. As much as constructs or media narratives or systems of oppression like patriarchy try to make people *Other,* we are *not Other*.

Any time I felt fearful about speaking out or engaging in disruptive civil discourse, I inhaled the wisdom of people who were experts in communal care, self-determination, and transformational change making. More often than not, I found that wisdom embodied in Black, brown, Indigenous, and queer artists, friends, thought leaders, and spiritual teachers, who once again forge ahead in breaking down systems of oppression because their survival depends on it. Because they know all of our survival depends on it.

Bringing people together in shared creative community was usually my antidote to despair, but physical gathering was not an option. So instead, I hosted digital conversations with friends who were offering necessary medicine for a sick society: discussions around witnessing Black grief, exploring what it meant to be a good white person (spoiler alert: It's not about *nice*, it's about dismantling systems of oppression), and talking about what we could learn from the resiliency of the Indigenous community.

I had just finished posting my third conversation of the week when Alex texted me from my dad's downstairs office.

Hey, Ker, I support what you're doing, but Faherty's Insta isn't just yours. Can you run these conversations by me and Mike before posting?

This was a valid point: Faherty's Instagram was not my personal account. And yet, I wanted to post what I was posting. Social media was part of my job, and I wanted autonomy in what I was posting, much like Mike designed the clothes he wanted to design and Alex made the financial decisions he thought were best for the brand.

Can't I talk about inclusivity, grief, and healing without needing permission? I texted back. I thought the posts were uncontroversial, loving, true, and insightful. I was becoming increasingly confused about the way that intrinsically basic values around equality, kindness, empathy, and communal accountability were now being politically co-opted into something bad.

You can, but we're getting backlash.

While the majority of our customers appreciated the posts,

Alex was right that some others were not so happy. Our warehouse had recently alerted us that some customers were sending back their Faherty clothes in large boxes with angry handwritten notes: *You lost a customer, you woke idiots!* One of our wholesale partners who was of the exact race and gender you can imagine had written Mike an email saying, *How can you let Kerry talk about these things?* Others wrote beneath our posts: *Unfollow! Stay out of politics!* Another man commented that I needed to brush my hair. I could at least agree with him on that.

But I never understood what people meant about *staying out of politics*. Politics shaped nearly every aspect of our business: environmental regulations, how we sourced product, corporate governance requirements, tariffs, and, most important, the rights our teammates had or didn't have. We had team members who were denied healthcare for life-threatening issues, who were formerly incarcerated, whose family members were victims of gun violence, who were verbally or physically assaulted because of their race or gender identity, who grew up on a reservation without access to running water, who were afraid for their lives when they were pulled over for a traffic stop, whose families were at risk of deportation, whose kids needed access to hormone therapy, who needed to have an abortion. And someone was telling me that brands should *stay out of politics*? Huh? We were an American-born brand, and the only reason we were operating and successful was because of our team members: individuals who faced real American problems day in and day out. So no, there was no clear distinction between politics and business; no compartmentalization of our team's health and the brand, the individual and the whole.

I don't care if certain people are angry, I texted back from the bedroom.

That I didn't care if people were mad at me was an incredible indicator of my personal growth, years of therapy finally paying off. I used to hate it when people were upset at me. My whole life I had wanted to be likable. And I had been. I was literally one of the most likable people I knew: agreeable, optimistic, service oriented, self-deprecating! But being likable doesn't always mean you feel good, and I felt *good* rallying around incredible people envisioning a better world even if it meant hundreds of people were mad at me. I could be disliked and still feel steadfast, tender, and resolute. This was progress!

I didn't want approval anymore; I wanted authenticity. I wanted to put a stake in the ground on what I cared about: truth telling, community building, ending the patriarchy, cultivating creativity. What was the point of having a company if we didn't have the freedom to share what was important to us? I didn't join Faherty because I was obsessed with clothes; I joined it because I believed it could be a platform for the things I believed needed changing in the world.

I completely agree with you, Ker, I'm just worried about how it could affect the rest of our team. I could hear Alex's concern from a floor away. I appreciated how he was always thinking about the health of the team. He took his leadership responsibility seriously, albeit through a different lens. I thought about the social issues I wanted to support on behalf of our team members, and he thought about how specific stances on those social issues could affect the financial livelihoods of our employees. We also had concerns about their safety. We'd had an incident in which some people had walked in off the street and threatened our store team for having a "Love Is Love" decal on the store window. It had shaken everyone up. The world was becoming increasingly volatile and guns were everywhere.

I understand that everyone may not agree with us, I added, *but people deciding to not buy our brand because they don't align with our values is actually a form of conscious capitalism. It's a good thing. People should be intentional around who they buy things from and why.*

Yup, Alex agreed.

And I know some of these people, even if they hate some of the things we believe in, love their soft Cloud Cotton Henley so much they ain't sending it back.

LOL, Alex said.

Good talk. Let's eat.

Twenty-six

Beau checked in on me: *How are you and Al doing?* The text felt weighted.

Hanging in there, I responded. I had so much more I wanted to share with him: a couple new meditation podcasts and a new chanting song for his morning journaling. I wanted to tell him that one of my friends had played his band's music at her parents' funeral, and that there was recently a study of how kids all around the world could speak a language they had never been exposed to—fluently. Proof of past lives!

But I didn't tell him any of that. We didn't share as much about our lives as we used to.

How are you and Annie doing? I asked obligatorily, sensing this was what I was supposed to write back.

Well . . . we're planning on getting married soon.

I paused before I responded, watching the three dots appear below his text.

Just family and a small group of friends, he added. I cringed at the word "friends."

A few years before, the two of us were walking down a narrow brownstone-lined street through Brooklyn Heights. Beau had paused to peer over a wooden fence to watch two families having a barbecue in a small backyard: The kids were playing with a ball; the wives were talking together and drinking wine; and the husbands were both standing over the grill.

"Can't you imagine our families doing this years from now?" he'd asked.

I thought about it for a moment. But then I shook my head. I wanted to see the future he was imagining but couldn't. Maybe in the past I could have, but something had shifted between us by then, an unspoken sexual intensity, like a ticking time bomb awaiting the small, quick light of a match to blow everything up. Our relationship felt too flammable to be categorized as a friendship.

"Nah," I said, shaking my head. He frowned and stopped looking at the families, turning to look at me. "We're not friends, Beau," I said, sadly smiling. It would have been so much easier if we were.

"Yes, we are, Ker," he said matter-of-factly, as if daring me to believe it.

"No, we're not," I said, starting to walk again.

He exhaled, long and slow. He stayed a few steps behind me the rest of the block. When I got to the corner, I turned around to face him.

"Burger and a beer?" I asked, changing the subject.

"Yeah, I'm starving," he said, not looking at me.

I LOOKED DOWN AT Beau's wedding announcement text again. He wanted to give me the heads-up that he was getting married. And he also wanted to clarify that I wasn't invited.

It affirmed what I knew to be true. No matter how close we were, we weren't friends.

Congrats Beau, I texted back, and then added, *Make sure to sign a year-to-year contract.*

You're such a romantic, he responded.

I left it at that.

AVA CAME TO MY bed before the sun rose. She had lost her tooth.

"The Tooth Fairy left me something," she whispered while clutching a small envelope streaked with glitter. (Hint: I was the Tooth Fairy.) She thrust out her arm to show me the note inside:

Dear Ava, You will lose things in your life. Over and over. Trust that something grows beneath the gap.

I needed my daughter to know this truth, however young she was: We lose things. I thought of all the things I had lost: my jade Buddha necklace while swimming in Haiti, the yellow journal with one of my psychic readings I left on the plane to San Diego, hundreds of socks, a few friendships and lovers, and myself. I had even lost myself at times. Ava looked at me wide-eyed.

"But did she leave me any money?" she whispered. A crumpled dollar fell out of the envelope. She shrieked in glee.

I could see the spot in her gum where the tooth had fallen out: bright pink and almost bloody, faint ridges of a new tooth growing in. She had lost something that was a part of her, but in the gap where it had been, something newer, bigger, and stronger was growing.

One day she'd understand.

~

TO DIVERSIFY OUR FAHERTY Instagram feed from sun-washed tees and indigo jackets, social commentary and surfers (a classic non sequitur and dichotomous Insta feed), I reposted a picture of a whale swimming through the sea with a baby calf by her side. Underneath, I captioned: "I know things are hard right now, but somewhere, right now this is happening." Knowing that Nature seemed to be thriving while all of us were inside our homes helped to lower my cortisol levels. The only caveat to this was the fact that a nine-foot alligator, emboldened by the lack of activity around its lagoon, had recently wandered into my parents' yard and stared at our front door for hours, eyeing Ava and Riggs hungrily through the glass window panes. When I called the security guard from my parents' gated community to ask for help, he recommended we throw an orange at it to get it to move. Of course I livestreamed this standoff with the alligator because content is king, and man, does gator content go *viral*. Please note that after watching the alligator thrash upward on its back leg and violently open its jaws, we, and all of Insta, learned that one should never, *ever* throw an orange at an alligator.

But back to the whale photo with her calf: These types of images reminded me that no matter how stressed humans were, Nature—aka the *more-than-human world*—was largely unaware of our suffering. While we were in our freakouts and despair, the sunflowers still bloomed in an open field, the cacti stood stoic and prickly in the desert, and the eight-hundred-year-old redwood remained rooted steady in the forest. Instant perspective.

The morning after the whale post, I got an email from a children's book editor I'd met ten years earlier when I was teaching mindfulness to kids.

Kerry, it's time, the email said. Years ago, she had encouraged me to write a kids' book, but Faherty had hijacked any book-writing energy. Recently, however, she had switched publishing houses, and she was now looking for new authors.

"*Somewhere, Right Now* is the name of the children's book, and you are the author," she wrote. "You have six weeks to write it. I'm sending over a contract."

I was completely caught off guard and also euphoric. I had countless notebooks of unpublished and unshared mindfulness poems that had accumulated dust in the bottom of my bedside drawer, and now I had the opportunity to put some of these sentiments into a book for kids. The opportunity to share my work seemed both ten years (thirty years?!) in the making and also instant. *I ACCEPT!!!* I wrote back.

I spent the next four weeks writing it. I wrote one draft, my editor didn't like it, so I started writing again, this time about a family who, over the course of a day, had a series of big feelings (fear, anger, sadness, exhaustion) and how they supported each other through it. I made sure to put a dad who cried in it, and a mom who admitted how overwhelmed and tired she was. Each family member acknowledged the others' feelings, while also reminding one another that no matter how hard life can feel, *somewhere, right now,* something beautiful was still happening in the world. Whales were swimming through the sea, horses were learning to walk on a farm, giraffes were grazing on acacia trees. (I should admit with embarrasment now that I accidentally wrote that giraffes grazed on *apricot* trees, which is factually incorrect, because I am a flawed, non-detail-oriented person. *Kerbear, you don't read good.*)

When Ava asked me what my book was about, I told her it was about kids learning about nondualities. That two things can exist: We can feel pain in our individual bodies while also understanding that we belong to a world where, in every moment, beauty still unfolds.

She rolled her eyes. "Mom, everyone already knows two things can exist at the same time," she said.

"Not everyone," I said, disagreeing. *Not everyone.*

WHEN I MENTIONED MY children's book to my friend Kathryn, she recommended I join one of her classes at the Brooklyn Writers Collective. "Time for some adult writing too, Ker," she said, sending me the sign-up link.

The first class cracked me open. Over three hours on Zoom, fifteen of us—mainly women—shared our personal stories about grief and abuse and love and loss. Dear lord, everyone was *so honest,* excavating their buried feelings with the crude and sharp precision of the pen (or at least their keyboard).

Week after week, I accumulated snippets of entangled memories, weaving them into short stories. Molly, our instructor, pressed us, always, to go deeper: *What are you not saying? What is the unsayable that needs to be said?*

What didn't I want to say? What was I scared to say? And why?

Over the subsequent weeks, we shared essays on buried

dreams and sad brothers and dead mothers and babies that would never come to be. We cried over lost necklaces and lovers and laughed over blood and wine stains on white couches. We ruminated on the symbolism of ghosts.

"Isn't it crazy," Kathryn observed after one class, "how all of us are just walking around with broken hearts?"

~

AVA CAME DOWN THE stairs, her hair matted to the side of her face. She leaned her sleep-flushed cheek against my shoulder as she watched me write in my journal. Next week, we'd be returning to our apartment in Brooklyn after three months at my parents'. COVID wasn't over, but we were ready to get back to our life.

I had rededicated myself to writing at least three pages of stream-of-consciousness thoughts each morning to empty out the clutter in my brain before filling it with fresher ones.

"Who are you writing to?" Ava asked.

I paused. This was a good question. I flipped through my crinkled and wrinkled pages of hopes and sadness and dreams. I thought I was writing to myself, but I also felt like I was writing to someone more than myself.

"God, I think?" I talked a lot about God with my kids, indoctrinating them with all the spiritual teachings. We thanked Jesus for our food at dinner, lit incense and did tarot cards before bed, listened to Hare Krishna chanting on the way to soccer, talked to our ancestors on beach walks, yelled for Gandhi when we needed to stop fighting, apologized to Mother Earth when we stepped on ants, started natural burials in our backyard for dead worms, brainstormed all the different ways we'd come back to life after we died, and asked Buddha for great Easter baskets (sometimes things got confused).

"God," I confirmed. "I'm talking to God."

"Oh," Ava said. She seemed almost satisfied with that answer. But as she walked back to the kitchen to get her bowl of Cocoa Krispies, she paused and turned to look at me. "Shouldn't you just zoom?"

Twenty-seven

"Damn it," I muttered out loud as we walked into our Brooklyn apartment and saw my limp, brown banana plant in the kitchen. We had been gone for a full three months. I had let a friend of a friend who was a nurse stay in our apartment for free, as he volunteered in hospitals around the city. *Your only task is to keep my plants alive,* I had texted him before mailing him the keys.

The small succulent plants left over from Riggs's baby shower were dead. Two bamboo stalks propagated from our babysitter's tree were yellow. The Trader Joe's orchid looked bare and sad. The only sign of victory was that my large cactus had somehow birthed four bright pink-and-yellow flowers. For years, I had been watering it weekly, and all I got were green prickles. Left alone for months, however, it had bloomed flowers. If that wasn't a metaphor for the gifts of solitude.

My stomach dropped when I saw my beloved orange tree. When we'd left the apartment months before, it had been thriving, filled with sweet, fragrant white flowers that made the whole apartment smell like a rich person's bathroom. Twelve tiny, sour oranges had hung from green limbs. But now? It was covered in a white powdery substance that meant it had been infested by pests. I had been convinced that if I could grow an orange tree successfully in the confines of our apartment—if I could keep it alive, surely it was proof I could keep *anything* alive.

In the following weeks, I did everything I could to resuscitate that orange tree. I took it out of the pot, shook out the roots, and replanted it in new, fresh soil. I washed its leaves with hot water and soap. I sang to it. Stroked its leaves. Prayed something would grow back. I brought it out to our tiny four-by-ten balcony so it could feel the cool breeze on its leaves, placing it next to the dead puffer fish I had found on a beach cleanup with Surfrider in the Rockaways. It had washed up on the shore fully blown up like a balloon, beautiful, spiky, and dead. Ava had been asking for a pet for years, so I was thrilled to be able to bring her home one: one that she didn't have to feed or clean; one that would never swim away. I housed it in a bucket filled with bleach. Ava didn't seem to appreciate the benefits of having a dead pet that you could look at and admire without *doing anything*. No feeding, walking, cleaning, or worrying about when it would die because it was already dead! The only downfall was sometimes I detected its decomposing fishy flesh in its Cloroxed habitat wafting through my window.

I hoped orienting the orange tree next to a rotting fish

wouldn't heighten its despair. But maybe it did: The white powder came back. I brought the tree back inside.

Someone told me that ladybugs eat plant pests, so I ordered three hundred ladybugs on Amazon for $19.99 and unleashed them in the apartment with a single cut of a net. For three days, ladybugs cloaked every part of the living room: walking on the orange tree leaves, of course, but also landing on my coffee mug, on Riggs's backpack, on the remote control, on the toaster. I swore I felt one on my forehead as I slept one night. And then suddenly, on the fourth day, all the ladybugs were gone. Mysteriously, not one red-and-black carcass could be found. They looked to have done their job: Most of the powdery substance was gone. But weeks later, like dandelions rebelling against a manicured lawn, the pests came back stronger than ever.

"Orange trees belong in the wild, Mom," Ava told me matter-of-factly after I yelled out in frustration. I wanted to blame someone for this defeat. But who was to blame? I forgave our houseguest's plant-prioritization inadequacies: He had been too busy keeping humans alive. I forgave the pests, who, like weeds in soil, appeared with no malicious agenda but to survive. I forgave the ladybugs, who ate what they could before they too died.

The next day, I put the orange tree on our Brooklyn stoop with a note that said, "It tried its best."

By morning, it was gone.

~

THE DAY THAT BEAU got married two thousand miles away, my writing teacher announced to our class that next week's assignment was to write a letter we would never send. "Epistolary form," Molly instructed, "is a way for the narrator to speak a truth that normally would not be shared in conversation. It allows for the truth to exist in ways that other forms do not. Kerry," she added, "your letter will be workshopped first. See you next week."

Later that night, I opened Microsoft Word and began writing a goodbye letter to Beau, recounting the entirety of our relationship over the past six years: How the first time we met, we had made each other cry. How I sent him the poem called "When You Accidentally Kill The Things You Love." How I wasn't sure if he ever even read it, but maybe it was foreshadowing. How he said he hated poetry, but that he served as the key to unlock an inner poetry inside me that had lain buried deep in dry soil. How he entered my life at a time when I needed to remember I was more than just Faherty Brand, more than just a Faherty family member. How he helped me awaken a part of myself long forgotten: the part of me that was an artist too, yearning to speak her truth. I recounted in the letter the night we lay next to each other side by side with a child that wasn't his in my belly.

I wrote that I was finally ready to let him go, but that even the phrase "letting go" felt forced. The act of letting go felt like so much *doing*—or undoing—like cutting the cords, psychically disentangling, carving out a portion of my heart, and giving it back to him. I didn't have the energy to let him go, I wrote, but I could let him *be.* I wrote about how, growing up, we think there is only one type of love, but there are so many types. There is a *doing* love and there is a *being love,* and our love was a *being love.*

Alex was my *doing love:* my beloved life companion. My business partner. My support network. My coparent. It was an active love wherein we both tended to a shared fire to keep each other warm. But with Beau, we tended to separate fires in separate houses, and nothing more was required: no physical contact, no emotional correspondence, no expectations. Knowing his presence was somewhere on this earth was simply enough, and when I thought of him, I could be grateful that his presence on earth infused me with some type of creative spark. But I didn't need him the way I used to. Sometimes there are love stories not meant to be written: a thousand unmade memories that belonged to another time and space. Sometimes people are not meant to be owned or kept, like the toads I put in a plastic bucket. I rewrote the poem from the weekend after we first met: *some things belong to the wild / running freely in the sand / it takes time to understand / I must love from where I stand.*

I ended the letter: *I am setting you free. I am letting you be.*

After I read the letter out loud to the Brooklyn Writers Collective group, there was silence for a few seconds. Scarlet-letter shame flushed into my cheeks as I judged the reaction: *I was a bad writer. I was a bad wife. I was a bad person.*

"Damn," someone finally shared. "I felt that."

Before the end of the class, a woman named Beth reached out to me via a private chat. *Hi,* she said, *I know we haven't met yet in person, but that piece was really triggering to me. Can we meet for coffee?*

TWO WEEKS LATER, SHE and I sat down in Battery Park, not for coffee but instead for pasta and a glass of wine. Beth shared with me her husband's not-quite-friendship, not-quite-lover relationship with another woman. As I twisted heaping portions of pasta into my mouth, I felt equally deep compassion for her, for her husband, and for the other woman, and sort of sick to my stomach about the dynamics of it all.

And then my phone buzzed.

"Let me get this," I apologized, reaching into my bag. "Alex is at home with the kiddos, and I'm pretty sure we have no food in the fridge." Sure enough, the text was from Alex, only it wasn't about what to feed the kids for dinner.

Hi, the text said. *I read your letter to Beau.*

I inhaled sharply. Beth asked if everything was okay. I felt the cruel irony of the moment wash over me. What were the chances that Alex would read the letter while I was with a woman who was simultaneously telling me the pain of being in her position?

But it was an even crueler irony that Alex had even read the letter itself. For months and months, I'd sat at my computer in front of him, typing my heart out, and he had never stopped to ask me what I was writing about. He had walked by me countless times during my Zoom classes and watched the kids when I was at a writing retreat. I had pages and pages of ruminations and essays on mothering, on being a business owner, on childhood memories, on psychic encounters, on dead things.

And now, after never having read any of my work, he stumbled upon *this* piece? In the way that he did? It turned out that Ava that evening had asked if she could practice writing her letters on a computer, and because his computer wasn't charged, he had opened mine and then opened Microsoft Word, only to see the last thing I had recently written.

Coming home, I texted back frantically, excusing myself from the table and apologizing to Beth for the abrupt ending.

On the fifteen-minute drive home over the Brooklyn

Bridge, I went through every possibility of what could happen next. And yet I also felt a strange calmness, a release of pressure now that my secret was out. I'd heard that mini tremors help release the pressure of impending earthquakes, decreasing the magnitude of bigger future ones that may cause seismic damage. I wondered if him reading the piece released some of this pressure.

I texted Molly, my writing teacher: *Alex read the letter.*

Congratulations, she wrote back. *You're free now. No more secrets.*

When I walked through the door of our Brooklyn apartment, Alex was sitting in a chair with his hands on either side of his forehead. Half-eaten chicken nuggets and toys were strewn everywhere. The arts-and-crafts box was open, and the kids were on the floor drawing something in Magic—maybe even permanent—Marker. The apartment was a mess. We were a mess.

I can't remember who said what first. But I remember us hugging, me crumpling into his arms, the first real hug we'd had in maybe weeks. My tears accumulated in his collarbone. His tears wet my hair, messy and unbrushed. As we stood holding each other in mutual grief, I stared at the windowsill where my new replacement orange tree had been growing. I hadn't wanted to give up on growing a fruit tree inside our apartment. And there it was, tilted to the right, toward the sun. Small, sour, green oranges protruding from fragile branches.

Alex let go of our embrace and looked at me with weary eyes. It was the most present I had seen him in months. It brought me a strange relief. *He was still in there:* a deeply feeling human being who I could hurt and who could hurt me, his buried humanity rising up from the layers of Excel spreadsheets and financial forecasting and emails and revenue targets. A little boy who had needs and feelings and wanted only to be loved. I had hurt him. *He was still in there.*

I didn't know if we as a couple were eroding or evolving. Maybe we were doing both. Wasn't this how nature was set up anyway? Weren't the orange tree's roots going deeper into the darkness so that the branches could sprout upward to open skies? Weren't we all destroying ourselves and saving ourselves at the same time, every day, over and over? Weren't we alive only because we inhaled and exhaled in one singular breath? Wrapped in each other's arms, Alex and I inhaled, then exhaled in one long, devastating breath.

Twenty-eight

The next morning I woke up alone. Alex's side of the bed was empty and cold. Where his body should have been was a letter, folded in half and waiting for me to find it. A single strand of his chest hair was coiled around the corner of the paper. I opened it.

Dear Alex, it began, *I need you to know what the relationship with Beau meant to me because I was really struggling in our marriage.* Alex had written a letter addressed to himself from *my* point of view. He wrote about how I needed support and was longing to access my own creativity. That I hadn't meant to hurt him. He signed it *Love, Kerry.*

How had Alex known to do something like this? He wasn't in therapy and yet this was the most moving therapeutic exercise I had ever experienced: to put himself in my shoes and to write a letter back to himself from my perspective.

I never questioned my desire to get married, growing up. I always saw it as a step forward on the predictable path of life: Get married, have kids, raise kids, retire, and die. As I held the letter there in bed, I pictured us standing over the mudpuppy grave on our wedding day, exchanging our vows, swearing we would be together forever, through sickness and in health. Alex and I had exchanged handwritten notes: I promised I would never stop working on myself to be a better individual and partner and thanked him for never reading my journals. He promised me he would always bring me coffee in bed and remind me to work out and have fun.

I realized it is a disservice to new couples everywhere to proclaim that a wedding is a celebration. Weddings are an *initiation:* the start of a partnership that navigates codependency and sacrifice and childhood wounds and autonomy. It is a journey to freedom through the foothills of heartbreak and repair, laughter and pain. So often in exchanging vows, we name what we love about the other. Yet while marriage is surely the act of choosing someone whose traits you love, it is also, and maybe more fundamentally, choosing to live with another's flaws for the rest of your life. So much of marital success is based on whether any of those flaws are deal-breakers to the other partner. Had Alex and I ever shared what our deal-breakers were? Because it sure seemed like unspoken deals were being broken.

After reading his letter, I wrote him one back from his point of view: *Dear Kerry,* I began, *my whole life has been trying to care for and provide for the people I love, and this is why I'm working so hard. I want to feel loved by my family. I want to feel like you care and value me. I feel betrayed and I am hurting. Love, Alex.* I left it by his bedside before going to work.

WHEN I GOT TO work, I looked through the Plexiglas that separated my office from his, watching him in meeting after meeting making decisions about cash flow and inventory allocation. Alex's shoulders were hunched forward and down; his eyebrows were furrowed. He wasn't okay.

I finalized an upcoming PR event and completed a performance review. I wasn't okay either.

LATER THAT NIGHT, ALEX read the letter I had left him and asked me if I would cry if he died. What a question to ask your wife.

"Yes," I said. "Of course I would cry."

He shut himself behind our bedroom door, leaving me to do bedtime with the kids alone.

"Tell us a story about when you were bad," Riggs said as I walked into their room trying not to cry.

I panicked. Did Riggs know something? Don't kids always know something?

But then I remembered how earlier that night, after purposely knocking down Ava's Magna-Tiles, Riggs had thrown himself on the floor yelling, "Just punish me! I'm bad. I'm a bad kid."

I had scooped him up as he cried, whispering, "I love you. You're not bad," till he calmed down.

I scanned my memory for a child-appropriate story from my past.

"Well," I began, "once, I had a nest of baby mice in my NYC studio apartment."

"Gross," Ava said.

"Yes," I said. "So my landlord came over and put down a trap made from thin strips of glue. When I came home from work, there they were: three small baby mice stuck, shaking, their mangled ears and tiny paws stuck to the glue. Their mother was on a separate strip, mouth to the side, eyes open, facing her babies. They were all still breathing."

Riggs's eyes widened. "What did you do?"

"I didn't know what to do. If I tried to pry them off the trap, it would have pulled their limbs off. If I threw them in the trash, they would have died a slow and painful death. So I put them in a paper bag, placed them on the ground, said a prayer, and then dropped a seventy-five-pound potted fig tree on the bag. Then I sat on my steps and cried."

"You smushed them?" Ava cried, her eyes welling with tears. Certainly if *The Giving Tree* made her cry, so would the bedtime story of me murdering a mouse family.

"That's really bad," Riggs confirmed.

"You know," I said slowly, "part of being human is that sometimes we harm and even kill things to benefit our own lives." I thought of the chicken I had eaten for dinner, willfully ignoring what its life was like as I chewed through its breast. Of the countless takeout containers that would end up in the ocean and maybe be swallowed by a sperm whale. Of the toads I had caught on the shores of Lake Erie that lay limp and cold on the bottom of my pink plastic bucket. I'd never met a wildflower I didn't want to cut and put in a ceramic vase, as if I owned its beauty. I did not let things be. Even myself—half wife, half wolf—howling at a blood moon through the closed kitchen windows at dusk, trying to balance my wildness and domesticity.

"Sometimes we do good things and sometimes we do bad things, and sometimes it's not about being good or bad but knowing that whatever we do has consequences."

I kissed Ava and Riggs on their cheeks.

"And sometimes you can be good and bad at the same time?" Riggs asked, turning to his side as his eyes began to close.

"Yes," I said. "Sometimes we are both."

"Mom, we know about nondualities," Ava said, rolling her eyes. "You tell us all the time."

I kissed them both, then turned off the light.

~

ALEX AND I KEPT going. What else was there to do? We saw one couples therapist, but in our fifty-minute time slot, she somehow made us dislike each other more.

"Let's not go back," Alex said. I agreed.

Someone recommended we see a local intuitive woman named Iris who did past-life regressions and inner-child work in her cottage.

A few minutes into her session with me and Alex, Iris stopped us.

"I see a little boy standing behind you," she said to Alex. "Age twelve, perhaps." Alex burst into tears. When he was twelve, he explained, he had heard his parents arguing and was afraid his mom was going to leave his dad. He had begged her to stay.

My twelve-year-old self showed up too, wanting me to acknowledge that sometimes, like Riggs, she wanted to throw temper tantrums; that she wasn't always fine; that she needed me to scoop her up like I did my kids and say, *I see you in all your messiness. You're not bad.*

Iris printed an illustration of a wheel that had a hundred different emotions on it and gave us homework: Identify how we were feeling. Alex was good at articulating when he was feeling generally *stressed* or *mad,* but the wheel offered more nuanced feeling states that he found harder to pinpoint. The next day he pointed to the wheel and said: *insignificant, betrayed, furious, sad, hopeful.* I looked at the wheel and pointed to *defeated, withdrawn, vulnerable, resentful, hopeful.*

There was hope.

~

A FEW NIGHTS LATER, Alex and I ranked each other from one to ten, ten being the best. He ranked me a two. I ranked him a seven.

"I don't trust you," he said.

I understood.

"But I still love you," he added.

"I still love you too."

~

A FRIEND RECOMMENDED THAT I do a guided psilocybin journey. I had never done drugs before, but I thought now was a great time to try.

I sat in a small apartment in Queens as a woman named Tonya watched me eat a bowl of applesauce with crushed-up mushrooms in it. A soundtrack with lots of drumming played in the background.

"Here's hoping I wake up healed!" I said to Tonya as I put a black eye mask over my face and curled up in the fetal position on her futon.

"The medicine will give you what you need," Tonya assured.

Minutes went by. I watched as my brain's synapses turned from numbers and words into a kaleidoscope of colorful dancing shadows.

"Heal me," I serenaded the shadows.

And then I heard a Voice respond, loudly and matter-of-factly: "There is no you to heal. There is no You."

I sat up in a panic and took off my eye mask. I touched my body. I saw my Faherty bag in the corner that held my iPhone and the names and numbers of everyone I loved. Of course there was a Kerry. Of course there was a Me.

"If there is no me, then who is listening to you?" I asked back. This was a trick question: If I could hear the Voice, certainly it meant that someone (Me) existed somewhere to hear it?

"Not you," the Voice said back, laughing.

I lay back down, confused and sweating. When would the healing start?

The Voice repeated again with matter-of-fact authority: "There is no You."

I silently fought back, repeating in resistance: *There is a Me. There is a Me. There is a Me.*

And then . . . I had had a vision of myself stripping down naked, but instead of taking off my clothes, what came off were my identities: Kerry. Sister. Mother. Wife. friend. Chief Impact Officer. Faherty founder. Athlete. Dreamer.

Off. Off. Off.

I observed myself from a distance in my nakedness and then I watched my skin start to melt, then my flesh, my veins, my bones. I was melting into nothingness. I became nothing but a void, floating in a weightless and empty darkness.

In that void, I understood—really understood—the meaning of the scientific law that matter cannot be created or destroyed. I was gone, but I was not destroyed. I didn't have a Self, and yet there was a part of me that still existed and that part could be referred to only as the Soul. I belonged to eternity, and it felt like never-ending peacefulness.

"There is no Me," I said. I wanted to cry in relief, but there wasn't even a Me there to shed tears.

And then I felt myself floating back to earth, watching as stardust turned back into my human flesh, my fingers, my arms, my breath, my face. All of my identities returned to my body as thin layers of clothing around naked skin: Back to Kerry. Back to Faherty. Back to my house. My children. My obligations. My memories.

"It's all for You," I heard in satisfaction.

It seemed to contradict the Voice's prior statement, but I also believed it was true: that everything—the pain, the longing, the suffering, the joy, the ache, the laughter, the musing—all of it was also *for us*. All of it was a gift.

I woke up, hearing the echoes of the journey's wisdom whispered angelically between my ears:

There is no Me. It's all for Me.

Twenty-nine

A month or so after Alex read my letter to Beau, we were leaning against our wooden headboard in our queen-size bed when I chose to bring it up.

"Al," I began, moving my pillow closer to his, "I know it's never the right time to talk about this, but now is the right wrong time. I need more equity."

Al nodded, unsurprised. We had talked about this in one of our sessions with Bruce. He had hinted I would get more one day, but I still had way less equity than him and Mike.

My close friends were shocked when I told them the current math.

"You guys don't split ownership three ways?" they asked in awe.

"Nope," I said.

"How much more do they have than you? Double?"

I shook my head. "More than that."

"It's not right, Ker," they gasped. "It's just not right." Friends who get mad for you, let me tell you, they save your life.

"Al," I continued, "the work I do matters and I need to be valued for it."

Alex listened to me as I continued my justifications: I didn't need the exact same amount of equity as them—because I knew this was their lifelong idea—but I needed more. I had poured my heart and soul into the brand; I had offered every one of my gifts; I had allowed my life to be engulfed by his and Mike's dream; I had let family boundaries be broken; I had sacrificed my mental health. Friends had slipped away. I didn't take my two maternity leaves. I had looked for love elsewhere. I didn't say these things to connote I was a victim, because I wasn't. I had cocreated this reality.

I continued. While the things I brought to Faherty were not as quantifiable or tangible as business acumen or creative strategy, they were just as important to the impact and the brand's culture: our sustainability, the reputation of how we showed up in the world, the *soul* of the brand. We had recently done an employee engagement survey, and while we received a lot of feedback on how to get better, there were two statistics that made me so proud: 94 percent of our team was proud to work at Faherty and felt like they could bring their true self to work. These were the statistics that mattered to me; these were the parts of Faherty I had fought so hard for. Getting more equity was not only about being adequately rewarded for that work but also an affirmation of my past and present worthiness.

Alex stared back at me, quiet.

Now I was getting more flustered, more righteous, more angry. Now I was crying. Why was he not responding?

I needed a reaction. "Listen, if you don't give it to me, I'll quit. And then good luck with Faherty. The last thing this world needs is two white guys who aren't in therapy running a company."

Alex yelled one loud, guttural "FUCK," then ran out of the room.

I'd clearly hit a nerve. Finally. I felt some satisfaction at being able to penetrate through the fortress that protected his feelings.

The way Alex yelled and ran away made me think of Riggs and his temper tantrums, which were still big and common. Once, I told a friend that Riggs's tidal waves of emotion overwhelmed me, and she responded: "Ah, what a gift to have men who can feel." She then added, "Until Alex is able to deal with his repressed childhood emotions, Riggs is gonna have a hard time regulating his."

When I told Alex this, he shrugged and said, "Maybe?"

Recently, when we had been at Ninie's house, one of the Faherty family members said, "Oh, stop crying!" when she witnessed one of Riggs's outbursts. She glowered at me as I picked him up into my arms, then scolded, "He needs to know he can't act like that."

"Can't act sad?" I questioned, before adding, "No one stops crying when you yell at them to stop crying."

I was hell-bent on making sure my kids could express their feelings. And I celebrated the small wins. Like when Riggs, after being denied another cookie, had run into his room to scribble, I HATE U MOMMY on a piece of paper before taping it to his wall. When Alex walked into the room a moment later, he saw the paper and asked Riggs what was going on.

"I'm so proud of him," I interjected before Riggs could respond.

Riggs looked at me suspiciously.

"You know how I write down my feelings in my journal every day, all the things that make me frustrated and upset? Instead of hitting someone or throwing things, Riggs is writing down his feelings too."

Alex looked at Riggs. "Wow, good job, buddy."

I watched something register in Riggs's eyes, anger alchemizing into something softer, and then Riggs ran to me, tucking his little head between my neck and my ear.

"I don't hate you, I love you, Mommy," he said.

"I know, honey, I know," I whispered back.

I thought of little Alex, emotions swelling inside of him, trying to feel the things that made him human. *Stop crying,* I heard echo across his childhood. *Stop crying,* I heard echo across my own childhood.

All of us adults and kids still learning how to feel.

FROM THE BEDROOM NOW, I could hear Alex's muffled yells into a pillow. A part of me wanted to run after him, to tell him I didn't need the equity, that everything would be okay. I thought of my fourteen-year-old self, the one who didn't want anyone to feel pain; the one who didn't want to burden anyone with her needs; the one who was always fine.

But I didn't run after him. I didn't tell him it was fine. Instead, I lay on our bed with tears streaming down my cheeks, considering my options. If I didn't get more equity, I could quit Faherty. I could go back to teaching mindfulness. I could clerk for a judge again. Or work in a greenhouse. I could leave

Alex and still be okay. Maybe one day Beau would get a divorce, and I would reconnect with him. Or maybe I could find an Irishman who lived on the shores of Connemara and wrote poetry. Or maybe I would fall in love with a woman. I could leave. I didn't know if this realization was an outdated survival mechanism or a sign of strength. Maybe both. But something brewed inside of me and it felt dangerous: There is nothing scarier than a woman who believes she will always be okay. There is nothing scarier than a woman who is willing to leave.

A few minutes later, Alex reemerged, shaking his head in defeat. I didn't know who was defeating him, his ego or my ego.

"Ker, you know I love you and value you. But I can't give you more equity. A lot of other business owners would agree with me. Faherty was Mike's and my idea, and we deserve more. You came onboard two months after we started it. Plus, you signed a contract when you joined and that contract is still valid."

I felt like I was going to throw up.

This was not about the money, not really. I was a lawyer; I understood that I had signed a contract agreeing to the terms of my equity when we started. I also understood New York state marital law 101: I was already entitled to half of his equity anyway if we got divorced. Rather, this was about partnership, about what we prioritized, about who we prioritized. This was about value. And even more than that, this was about love. And he loved Faherty so much that he couldn't let any of it go, even at the cost of hurting me.

If the business was his mistress, she had won.

~

USUALLY I COULD MINIMIZE my feelings enough to keep moving, but the pain of betrayal was too hot in my body. My body demanded I stay with the feeling of grief. I spent two days in bed. Ava came in and asked what was wrong.

"I'm sad," I told her. I don't believe in parents dumping their problems on their children, but I also believe it is important that kids know that their parents have desires and disappointments too. This is a part of being human.

"Imagine that three people show up to work every day for eight years, but when the job is over, two of the people get seventy dollars and the other person only gets twenty dollars. How do you think that would make the third feel?"

"Bad," Ava confirmed.

"Exactly," I said. "That's how I feel. I feel bad." I smoothed out her hair with my fingers.

"What would you do if you were in that scenario?" I asked her rhetorically. I knew I was parentifying her by asking her this question, but she often had a refreshing perspective on things from her curious and innocent mind.

"What would I do if I was who?" she asked.

I gasped. What a question back to me: *What would I do if I was who?* She intuitively grasped that each person's actions in this equation were shaped differently—each one coming from a unique perspective based on context. That maybe no one was inherently right or wrong, but rather had specific desires they needed to be met based on who they were.

"What would you do if you were *me*?" I clarified.

Ava bit her lip. "If I were you, I probably wouldn't say anything, because then it would start a conversation you'd probably have to bring up and over again, and probably nothing would change anyway, and then you'd get even more mad. So I'd get over it?"

I looked at her. She had a lot of younger Kerry inside of her: this desire not to cause conflict or discord, to sacrifice her feelings for the ease of others. I had seen it in the way she handed Riggs the bigger ice cream cone when he started to cry. "Just take the ice cream," she would say, shoving the cone into his hand. "I can't deal with the crying!"

"Well, Ava," I countered, "I don't want to get over it, and this time I did say something. I yelled and cried, and you know what? You were right that nothing changed. But here's the thing: Even though I felt betrayed, I didn't betray myself. I advocated for myself. And that's important."

"Okay, Mom," she said. "Do you need a hug?"

"Yes," I said, opening my arms. "Hugs make everything feel better."

Thirty

A few weeks later, Alex and I were visiting a Faherty store off the coast of Massachusetts. Summer was our busy season, and we spent hours helping the team restock the floors, giving them product knowledge, and introducing ourselves to customers. This year, my parents had come too, and as my dad walked our kids around town, my mom cleaned our store bathroom on her hands and knees.

"Look at this!" she said, as per usual, showing me the clumps of dust that had accumulated underneath the sink cabinet.

"I know, Mom, I know!" I said, rolling my eyes. We were all so consistent, weren't we?

The second day on the island, I walked past the local community theater and saw a sign on the door advertising an intimate solo acoustic concert that night at 6:00 P.M. And the performer? None other than Beau.

You have GOT to be shitting me, I texted Kathryn. It was going to be Beau's first live performance since COVID. I hadn't seen him in person in two years. And now he was in this small town the very same weekend we were?

The universe, she texted back.

Beau was blissfully in the dark about the letter I had written him and the subsequent fallout from Alex having read it. Instead, he was living his best newlywed life, as he should have been. And good for him. I debated whether to reach out, but there was a 98 percent chance we would run into him on this small island, and if we saw him, Alex would not be greeting him with a hug.

"Happy New Year, Happy Birthday, Happy Fourth of July," Beau said when he answered my call. We hadn't spoken on the phone in months.

"Hey," I said, which was way more serious than my usual prolonged five-syllable "Hiiiiii."

"Uh-oh," he said.

"Yeah, um, long story short . . ." I filled him in on the letter, how Alex had read it, how it had been painful and hard for us.

Beau was silent for a minute: He was a slow digester of drama and details.

"I mean, I thought we were pretty ethical considering the circumstances. That should make Alex feel better?" he said.

"Alex doesn't feel good about this, Beau," I said. "He feels like I betrayed him and that for years me and you were just friends."

"We are just friends," Beau countered.

"We're not just friends, Beau," I said, sighing.

"Dang, I admire Alex so much," he said. "Should I text him to grab a beer and apologize?"

"I thought you were sober?"

"Kinda," he said.

"Well, whatever." That wasn't my problem, thank God. "And no, Al won't want to grab a drink with you."

"Damn," Beau responded. And then his voice dropped, the weight of reality kicking in: seven years of our memories and triangulations crumbling like a sandcastle at high tide.

"I'm sorry, Ker," he added. "I do want us all to be friends one day."

"I'm sorry too," I said, although I wasn't sure what I was apologizing for in that moment, but pretty sure it was everything to everyone.

When I told Alex about Beau's acoustic set, he took a deep breath and told me I should go and take the Faherty store team with me for a morale-boosting team outing. He would stay at home with the kids and my parents. He was always thinking about the team.

"Seriously?" I asked. The suggestion seemed too Buddha, too gracious, too selfless, too repressed, too illogical.

"Yeah," he said, "I'll be fine."

The team was thrilled at the invite. Right before we all walked in, Alex texted, *I'm coming*. I reserved a seat for him, and as the concert started, he grabbed my hand as we watched Beau sing harmonic melodies with vague lyrics of unrequited love onstage.

"I want to thank my friends the Fahertys for being here tonight," Beau said, looking out into the crowd, trying to spot us. Our teammates cheered. I squeezed Alex's hand, and he squeezed mine back.

Alex sang along to some of the tunes, while I felt like I was going to be sick. It was too much.

I felt like a dizzying kaleidoscope of voices and needs. All parts of my inner self screamed for attention: the woman who wanted to live the rest of my life with Alex, the bohemian poet who craved creative expression at every moment, the responsible and selfless mother who put her family first, the little girl who didn't want to make anyone upset, the wild, righteous, sensual woman who chased pleasure.

Everything belongs, everything belongs, I whispered to myself.

AFTER THE SHOW, EVERYONE went to a local karaoke bar, and Beau's wife came out and gave me a quick hug, and then Beau came out and hugged Alex, and then Beau hugged me too. I noticed that he had gotten his ears pierced, which I thought was a poor decision. We all stood awkwardly. The music was loud and a dude onstage was screaming the lyrics to a country song: *I'm proud to be an American where at least I know I'm free.*

"I gotta get out of here," Alex said, pulling my elbow toward the bar's exit.

"Yup," I agreed.

When we got back to our rental, my parents had put the kids to sleep and their door was closed. As we lay in bed, Alex said it had all been too overwhelming, and I said I understood. He cried while I hugged him from behind, saying, "It's okay, it's okay," until he fell asleep. Then I turned onto my back and stared at the ceiling and replayed every moment of the past seven years.

Beau texted a few weeks later asking if we had any linen shirts, size large, in lavender for a wedding he had coming up.

Sure, I said, putting in the order for him. I wouldn't talk to him for a year after that. Because what else was there to say?

~

A MONTH LATER, I was making a sandcastle on the Jersey Shore with the kids when I saw two lifeguards on ATVs fly by. Then two more. I looked up. There was a swarm of people standing by the edge of the shore, staring out to sea. I heard someone yell, "Young kid! Missing! Riptide!"

No.

I frantically told Ava and Riggs to go up to the pool, then joined the crowd of people standing by the shoreline, arms to their foreheads, looking out at the water. We watched the lifeguards—kids, really—lock arms and walk slowly from jetty to jetty searching for the fifteen-year-old who had been swept out into the waves. Every minute that went by, more panic. *Please, please, please,* I prayed as we stood on the edge of the shore for longer than the length of time that would ensure his survival.

More minutes went by. Then more. Slowly, one by one, each of us bystanders walked back up to the boardwalk in shock. I held back my sobs as I pulled my kids out of the pool, clutching their warm, wet skin in devastation.

The boy washed ashore three days later. He had been at the beach with his grandmother that day. He and his sister had gotten caught in a riptide. His sister had been saved. He had not.

For a full year, whenever I took my beach walks on the weekend, I would find a stone and rub it between my thumb and index finger—the way my grandma did when she was anxious—and think about that day.

I wondered if there were only two metaphorical ways to die: some of us slowly eroded by the elements and others swept out to sea in an instant.

Most times, I didn't cry for the dead, I cried for the living. It's just harder and denser down here, you know?

Thirty-one

It was fall and the leaves were bright red, and Alex and I were on the Taconic State Parkway driving up to Woodstock for the weekend to go hiking with the kids. It was rare that just the four of us were together as a unit: no added family member—from my side or his—no extra friend, and no store visit, trade show, or Faherty event.

I drove so Alex could crank out a few hours of emails even though it was a Saturday. My cracked iPhone lay on the dashboard, plugged into a charger, for directions and music.

"Play Taylor Swift," Ava requested from the back seat.

Alex grabbed my phone to open Spotify.

And then, there it was, aggressively displayed on the dashboard screen: the name of Beau's band on the "most recently played" list. Alex looked at me as I stared at the double lines in the middle of the road, then put his head down and started to shake. Was it rage? No, it was silent sobs, tears ricocheting off the strap of his seatbelt.

"Dad?" Ava asked. She could see his arm between the passenger window and his seat. He didn't answer.

"Dad?" she asked again.

He looked at me. His eyes brimmed with pain and betrayal. "Why are you still listening to his music?"

I looked at Alex and then looked back to the road. I shook my head as if to say, *I don't know.* But I did know. Doing so provided me with an escape; it reminded me of a part of myself that didn't belong to anyone or anything. It was almost a form of chanting to hear his music, a conduit for creativity and lowered cortisol. But I also knew it was an act of betrayal. Of choosing to hold on to something, even emotionally, that caused Alex pain.

"I'm sorry," I said.

Ava leaned forward from her car seat and stroked the top of Alex's hair. Alex cried for the next few moments as Taylor's "Karma" played in the background. Ava was comforting him the way Alex wanted me to.

Riggs sat in the back seat, staring out the window. From my perspective through the rearview mirror, I couldn't tell if he knew what was going on, but I think he could. I think he too was trying not to cry.

I felt shame. I also felt anger.

I thought of the equity: how Alex couldn't give it to me, no matter how much I pleaded.

We were doing the same thing to each other.

We both wanted the other to give something up. We both *needed* the other to give something up. And we both didn't want to.

~

WE WERE VISITING MY parents in South Carolina again and had driven to a nature preserve known for its bird-watching. So far we had only seen two blue herons. The kids were getting bored. But as we turned onto a small enclave of sand, we stumbled upon hundreds of fiddler crabs: blue and red, the males distinguishable by their one disproportionately huge claw. I wanted the kids to get a closer look, so I picked one up with my index finger and thumb and put it in my hand. And that's when it pinched me, hard.

"Ouch!" I yelled, trying to fling it off me but not able to. The male fiddler's large claw clamped around the thin skin of my palm, drawing blood.

"Ouch, ouch, ouch," I said, yanking it off me firmly and then tossing it down on the sand. "Stupid crab," I said as I watched it crawl away, unscathed.

"You shouldn't call the crab stupid, Mom," Ava said.

"You're right," I agreed.

"'Cause you were the one who picked it up," she added.

I raised my eyebrows.

"So it's kinda your fault."

I thought of all the pain I held in my head, heart, and hand. Picking up things that didn't belong to me: crabs and people and shame.

"You're right," I replied. "You're right. It's kinda my fault."

Thirty-two

Business was good. Our men's sales were thriving, women's were slowly increasing, and we had over fifty brick-and-mortar stores across the country. Alex, Mike, and I weren't outwardly fighting at work, but there were still some tensions between the three of us, buried under the busyness of endless tasks and swallowed beneath the seams of repressed frustration. It was clear we needed therapy: family or business; it was one and the same. People say there is the personal Self and the work Self, but I don't believe there are clear boundaries between the two: Our moods, relationships, and experiences outside of work inform our perspectives, decisions, and interactions at work. We bring our personal strengths and weaknesses into our workday much like we do our laptop and lunch box. If you're a bad communicator at home, you're likely a bad communicator at work. If you believe you are the victim in your personal life, you'll likely feel like the victim at work. If you are chaotic and controlling on the weekends, you're likely chaotic and controlling Monday through Friday. The flip side is, of course, also true: If you are a problem solver in your personal life, have a can-do attitude, and believe the people around you are inherently good and trustworthy, you'll radiate that energy outward at work.

Sometimes when Alex, Mike, and I were in meetings and we disagreed about something, I could see all of the wounded versions of ourselves unzip themselves into the room, children begging for attention. We were united in our shared mission for the brand, and also constantly complaining about one another: Mike was mad at me because he didn't think I was innovative enough in my impact strategies, I was mad at Mike because he never asked my opinion on the women's business and cared more about being an aspirational brand than a conscious one. Alex was mad at me because he didn't like it when I vented my frustration about Mike, and I was mad at Alex because I wished he stuck up for me the way he stuck up for his brother.

Even though we worked together in the same office, it was rare that the three of us met all together to discuss how we were feeling, what our needs were, and how things could get better. We needed help, and yet there were obstacles in getting the family into therapy, which was to say that Mike and Alex weren't interested in it. I thought of the endless hours I had spent in a chair talking about family dynamics, and I laughed every time I heard the line "I go to therapy to deal with the people who don't go to therapy." Of course, I knew I was the problem too: still righteous, still inconsistent, and still creating messes in the business with my delayed feedback—ideas that the team didn't have the bandwidth for—and my inability to delegate. I was still trying to minimize my own needs at times by catering to others' feelings.

To persuade Alex and Mike to show up for professional therapy, I would need to get creative, which is why I was thrilled to find a corporate coach named Una who not only specialized in executive coaching but also was a clinical therapist who centered on existential therapy. Perfect.

On the initial phone call with Una, I shared my psychoanalysis of both of them.

"I don't need to change them," I noted, "but everyone does need to be different than who they are for this to work."

"I hear you and see you, Kerry," she said. I could hear her taking notes on the other end of the line, maybe about Alex and Mike, or maybe about me. I had a feeling that she had already psychoanalyzed my holier-than-thou pre-enlightenment syndrome and my need to control social situations. She recommended we do six sessions, some all together, some in one-on-ones. I sent Alex and Mike the calendar invites with the subject line "TIMELY: Leadership Development for Entrepreneurs." They accepted.

At our first "corporate coaching session," Una started by congratulating us on what we had created, which was an affirming way to kick things off. We never stopped working long enough to acknowledge that Faherty was growing and in the best place it had ever been: We had an incredibly talented team of passionate and smart employees, a spacious new office downtown, and lots of enthusiastic, supportive customers. We were working on getting B Corp certified, which was a rigorous certification process for companies that met social and environmental standards that proved the business cared about more than just profit. I was working on launching a reuse-and-recycle program titled Second Wave so that people could buy and sell their preloved Faherty clothes to ensure that no old Faherty clothes ended up in landfills. And recently I had hosted my first Faherty Impact Retreat, bringing together amazing artists and activists in upstate New York for rest and rejuvenation. Faherty, as a business, was doing great. But were we as a family?

When Una asked us to go around and share how we were feeling, Alex shared he was *stressed*. I felt *defeated*. Mike felt *frustrated*.

We spent the next few sessions complaining, accusing, and crying, but also giving one another compassion and acknowledgment. Alex told me I was sometimes unreliable and inconsistent, and I agreed. I told Alex he was a workaholic with an unhealthy definition of success, and he agreed. I told Mike he was a bad communicator, and he agreed. Mike said he felt deleted by me, noting that he didn't feel like he and I were friends anymore. I told him that I was worried that one day he would want to delete *me* from the company. Each of us shared that we didn't feel valued and appreciated or, more succinctly, we didn't feel loved.

Could I see that Mike was the creative visionary and without his dream to start this business, I wouldn't have had this platform to do some of the work I loved? He cared about this business more than any of us and was always thinking about ways to make it better. He traveled the world visiting our factories to form relationships that ensured the products were ethically made and high-quality. He was always innovating and experimenting with new fabrics and new designs, and his high standards were the reason why our customers trusted the brand.

And then there was Alex: His leadership and business acumen were the reasons the brand was still afloat. He was the one who bore the brunt of the financial stress, and despite its taking a heavy toll on him, he never stood in the way of Mike or me in creating what we wanted. Time and time again, Alex's decision-making prevented us from going under; he helped us secure last-minute loans and restructured the budgets so one day we could be profitable. He also protected us from having to take on outside investors who might not share our vision of the brand. He was, simply put, an incredible CEO, and while sometimes that meant he didn't have as much energy to give back to me, I could acknowledge the fruits of his labor at work. One of the traits I find most commendable—the trait that draws me to people the most—is passion to create something that aligns with one's dream. I had, in some ways, been resenting Alex for the very thing that made me attracted to him: his desire to create the best company he could. Didn't I too prioritize my needs over others' sometimes, even his and our kids'?

Alex acknowledged that he was the leader he was because of how I encouraged him to expand his definition of success. How individual success needed to be tied to emotional growth and serving others, or else what was the point? How my desire to make Faherty a place where people loved working helped ripple outward to our customers, a key component in why the brand made people feel good.

Toward the end of our time with Una, she told us we were "prognosis positive." Nothing was fully solved, but each of us cried and admitted a simple truth: We simply wanted to feel loved, and we believed in what we were creating.

I had spent so many years creating narratives around Alex and Mike as to what they were *doing to me,* when the truth was we needed one another. They were not the enemy: We were a family, and we were business partners. If the Faherty Brand ship went down, we were all on it. None of us had the skill set to make it on our own; it was clear that we were better together. I realized that the kindest thing I could do for myself and for others was to love people for exactly who they were, right here, right now. Changing people never worked anyway, and it was too exhausting. Maybe I could hold the nonduality of both love and acceptance; of meeting them where they were, and meeting me where I was. Maybe we were all healing in all our different ways: all in perfect timing.

At the last session we told one another we were sorry and made promises about how we would be better: Alex and I enrolled in a Vedic meditation course to better deal with our stress. Alex and Mike joined a yearlong "conscious capitalism" class that explored a purpose- and people-driven mindset and taught tangible skills for individual leadership and organizational health. I agreed to be more clear and consistent in my role at Faherty and less judgmental about how everyone else was operating.

That weekend, I walked the Jersey Shore and drew a heart around every dead thing I could find: a crab shell, a corpse of a seagull, a fish head. I would not let anger corrode my tender heart. I would bring love to places where resentment had lingered.

We might not be fully healed, but we could love each other and tell the truth.

Maybe we would be okay.

Thirty-three

Alex got a Zillow alert that an 1890s Victorian house was for sale in his childhood town. We had no plans to move out of Brooklyn, but we were avid voyeurs: Why not snoop around? The second I walked into the open house, it reminded me of our summer cottage in Canada: old and drafty, creaky wood floors, a funny layout, no closets, and a lived-in charm that felt old but not haunted. I couldn't sense any Dahlias here.

As Alex walked through it, his eyes welled up.

"We need to buy it," he said with more intuitive clarity than I'd ever heard from him.

It was rare that he articulated a desire so clearly and firmly, and I knew immediately this was important to him. The house sat a mere block from where he and Mike grew up: a time when Ninie and Roger were still married, their family still intact, a time filled with possibility and optimism. We couldn't afford the house on our own, but Ninie agreed she would go in on it with us again, selling our current shared home for this one. Months later, it was ours.

The new house felt symbolically like both a redo for Alex to create the life he wanted as a kid and a restart for us as a family. At first, we lived there only on the weekends, but at the end of the summer Alex suggested we move down to the shore full time. I was hesitant. I loved my life in Brooklyn and the long dinners with friends, live music, local restaurants, and walks by the pier. My community of artists and musicians and writers and activists was here. Was I ready to move ninety minutes away, live with my mother-in-law full time, and have very few friends nearby?

Yet I also liked the idea of having a house with a backyard and a real garden and being close to the ocean. And I knew how much moving out of the city would change Alex's life. He would work less. He could surf more. His childhood best friends all lived close by. He didn't have a community of friends in Brooklyn.

"Let's do it," I agreed.

Months later, we packed up our apartment in Brooklyn and left 60 percent of our life on the stoop: preschool art, old phone chargers, IKEA place mats, the puffer fish bucket, self-help books, and twenty-seven lightbulbs that I had amassed via an Amazon subscription that I didn't know how to unsubscribe from. One of the movers accidentally put a ceramic bowl we had gotten for our wedding on the stoop, and someone picked it up before I could retrieve it: *a practice in nonattachment,* I whispered to myself.

My mom came to help with the purge—her specialty based on years of sneakily throwing out my dad's tchotchkes—and found my wedding dress crumpled in a plastic bag outside. Halfway through the ceremony, I had cut it from the knees down so I could dance better in it, and the grease from the caterer's scissors was still on the frayed seams.

"You're throwing out your wedding dress?" she gasped. "Have you no heart?"

"Mom!" Ava cried when she saw her self-portrait from the day before in the recycling bin.

"What are we going to do with all this stuff?" I asked. I psychoanalyzed my lack of sentimentality: Maybe my heart was slightly cold, but at least it was clutter-free. "We can't hold on to it all. It needs to go away."

"But where does it go?" Riggs asked, holding up a ripped box of puzzle pieces.

"Well, the stuff people don't take home will go into a garbage truck."

"And then where?"

"To the dump."

"Like a hole in the ground?"

"Yeah, kinda," I said, thinking of the landfills we passed by on Staten Island every time we drove down to the shore: a huge mountain of belongings, vestiges of memories and consumerism.

"Oh," Ava said, hearing my summary of the New York City sanitation process, "so all of this stuff doesn't actually go anywhere. It just stays here, but in the ground."

"Yes, it does," I affirmed. "It all just stays here."

I thought of the sperm whale, the mudpuppies, Queens Calvary Cemetery stacked with coffins, my dad's leather-bound books, Karl's bench, the shiny plastic shrines of grief on the highway, and now twelve years of my life in Brooklyn on a stoop.

There was no away.

~

"AL, YOU NEED TO get a vasectomy," I said one morning over a yogurt parfait. While I trusted the pullout method significantly lowered the odds of a third pregnancy, I could not bear having to birth one more thing with needs.

"Ker, I've heard about some crazy side effects," Alex said reluctantly. "Like swelling and cramping and light bleeding."

"Oh, really?" I said. If my uterus could laugh (and it could), it would.

"Plus, I already donated my kidney," he added, which was a valid point, but by doing the math in terms of sacrifice, I was still winning: My uterus got cut open twice, perforated once; I hemorrhaged every month; Ava and Riggs both chewed my nipples off at some point; and the patriarchy was now trying to convince me I need to stick needles in my face to appear sufficiently sexy. The thought of having to now put anything foreign in my body so as not to get pregnant, be it an IUD or the Pill, simply didn't seem like a fair option.

"Plus, what if we get divorced?" Alex added. "That means you can have more kids and I couldn't."

I had already obviously thought about that, and I agreed this was a nice benefit for me, but I didn't want more kids. I could barely handle two.

"Time for the snippy-snippy," I said, using my fingers to form scissors. "You got this."

"Fine," he said, shaking his head and laughing. "But once again, I'm a selfless husband."

~

ALEX AND I SETTLED into our new home on the Jersey Shore. The sediment was slowly falling back to the bottom of the shaken-up snow globe of our marriage. I built a ten-by-ten vegetable garden in the back corner of the lawn and threw in seeds: lettuces, carrots, radishes, snap peas. I grew two carrots that somehow tasted a little like soap, but it was a start. I learned to pull the weeds, knowing that for my tomato plants to bear bright red fruit, the roots couldn't be strangled by uninvited species. I placed three compost bins by the garden, watching as our food waste manifested into rich, fertile soil.

Next to the compost, I started our own natural burial ground: a dead cicada as big as an open palm, a dead mouse we had found flattened between iron pots, a dead vole stiff with sharp claws and two buckteeth, and a dead squirrel. Ava dug up the squirrel a few weeks after we buried it, and it was mainly just the tail left. "It's decomposing great," I assured her as she covered it back up with soil. Grandpa Bob—the cardinal—sometimes flew in and out of the yard to eat birdseed. I knew he was only one out of every four cardinals, but I greeted them all as if they were him, just to be safe.

Thirty-four

I sat in a La-Z-Boy across from Iris in her cottage on the Jersey Shore. She was about to hypnotize me so that, in a trancelike state, my conscious mind would quiet and allow my subconscious mind to access my "higher Self." Iris had explained that in this state, it would feel like I was in a vivid dream where I would be lucid and yet also capable of accessing past lives or even future ones.

Slowly, slowly, slowly, Iris offered prayerlike invocations and instructed me to relax as I watched the current Kerry fade away.

And then, with my eyes closed, I began to see a picture form, as if I were watching a movie on the screen of my mind.

There she was—the woman from my dreams, standing on a rocky shore, naked, hair cascading down her back, staring into a stormy sea.

I watched her wade into the water.

"No," I whispered to her. She didn't turn around.

"No," I whispered again, pleadingly.

"What are you seeing?" Iris asked.

I described the scene. Except this time, I somehow knew more about her. "She has two kids at home," I said aloud, watching as she walked deeper into the water.

"Who is the woman?" Iris asked gently.

"The woman is me," I said, starting to cry. "From a past life. She is me."

She was now up to her knees. Then her hips. The water was rough and gray. She didn't turn around. I watched her intently dive under the water and swim slowly out to sea until I could no longer see the flesh of her back. I thought of her children, alone. Without a mom.

"What do you want to tell her?" Iris asked.

"I want to tell her I forgive her," I said through sobs.

I wanted to forgive her for wading into the water to escape her life, for abandoning her own children, for leaving them behind. For her inescapable sorrow.

I heard Iris inhale. Then exhale.

"And what does she want to tell you?"

I waited for a response as I stared into the vast horizon of the human-less ocean, listening for her voice to whisper a truth from the other side.

"She wants to tell me I'm doing a good job," I said finally, tears still streaming down my cheeks.

As my sobs subsided, I sat in silence, waiting to hear or see another scene or image. But nothing came. Eventually I opened my eyes.

For so many years, she had been trying to contact me in dreams, to tell me something. *It's okay, Ker,* I self-soothed, hearing her whisper quietly again. *You're doing a good job.*

I would never have the dream again.

~

WITHOUT MY BROOKLYN SOCIAL life, the beach became my best friend. My walks on the shore reminded me of summers at Lake Erie, walking the same one-mile stretch day in and day out in search of small treasures: yellow northern flicker feathers, coral from far away, and then, shockingly, a dead sturgeon—one of the most ancient and also endangered species in the world. The night after I found it, Riggs and I pulled out his dinosaur book and found a picture of a sturgeon: bony plates on its back, a sharklike tail, and whiskers—called barbels, I learned—protruding from its mouth. The caption said that sturgeons have been in existence for 165 million years.

"One hundred sixty-five million years," I said aloud as I rubbed my index finger over the photo of the sturgeon. And then a tear dropped from my eye onto the page.

"Why are you crying, Mommy?" Riggs asked, still staring at the picture of the ancient fish.

I thought about how long the earth has been in existence, going through mass extinctions over and over; how so many species don't end up making it, and yet still, somehow, the earth endures. I wondered if we humans were on the verge of extinction too, and if proof of our existence would one day be encased in fossils in shallow sediment. I wondered if any other species had such a capacity for self-destruction.

"Time," I told Riggs, kissing his cheek and closing the book. "What is time?"

THE NEXT MORNING, CAN you believe I found another washed-up dead sturgeon? A local fisherman told me to alert the authorities. "No one sees sturgeons onshore," he said in disbelief. "And you've found two?"

This means something, my friend Lindsay texted me. She'd looked up its spiritual sign: *Sturgeons represent that life is not bound by time or space.*

I don't know where she got her information, but I believed it.

As the months went by, I found six more dead sturgeons washed up onshore. I wasn't sure if it was a warning or a symbol of hope.

MOST DAYS, HOWEVER, I didn't find ancient species onshore; I found sea glass—brown and white and green and turquoise pieces. I had to walk slowly in order to spot them, but I found that to be unhurried was an act of growth—a gift, as if my steps synchronized with the natural rhythms of the waves.

Every time I found a piece of glass, I squealed in delight, like a treasure hunter who finds pieces of gold. How was I worthy of such small pleasures? I once asked the Universe to prove her love for me by sending me a piece of blue sea glass. And now, though they are objectively rare, I find them all the time, in a disproportionate proof of magic. Sure, I could just be lucky, but as they say, *either nothing is a miracle or everything is*. To me, the blue pieces are a constant reminder that we are always receiving love—life force energy that comes to us for free. We just need to keep our eyes open, knowing that sometimes love appears through remnants of discarded and softened glass.

Recently Riggs and I found a blue piece whose jagged edges were still too sharp.

"It's not ready yet," I told Riggs as he examined it.

"But it's blue!" he exclaimed, tightening his hand around it, understanding the preciousness of the find.

"Throw it back in, lovebug," I encouraged. "It will cut you. It needs more time." I knew how hard it was to let go of something you wanted but that wasn't ready. "Trust in time, Riggs," I said. "One day it will be ready." He threw it back in.

Sometimes, of course, I find trash. Lots of it. After one particularly large hurricane swell, I took the kids to the beach and there was so much litter, it made my stomach churn. I told Ava and Riggs to use all the plastic pieces lying around to make an imaginary city so we could transform the waste into art. I drew a square in the dry sand and the kids got to work: Ava stacked bottle caps on top of one another to make buildings, and Riggs made a cemetery out of blue and pink plastic cylinder-looking things, declaring them headstones.

"What are these, anyway?" he asked.

"Tampon applicators," I told him.

"Is there blood on these?" he screamed, throwing them down. He knew what tampons were because I talked openly to him about my period and why sometimes the bathwater I soaked in was a hot, magenta red.

"The salt from the ocean kills the germs," I said, although I wasn't entirely sure of that as I cringed. I had a flashback to when I was a teenager and my mom cut off the tip of her finger while slicing fresh bagels. Bleeding profusely, she wrapped her wound with a washcloth and then returned to cutting the bagels, leaving smears of blood all over the dough before bagging them up and putting them in the freezer. Weeks later, on a spring morning commute to school, my siblings and I opened up our paper towel–wrapped breakfast to find *bloody* bagels toasted and smothered in cream cheese. We called our mom from our car phone, screaming in disbelief and disgust: "MOM, THERE IS BLOOD ON OUR BAGELS!"

"Oh, the blood?" She cackled. "You won't be able to taste it. You're lucky you have breakfast. Some kids don't even have bagels." And then she added, "Besides, the freezer kills the germs . . ."

I remembered each of our responses, and how reflective they were of our personalities. My brother quietly placed his bloody bagel in the glove compartment, opened up a granola bar, and turned up the volume to Queen. My sister said, "This is so fucked up," and threw hers out the window onto the side of the highway. I stared at mine for a while, debating. My mom was right: Some kids didn't have bagels, and the bagel *had* been frozen, so the germs were probably killed? I spent the rest of the drive slowly nibbling around the blood, minimizing my queasiness for the sake of my breakfast nutrition.

I supposed then that there were two types of moms: those who would feed their kids bloody bagels and those who wouldn't. I wasn't feeding my kids bloody bagels, but I was watching them play with used tampon applicators, and it was clear which category I would fall into.

"Yeah, let's not play with these," I decided, coaxing Riggs toward the driftwood instead, grateful to find something that wasn't plastic. On my beach walks, tampon applicators and those one-use floss sticks were more common than any other type of trash. I was proud to not use plastic applicators anymore, instead swapping them out for a reusable Diva Cup.

Unfortunately, I still hemorrhaged golf ball blood clots each menstrual cycle, but I finally knew why: During my C-section with Riggs, some of my uterine lining got stuck in the stitches as the doctor sewed up my uterus, forming a small sac that hung beneath my scar. I had since been diagnosed with a chronic condition called adenomyosis where the lining of my uterus grows into the muscle (not dissimilar to endometriosis), causing heavy bleeding.

After hearing about the diagnosis, a new doctor recommended I get tested for anemia, given that I had accumulated seven years of profuse blood loss. "Surely your past ob-gyn shared the likelihood of anemia with you?" she asked.

"No," I had said sheepishly. There was only so much a doctor could share with you in a four-minute appointment. She called me shortly after getting the results back.

"I've never seen iron levels this bad," she said. "I honestly don't know how you've been functioning. Do you feel dead and exhausted all the time?"

"Indeed, I do," I affirmed, both proud of myself for being able to function with basically zero iron and also embarrassed that for years I neglected my body's cries for help (and there had certainly been cries for help: I got breathless walking up the stairs, could not get out of bed in the morning or work out, and often had brain fog). I had unintentionally deprived my blood from pumping oxygen throughout my body—an essential life force energy I needed. I vowed to never minimize my bodily symptoms again. It's one thing to believe your wellness is determined by the number of clean beauty products you use and quite another to listen to the cues from your body indicating where you need physical (and emotional) healing.

Not only did my doctor prescribe me immediate iron infusions, but she also diagnosed me with a rare condition called pica that had been activated by my anemia, which led to a constant craving for hard, chewy things like ice . . . or carrots.

"You mean all these years I thought my addiction to carrots was a quirky personality trait, but really it was a mental disorder?"

"Yes," she confirmed.

After my first blood infusion, I immediately stopped craving carrot sticks. "I don't even know who you are anymore," my friend Lindsay said as I kindly refused her farmers' market box of vegetables. "Who are you if you're not an orange-tinted carrot-aholic?"

"People can change," I said while grabbing a muffin. "I'm living proof."

Days later, I took a jog for the first time in six years. All these years thinking I hated working out, when really the issue had been that I didn't have enough oxygen-producing red blood cells. To prevent myself from regressing back to being anemic, I also vowed to get a benign hysterectomy in the fall. I asked the doctor if I could keep my scarred uterus in formaldeyde in a mason jar after its removal. I envisioned placing it on Ava's bookshelf with a label on it that said *HOME*. My doctor looked at me suspiciously at first and then burst out laughing. I had a feeling she thought that this was genius.

"We can discuss that as the date nears," she said.

"Great," I said with a thumbs-up.

AFTER THE KIDS AND I dismantled our city of tampon trash and soda bottle caps, we threw all the litter into a garbage bin on the boardwalk.

"There is no away," I reminded them as I grabbed their small hands in mine.

"Mom, we know," Ava said, rolling her eyes, although I know she was thinking the same thing.

On the walk home, Riggs stopped for a second to pick up a worm writhing in the heat on the concrete sidewalk. He threw it back into the dirt adjacent to the sidewalk, just as I had taught him. Anyone who composts can tell you worms are *gold*. I watched him as he knelt down, observing the worm burrow back into the grass. He seemed to be reflecting on something.

"This is the life," Riggs said assuredly as he stood back up and started walking again, undoubtedly proud to have rescued a creature in distress.

I did not tell him about the things I had read in the news that week: the hungry children, the assault weapons, the bombs, the wildfires.

I just put his hand in mine, warm and pulsating, and felt overcome with gratitude.

"Yes, this is the life, Riggsy," I agreed.

Thirty-five

I was ready to be a poet. I didn't need to be a good poet. I'd even settle for being a bad poet, so long as it meant I was writing again. I began to feel brave enough to share my poetry on my real Instagram, not like the anonymous one I had created years before. I wrote bad poems, okay poems, and who-knows poems. Poems that were almost honest. Poems that were 100 percent honest. I wrote poetry on the subway and in bathroom stalls and in between Zooms and on plane rides.

My poems were love poems, and I was realizing I could be in love all of the time, whether in my marriage or with my friends or just with life in general. Anyone could be my muse. I started writing a series titled Tiny Poems for others, inspired by the lives of my friends—*my version of a nineties mixtape*—

that acknowledged a part of themselves often kept hidden. I wrote a poem for Noah, my meditation teacher. Now a seventy-year-old man with silver hair, he was sober and wore a beaded bracelet, but not a mala, around his wrist. He was also a photographer and once sent me back an eight-by-eight photo he took on film of a dead hummingbird with a flower next to it.

I'll cherish it forever, I told him.

I'll keep looking for dead things, he texted back.

I promise more dead things are coming, I said.

I will stay awake, he said.

This too was a form of lovemaking.

One evening, I was thinking about the Catholic tradition of naming godparents prior to a child's baptism, and I started to wonder about asking people to be guardian angels to my kids after they died. I texted Noah if he'd be my kids' guardian ghost one day, after he was dead, of course, and he said, *If I had a Magic 8 Ball it would say, YOU MAY RELY ON IT.*

Thank you, I said, my heart swelling in relief.

I HAVEN'T MADE LOVE to a woman yet, but all my female friends are my platonic lovers. We pour our hearts out over candlelit dinners. We pursue pleasure. We dance naked. Swim naked. Burn things. Write letters we'll never send, keep secrets, say, *Fuck it all, nothing matters; fuck it all, everything matters.* We are an ecosystem of beating hearts, a community of people with a common desire: We want to get free. We do not want to be entangled in society's fishing nets of obligation and fear; we do not want to remain in small boxes while others stretch out in their oppressive comfort. We do not want to give and give and give until we have nothing left. We do not want to live in systems that benefit some and punish others based on their skin colors, sexual or gender identities, or hearts' desires. We do not want to have to serve others when it is not serving ourselves or the collective. The question we ask ourselves is no longer *Can we do it?* Of course we can.

The question is *But do we want to?*

~

I DON'T TALK TO Beau anymore. He has his life, and I have mine. In one of the last exchanges we ever had, perhaps somewhat of an official goodbye, I texted him I got a book deal and he wrote: *You are a serious and talented writer. Your mind, a fertile garden.*

This acknowledgment—that I was a serious writer—completed something in me, as if all this time, that's all I ever wanted to hear from him. That I could be seen as an artist too. For a long time, I thought Beau was the personification of my creativity, that I had to swim in his presence to be artistically inspired. But now I can propel myself into *my* river of creativity. For so long, I thought he was the Muse. Now I realize I am the Muse. My own life, in all of its challenges and monotony, is my constant spring of inspiration. I used to think he was an escape, but now I am building a life that I don't need to escape from.

I will forever be grateful to him for reawakening something inside of me that lay dormant. And isn't that the point of all of us humans meeting down here on earth in preordained soul contracts, anyway? Aren't we all eroding our sharpened edges against each other to smooth each other out? Or, alternatively, aren't we destined to rub against one another like flint stones to start a fire? He restarted a fire in me, and that fire has brought warmth back to my family: to my children and to my husband. I used to think Beau almost drove Alex and me apart, but I wonder if he helped save us. I don't know.

He still makes beautiful music. I know he meditates now and is sober, which makes my heart full and happy. I root for him. Sometimes his music comes on in coffee shops and I think, *Hi, Beau, I love you and hope you are well.* And that's it. There's nothing more to be done.

~

FAHERTY IS STILL GROWING, still changing, still evolving. I am in the office less and Alex is at home more. We still have the same three problems at work every season: budget constraints and production delays and inventory stresses. Our mobile beach house on wheels—with its miles and miles of memories—recently caught fire en route to an event and burned to a crisp in a blaze of glory on the side of the highway. Sometimes chapters simply end, but Alex, Mike, and I have learned to deal with these metaphorical and literal fires with greater ease now. Proof that when we measure *growth,* it can be measured emotionally too.

Recently we had the idea to expand Faherty beyond just clothes to hospitality, and we opened up a small café in our New Jersey town called Sun & Waves, a place where people can get rotisserie chicken salad sandwiches on sourdough bread and organic smoothies and fresh carrot juice. It was Alex's idea, and I had, as per usual, originally nixed it, but Alex believed in the mission: a place where people could gather, have events, and eat good food. His instinct turned out to be a good one. The café has quickly become a meeting hub for book launches, crafts workshops, tarot readings, and garden clubs.

"Do you know what my book will be about?" I asked Alex one day in the café as I wrote in the corner. I was staying home to write, and he was grabbing a protein shake before taking the ferry to work.

It was such an obvious question, but sometimes I didn't know if he knew.

"Life?" he responded. Kindly. Sadly. Knowingly.

"Yes," I said. "I am writing about life."

"When can I read it?" he asked.

"Soon," I said.

BEFORE ONE OF MY drafts was due, I went to Ireland for a week. I read John O'Donohue's *Anam Cara* each night by the fire and walked in the rain and washed down fish and chips with a Guinness, and I was so happy I almost died. Years ago, all the females in my family had returned to my ancestors' home in County Mayo, and we did gravestone rubbings of the Celtic crosses above their graves, feeling the fortitude and resiliency around attempts to erase their Irish identity. I had only recently learned that during the *forced* potato famine, the Choctaw Nation sent the starving people of Ireland $170. This was just after the Choctaws had endured the genocidal Trail of Tears. Hearing such a generous act of compassion during such mutually profound suffering made me weep. Ireland has since erected a statue—nine stainless steel feathers—to honor the Choctaw act of empathy, compassion, and solidarity as if to reassure, *We are not other*.

On my last day in Ireland, I got a text message from Alex: *Back home, rumors are starting that we're getting a divorce.* I laughed. *Why would they say that?* I asked.

Because most women wouldn't dare leave their husband and children for a week to do what they want, he reminded me.

I think of all the men who travel for work trips, for "boys" trips, for golf trips. I think of the double standard, of the response to a woman traveling for her own pleasure while her husband tends to the home. How this still feels rebellious to many.

On the final day, I spent hours on my hands and knees on the shores of Connemara looking for sea glass between large gray rocks, battered smooth by waves. I didn't find glass, but instead found ten, maybe fifteen, unbroken, delicate yellow shells. I put a rock in one palm and a yellow shell in the other, and something about their juxtaposed weight made me weep.

~

AFTER SCHOOL ONE DAY, Ava asked me to take her to the park and I told her no because I needed to write.

"If I write a book, it's gonna be fiction," she said, "because I'm a private person and don't want people to know things about me." My heart constricted. I exhaled slowly. We are so different in so many ways: she with her red lips, curled hair, fake nails, pantyhose, and heels. She wants to win. And me with my tinseled, tangled knots, grandpa sweaters, and sneaks. I've declared defeat. But I let her be her, she lets me be me, and isn't that one of the greatest love stories of all time?

"How do you feel that I'm writing a book about our family?" I asked back delicately.

"Your book, your choice," she said matter-of-factly.

When I told her the title of the book, she had grinned widely, as if reconciling something within.

"You are a selfish mom," she affirmed, "because you always do what you want."

I hoped she too would be a woman who grew up doing what she wanted to do.

"Thank you for seeing me. When I die, Aves," I said, "the rock over my natural burial can say: Here lies a Selfish woman."

She nodded.

I knew she understood.

Thirty-six

On a Monday morning, Alex and I dropped the kids off at school and then sat briefly in our car outside Sun & Waves before heading in to grab coffee. Our seatbelts were off, and we both leaned against our respective car doors, looking at each other.

Over the weekend, on a ski trip with friends, Alex had read a draft of this book in full, not once but twice.

"I just can't believe you're doing this, Ker," he said to me now, shaking his head. His eyes were pained. "That you would write about our life."

I remained quiet.

"I'm so proud of you, I am. But you wrote about the hardest time of our lives: when we were in survival mode just trying to make Faherty work. When we were all at our worst. And I feel like you didn't include a lot of the great stuff about this journey. About all the amazing things about our life. About Faherty. Or our marriage."

I nodded. I understood what he was saying. And he wasn't wrong, because there are so many good memories and things I have failed to share thus far. Like how Alex and I never run out of things to talk about. How we make each other laugh: two decades of inside jokes and funny incidents and work debacles that crack us up. How even when we are annoyed with each other, there is no one else with whom we would rather spend time. How we are great parents: He plays with the kids and takes them on fun adventures, and I teach them how to garden and tell them stories about death and God.

"Can you imagine if you had to read an entire book on what it was like to be married to *you*?" he asked. "It's just insane."

I thought about that for a moment: if the tables had been flipped and I had to read his version of it all. Of course it would be brutal. I ached in compassion at the thought of it.

"Plus, I feel like a lot of things you share make you unlikable. And then to have so much of the book be about Beau . . ." Alex trailed off. "It's just painful. I knew you guys were close. I already had to read the letter. But why did you need to put him in there as such a big character?"

Why did I? Why would I share publicly something that would cause my husband pain? That would cause my family pain? Why would I share something about a relationship I had that would potentially make people judge me? Dislike me? Or call me immoral?

"Because, Al, I wanted to write as honestly as I could about who I am. So much of inner life has been hidden, and I'm done with that now. I believe that truth telling is sometimes the biggest act of service, both to ourselves, and to others. My whole life I've wanted to write a book where I put down all my thoughts and experiences—the shiny and the shadowy—to reflect on what it means for me to be human. This is what it's like to be seen."

"Well," he said, shaking his head and looking out the windshield, "I feel like I finally see you." He said it sadly. With heaviness. With concern.

I had been waiting to hear these words—*I see you*—for our entire marriage, to feel the truth of these words, and now he was saying them. Not in the circumstances I wanted, but he was saying them. And I believed him. He finally saw all of me.

I thought of Jenny with the green ribbon, telling Alfred that he could finally pull off her ribbon so he could know the entire truth about her. Only now, I had to bear the brunt of watching the reaction of my husband pulling it off from around my neck, my head still on my body, my heart still beating.

"You know," Al said, "growing up, I was taught that the worst thing anyone could do to someone was to have an affair."

I recoiled at the word "affair." I wanted to defend myself against that word. But I didn't. I nodded. I understood.

"And growing up," I said, quietly, "I learned that the worst thing that could happen in a marriage was never being fully seen by the person you loved." I thought of my mom, begging my dad to swim across the river to come meet her, to join her where she was.

We let silence fill the car, each of us lost in the weight of our respective wounds.

"It looks like we married our unfinished business," I said.

Tears fell down our cheeks. He finally looked at me, and I swear I could see more deeply into his dilated pupils, accessing a place I had not yet accessed. A doorway.

"Should we take a beach walk?" he asked.

"Yes," I said, holding out my hand, not knowing if he would take it. He reached out to me, and we headed to the beach.

~

AS THE WEEKS WENT on and Alex processed this book, we articulated our ten years of quiet suffering: all the small ways and big ways we have betrayed each other; not prioritized each other; ignored each other; resented each other. He told me that sometimes I was a bad wife and a bad business partner and a lazy mom. I cried. I told him that sometimes he was a bad business partner and a bad husband, but never a bad dad. He cried. He said that sometimes he hated me. I said sometimes I hated him, too. He told me he thought about leaving me. I told him I had thought about leaving him too, and I would have understood if he wanted to: We were never stuck. This marriage was a choice, every day, and if we wanted to stay in it, we actively needed to choose each other. I wanted to keep choosing the life we had cocreated.

One morning, when the kids were at school, Alex and I were in the shower. I was sitting down on the tiled floor letting the hot water splash on me by Alex's feet, and Alex stood under the showerhead. I was too tired to stand. There had been so many follow-up conversations, so many tears, so many more truths unearthed. More family members read the book, and some did not like it. I could taste their projected fear on my own tongue every time they asked, "*Why are you doing this?*"

As the water seeped off Alex's skin he said, "I know that it's been your dream to write a book, Ker, but you have to understand there are consequences. Having this out there hurts me and other people you love. And it could hurt Faherty: We're an aspirational brand with family values."

I know that the act of sharing my story feels like an act of betrayal to those closest to me. That it is *selfish*. They are not wrong. I am prioritizing my own desire for unbridled, creative truth telling over others' comfort and feelings. I am writing this book *because I want to.* Because I *need* to. Because the rest of my life depends on how fully I show up for myself every day. Because it has helped me come alive again.

"Al," I said, sighing, "I do not need to be aspirational anymore: I'm retired from trying to be anything that I am not. I need to be authentic. I need to be tender and vulnerable and honest. I need to be resolute that I am worthy of sharing my voice and my experiences and my life. And when it comes to the brand and family values, I believe that the most 'aspirational' ones are those who admit their complicated, messy, and imperfect dynamics and still work through them with love and honesty. If certain people don't want to buy the brand anymore, that's still a form of conscious capitalism."

I watched the shampoo suds spiral down the drain.

Alex didn't agree or disagree. "Ker, I'm trying so hard to move through this, but I don't feel like you have shame for how your relationship with Beau almost destroyed our marriage."

I could feel in my veins all the ways my choices had led to Alex's pain. For the ways I had betrayed him. But I would not feel *shame*—a tactic in the collective that prevents people from believing in their humanity, that strips people away from the belief that they belong, that stigmatizes others to separate them from the whole. Yes, I will feel all other emotions—sadness, grief, accountability—but I will not let *shame* corrode my feeling of worthiness.

I thought about the ways that in our relationship we created a hierarchy of wounds: how we ranked and weaponized pain. How we proclaimed that this hurt was *more than this hurt;* that *this pain felt worse than this pain.* Of course, we could argue about the degrees of our suffering, and those distinctions may be valid, but was it *helpful* for the healing process? Each of us, intentionally or unintentionally, will wound those we love; and if we're lucky, we can also heal with those we love.

Alex turned off the water. I stood up and hugged him.

"I know I've betrayed you too, Ker. For years, I prioritized my relationship to my family and the business more than you. For years, you cried out for help, but I was so addicted to building this brand, I couldn't meet you."

I felt a deep relief in my body. Despite the pain we are in, through sharing and feeling and apologizing and crying, we are *somehow* the best we've ever been. We are more of a unit than we've ever been. We are more emotionally and physically intimate than we've ever been. We are swimming across the river together, even if there is a current that sometimes sets us back.

I whispered the ho'oponopono prayer, hearing it echo off the damp shower walls. "I'm sorry. I forgive you. Thank you. I love you."

He said it back. "I believe in us," I said, now putting my ear to his chest. I could hear his heart. It was beating fast.

"Me too," he whispered back.

Epilogue

After the storm, I walk to the beach to assess the damage: Littered on the shore are hundreds of plastic bottle tops—the sins of every thirsty sip. I walk over tangled fishing nets, toothbrushes, tampon applicators, straws, a red balloon, a brown piece of glass, and a dead baby stingray. I think of the teenage boy on Labor Day, how he was swept away on a sunny day. I think of Jenny as a child—her green ribbon around her neck—having to bear the secret of her fragility alone. I think of the ghost of Dahlia, looking for a mother to hold her at night, to tell her she is okay. I think of my mom on the side of the river, waving to my dad; how he is now swimming toward her. I think of the unseen scars of my ancestors' suffering, how the apples of addiction and now sobriety hang from the family tree. I think of my siblings and our secrets and the mudpuppies and the pranks. I think of Karl's mom still missing her child. I think of the sperm whale and the woman swimming out to sea, how I forgive her. I think of Beau and his melodies. I think of my kids in their temper tantrums and in their laughter. I think of Alex in his pain and forgiveness and his joy. I think of the two wolves inside of me, both hungry. I think of the seeds inside of me and the weeds, growing side by side, and having to discern which plants to pull out and which ones to tend to so they bear fruit.

I am not solely any of these things, but I am not other than them. They all are a part of me. In all my reflections on the Self, I still cannot clearly define it. Each of us is part Soul, eternal, perfect, and connected to the vast, all-encompassing universe; and part Human, temporary, physical, flawed, and uniquely individual. I am everything: good and bad; stardust and dirt; lover and hater; taker and giver. I am wanderlust and anchor; satisfied and restless; creative and logical; whole and fragmented; selfless and selfish.

As I walk back to the boardwalk, I turn around to face the ocean one last time. I think about how tomorrow, all of the litter and glass and dead things will be washed away and the ocean will look calm and blue, but underneath the surface it all will still remain. How in time, everything corrodes, erodes, breaks down, and fractures, our sharpened edges smoothing into tiny, crumb-like grains of dust.

As the sand and sea glisten in the sun, all I can think is *See how it sparkles and shines.*

ACKNOWLEDGMENTS

First and foremost: This book is a memoir. While the stories are true to my experience, my memory is imperfect, and some details and names have been altered for all the reasons you can imagine.

For the past decade, I have had a very specific way of reading books. I read the first chapter, and then once I have the flavor of the author's voice, I stop and read the author's bio. If there is a photo of the author, I stare into their eyes for a bit, wondering, *Who are you?* Then I flip to the acknowledgments and wonder, *And who helped make you who you are?* Only after reading the acknowledgments do I return to chapter 2, reading each word with a deeper context of how the author's words came to be.

A book is a book, of course, but it is also a communal sculpture molded from the fingerprints of many. Thank you to all who warmed my clay and pinch-potted this book. To Amy Hughes, my agent: You believed I had a book in me before I even knew exactly what the story was. Thank you for being a thought partner, business advocate, and friend. To Marnie

Cochran, my editor at Harmony, thank you for seeing me in my story, offering insightful and wise commentary, and sharing unending support as I navigated life on and off the page. Thank you to everyone at Harmony and Penguin Random House for stewarding this book into the warmth of the hands of people. And thank you to Mr. Stratton and Mr. Desautels, two of my teachers in high school who helped me fall in love with writing. Thank you, Margaret Anastas, for helping me bring my children's book, *Somewhere, Right Now,* to life and lubricating my psyche to show me that writing books was an option.

This book-writing journey very much started at the Brooklyn Writers Collective, where fellow writers first heard my essays in 2020 and encouraged me to keep going. To the BWC community, I hold all your stories in my heart. Thank you to Emily Stone and Rachel Bertsche for reminding me that my life has a plot and a plot has structure. Thank you to Molly Rosen Guy for being my smoky quartz writing doula, whose words of affirmation catapulted me into saying that which cannot be said, and to Natalie Ponte for her precise and profound feedback, which kept me going in my early (and final) stages. Thank you to the soul sisters who read this book in its early stages and who gave (and give) me endless honest feedback and spiritual support, specifically Kathryn Everett, Lindsay Branham, Ilea Dorsey, Noor Tagouri, and Mo Mullen. Thank you to Herbie Huff, whose insights I cherish and who was the first family member to read a draft of the book. Thank you to my 716 Nichols girls and my Yale and Peach (+Jana) crew: Our decades-long friendship has brought me ongoing laughter and reminds me of who I am. DSquaredS4ever. Thank you to those whose love has kept me afloat in so many different ways: Abby Gerow, Arum Rae, John Christian, Sami Freeman, Bri Delamarter, Azita Ardakani, Sam Dumas, Lyle Maltz, Laura Ruof, Amie Valpone, Bethany Yellowtail, Kim Smith, Ashley Combs, Joel Leon, Paul Beaubrun, and the Ballaines, Shraders, and Bouchers. Your friendship is the life force for me.

To House of Starks (Tootie, cousins, aunts, uncles, and spouses): You were my first imprint of what it means to be family—big, messy, fun, sandy, and sticky. I love us.

To the extended Faherty family: You expanded my idea of what it means to join a family with its own different but loving blueprint. Special thanks to Mike and Ninie: I am very proud of what we have created together from fabric, blood, sweat, and tears.

To all those who work and have worked at Faherty: Thank you. I see you.

Thank you to my spiritual and meditational muses, Dr. Jacqui Lewis, Constantina Rhodes, and Jeff Kober. A deep bow of appreciation to Elisabeth Youngclaus and Carrie Cegelis. To Iris Krstanovich, words cannot express the depth of my gratitude for your soul companionship. To Aimee Johnson, your constant truth-bomb reminders remind me not only that I am not crazy but that my soul has a mission and to trust it.

I want to thank all my ancestors who for a long time I failed to acknowledge and failed to feel. I can feel you now, both as the wind on my back and as the breath in my cells. The shores of Lake Erie and Spring Lake, the quiet and constant snowfall in Buffalo, and the land in the Hudson Valley have shaped me just as much as humans have, and their companionship held my tears and my hopes.

I want to thank all the babysitters who have opened their arms to my kids so I could work and write or escape. Particular thanks to Pam Cools, who joined our family at a time when we were all in need of some love, laughter, care, and discipline. Thank you for shaping my kids into what they are today and loving me as a chosen daughter.

Thank you to the Spring Lake community and Mountz parents: It takes a village.

To Shannon and Brendan, the people who I still laugh the most with. What a gift to share decades of inside jokes and pranks, commercial and video game jingles, long beach days, Christmas escapades, and beyond. I could have filled another book with the stories we collected over the years. I cherish you. Shan, thanks for always telling me when things are fucked up and helping me access my true feelings, and Brendan, thanks for decades of making me laugh and reminding us all how important it is to keep *play* alive. Herbie, your mind is one of the minds I love most in this world. Lauren, the way you love Brendan and the Docherty clan has been such a gift to us all.

To my mom and dad: Thank you for being the rich, fertilizing soil in which my specific specimen of seed could grow. Your support and encouragement have been a safety net, and because you taught me the art of unconditional love, it put me at an advantage to learn how to love myself. You are the best Pop and Isa and best friend to Alex. No amount of thank you feels sufficient. My soul feels at ease in your presence, and I love you so much.

To Ava and Riggs: You are the great joys of my life. I will forever hold you in your tears and happiness. As I say every day: I love you forever; I think you're incredible; and even when I'm dead, I'll find you and be with you.

To Alex: Where do I begin? There are very few partners who could read a book of this kind, go through the journey we just went through, come out on the other side, look around, and still say, *What a beautiful life we have.* We've cultivated something special and unbreakable: You help keep my feet in reality so I don't fly away, and I remind you that sometimes reality is more than what we're seeing. This book has many chapters, but I'm most excited about the future ones we're writing together. We got this. I believe in us.

To those of you who have read this book. I carry your hearts too. We are not other.

ABOUT THE AUTHOR

Kerry Docherty cofounded the lifestyle clothing brand Faherty with her husband and his identical twin. A graduate of Yale University and Pepperdine University School of Law, she is passionate about community building, sustainability, and creativity. Kerry is also the author of the children's book *Somewhere, Right Now,* featuring art by *New York Times* bestselling illustrator Suzie Mason. She lives with her husband and two children on the New Jersey shore, where she is constantly looking for sea glass.